WITNESSES TO JESUS

WITNESSES TO JESUS

The Stories of Five Who Knew Him

MIECZYSLAW MALINSKI

Translated by Lucy Mazareski

CROSSROAD · NEW YORK

1982

The Crossroad Publishing Company
575 Lexington Avenue, New York, NY 10022

Originally published as *Świadkowie Jezusa* © 1978

Library of Congress Cataloging in Publication Data

Maliński, Mieczysław.
Witnesses to Jesus.

Translation of: Swiadkowie Jezusa.
1. Jesus Christ—Fiction.   I. Title.
PG7172.A3855S913   1982   891.8′537   81-19440
ISBN 0-8245-0088-1   AACR2

CONTENTS

Pilate   3

Judas   49

Annas   97

Mary Magdalene   169

Simon Peter   227

WITNESSES TO JESUS

PILATE

When the Jewish informer rushed breathlessly into the palace late in the evening to report what he had seen in the Garden of Olives, Pilate listened with concern but little surprise: he had foreseen this long ago. If there was anything in the whole affair that surprised him, it was that one of the Twelve had turned him over.

"For thirty silver pieces," the informer sniffed contemptuously. "Like the price of a slave!" He was panting from his headlong rush.

Midway through his report, Pilate stopped listening. Swiftly, he reviewed in his head all the garrisons stationed near Jerusalem from which troops would have to be brought in to reinforce those in the city. The decision of the chief priests had taken him aback: to arrest Jesus on the eve of the festival days, when the city was seething with pilgrims—his followers—from the provinces was sheer madness. Why, they would reduce the prisons to dust to get their master from Nazareth back. And if they release him, he mused, then from tomorrow on, we can expect to have a new Jewish king, and with him, Annas, Caiaphas, and the whole ruling power of the priests and Pharisees will disappear. Palestine had never experienced anything quite like it. Yet surely the priests knew all this. They must have some trick up their sleeves. But what could it be? On the other hand, he had to concede—they did not have many chances left. After those events in Bethany involving Lazarus, Jesus had virtually won all Jerusalem over to himself. In such a sitation, he could do just about anything he pleased. And they still were not sure what it was he wanted.

He ordered the informer generously compensated for his pains. Then he turned to his centurion with the terse command: "An officers' council."

They assembled quickly, as if they were just waiting to be summoned. Pilate sensed that they already knew about Jesus' arrest and understood perfectly the seriousness of the situation. He made a short statement on the state of affairs and the developments that might occur. He ordered all detachments put on a state of alert and all defense points reinforced. He smiled faintly. "It sounds as though I'm preparing for a state of siege," he said. Half to himself he added, "Except that it's not really very funny." Out loud to his officers he said, "Don't let yourself be provoked. If the Jews begin fighting among themselves, you will not get involved on any side. You will not engage in any actions independently. You will await my orders and report every incident." The chief priests, he told them, may try to transfer Jesus to another town in the provinces to avert a riot in Jerusalem. "That's why a state of alert will be in effect over all of Palestine, and not just in the city," he added.

After the officers had left, he considered what to do. He thought he should remain in the Praetorium; it was late. But he could not resist the impulse to go home and tell his wife about these latest developments, and seek out her opinion. He ordered a litter and escort. "I'm going home," he told the centurion. "Take charge of everything. I'll be back shortly."

He saw the centurion's surprised reaction. "Tonight I will sleep in the Praetorium," he offered by way of explanation.

He mounted the litter; the porters swung forward. He listened a moment to the rhythm of their steps. Welltrained, he thought. At least he was able to teach them that much. He pushed aside the curtain and peered out into the night. It was dark, and a foul stink hung in the streets. "And it could have been so different here," he muttered bitterly to himself. "I wanted to do them a good turn, but they didn't want it. So, if it is no, then it is no. Let them live on their own dungheaps." He dropped the curtain in disgust.

There was a time—and he returned to it often when entertaining guests from Rome and telling them about his activities here—when he had wanted to turn Jerusalem into a little Rome. This was where he saw his calling—to give Roman culture to this poor, backward, superstitious nation. To build them roads and bridges; tear down the hovels, the dark, cramped, filthy mud huts that bred every possible disease; construct decent houses of stone—solid, spacious, light. But especially, he wanted to build hot baths. To accustom these people to water, these people who wet the tips of their fingers in water before eating. To teach them to wash, to bathe, to relish water—the source of life. That was what he wanted to start with, with water, with aqueducts. Without them, he couldn't make a single move. That was the first investment that had to be ventured. But Rome wouldn't give him any money for it. He petitioned, explained what he wanted to do. The answer was a disdainful silence. Later someone confided to him that it had been a tactless indiscretion on his part to approach Rome with such matters while she was waging exhausting, costly wars. It was then that he turned to the place where he knew there was gold in abundance: the temple. He consulted the chief priests; the consultations were endless. He elaborated, submitted plans, drew up sketches—all at his own expense. Now when he thought about those times, he felt like laughing at what a fool he had been, as excited as a small boy. And then he condescended to the point of asking for money. He, a Roman, asked them, the Jews, for money. But he only had their welfare in mind. He wanted to build them hot baths, great expansive ones. Let them have a place where they could not only wash off their dirt, but also meet to talk, socialize. He dreamed of even more: he dreamed of sports stadia. Let them have something more to do than just work and pray in the temple. Let their youths have a square where they could run, play, throw discus, wrestle. He wanted the Jews truly to join the family of nations in the Roman Empire, to grow in wisdom, health, happiness—to take satisfaction in the Pax Romana. He had only their welfare in mind. At one point he even thought that the priests understood him, that he had found acceptance among them, won them over. They nodded their heads, admired the plans, expressed their greatest esteem—until the question of money arose. Then they dodged the issue with a thousand excuses. They had no authority, they said; they had no resources. They pleaded expenses for the poor—especially for those unfortunate families whose breadwinners had been killed by the Romans. Only then had he understood that nothing would ever come of it. Those expenses of theirs for the families of Jews murdered by the Romans were nothing less than spitefulness on their part toward him. They deliberately goaded him, insulted him to his face, tried to make him explode. He pretended not to notice, not to understand, hoping that they would come around, see his goodwill, trusting they would appreciate the benefits such an investment would bring to the Jewish nation. Only later did he come to realize how he had been deluding himself; only later did he understand fully that they wanted nothing from him. Not only would they give nothing, but they would take nothing. Between him and them there was an abyss he could never bridge: he was a pagan, and they were the chosen nation. Everything was contained in that one statement of fact. "Whoever fails to understand that, will understand nothing," he liked to tell his guests from Rome. He grasped it, however, only much later. And then he lost all his control. He tried to take the money from the temple by force. That was a mistake that he later deeply regretted.

He dismissed the memories with distaste; he did not want to dwell on them any longer. They offended his pride. He felt like turning back to the Praetorium; he was sorry he had even decided on the escapade. He wriggled impatiently in the litter: this whole night ride home was senseless. Especially since his presence in the Praetorium might become imperative at any moment. And his wife had probably long since retired to bed anyway. He was angered by his own impulsiveness. He wanted to order the porters to turn round, but that would make him appear ridiculous to the servants and the soldiers, and to the centurion—"What, he's just left and he's back already?"

Finally they came to a halt. He sprang lightly from the litter. There were lights in the windows—perhaps she was not asleep yet after all. Halfway up the stairs, his wife appeared in the door, looming in white robes like a moth against the luminous marble walls and columns aglow in the moonlight. She ran down the stairs to meet him. He saw the joy in her face at his arrival. How could I have failed to notice that woman in Rome? he thought to himself. She clasped his arm.

"I was waiting up for you," she said. "I was sure you would come. I was so afraid for you. What's happening in the city? What's happening with the teacher?"

All the tension only moments before, tightening inside him like a knot, suddenly unwound. He answered her almost good-humoredly. The problems that had been hanging over him like cliff rocks instantly seemed to take on new dimensions.

"What have you decided?" she asked him.

"Nothing. For the moment I have ordered all garrisons put on a state of alert."

"What about the teacher?"

"He's not my concern," he shrugged, pretending indifference. He only said it to watch her reaction. She reacted exactly the way he had expected: she grew thoughtful and serious.

"You know," she began, "I've been thinking a great deal about him and the situation that has arisen."

"And what have you concluded?" he asked, with outward casualness.

"I'm convinced that it's not simply a local Jewish affair, but altogether a Roman, or even a universal one."

"How do you understand that?" Now he was genuinely surprised.

"Well, why are we really here? To add one more nation to the Empire? To have one more nation pay taxes and enrich the coffers of Rome?"

"Now wait, let's not exaggerate," he interrupted, his tone ironical. "The taxes they pay amount to next to nothing."

"We're here," she continued, "to create a modern cultured state out of this backward people. To pull them out of ignorance and superstition. You've always said as much yourself. This is your argument."

"Yes, you are right." He had already guessed what she was driving at.

"So then why shouldn't we at last find an ally in this teacher from Nazareth. Why must we always insist on doing everything with our own Roman hands—and always with the same lack of success because everyone thoroughly detests us. Here we suddenly find a man who thinks like our greatest philosophers, who is achieving goals we set up for ourselves. I agree, he expresses himself in a different language, one that is nearly unintelligible to us, or at least unintelligible to the people of Rome. But you yourself always said that they can't be taken seriously."

Pilate agreed with her arguments, but could not resist the temptation to tease her.

"But he doesn't wash," he said in a solemn voice. "And he even encourages others not to."

He saw the uncertainty flicker in waves across her face: she wasn't sure if he meant it as a joke or if he was serious.

"He doesn't wash?" she repeated softly. "Where did you get that idea?"

"Well, don't you remember what the Pharisees said about him? Among other things, they accuse him of breaking the laws of their elders and not washing his cups and hands before eating. He and his followers."

"Oh, is that what you mean? You were simply teasing me." She burst into relieved laughter. "And do you remember how he answered them? That those were not the things that make a man unclean, but hatred, jealousy, and revenge. You know it better than I do. Anyway, you're quite right. That's the whole point. He knows that it's not enough simply to talk to a man, not enough to make him wiser, but that he has to be disposed to take action. It's not enough for a man to know; it's necessary for him to decide and act. And in this respect, he is wiser than Socrates. Because look, they have already stopped living in dread of their sacred rules and regulations. They have already overcome their fear of violating every custom. With his help, they have managed to throw off the fetters that those 'commandments of their elders' threw on them. He educates them as if he were a wise old sage, although he's only thirty years old. You know, when I think about him like this, I get the impression he was a disciple of Plato. Or no, as if Plato wrote his reflections—or at least certain ones—with him in mind."

"Don't you think you might be exaggerating a little?" Pilate interrupted, vaguely annoyed.

She hesitated, then went on. "Take the problem of the *Phaedo*. It's the same thing. Plato keeps on telling us that man exists in darkness, that he is as if bound, almost paralyzed; that another man must bring him truth—a philosopher. He says that it is necessary for a man to begin to imitate the philospher whom he had the good fortune to find. That's not a duty, but the result of the rapture that comes over every weak and ignorant man when he suddenly sees the light. Such a man begins spontaneously and joyfully to live like a philosopher. He starts learning how to live in freedom. You remember the word Plato likes to use, mimesis—imitation, mimicry. And the other word, participation, which is accomplished through imitation. Participation in pure Good, in God."

"I think I can still remember a few things Plato said," Pilate remarked with a hint of sarcasm. "But how do you connect him with the teacher?"

"I'm sorry. I didn't mean to offend you." He could see the tears welling in her eyes. "It's my talkativeness, as usual."

He softened. "Never mind. Go on."

She resumed shyly, then went on more and more enthusiastically as she worked out her ideas. "I am convinced that the principles expounded by Plato are being fulfilled by the teacher from Nazareth. Notice, he even said about himself: I am the Way. The same thing Plato said. Even more: I am truth and life. Further: Whoever follows me will not walk in darkness. He keeps repeating to the people: Learn from me, take my example. He constantly calls himself the shepherd, and he likens his followers to a flock of sheep that follows him. He says he is the door. He is supposed to have told one of his disciples: Whoever sees me, sees also the Father."

"How do you know so much about him?" Pilate asked, his interest aroused.

"Oh, from your specialists on Jesus." She smiled. "They know exactly what he says and what he does. They either observe it firsthand, or they find out from the Pharisees and priests. But tell me, isn't it just like Plato? Isn't it just like his *Phaedo*?"

"Perhaps he really does draw from Greek and Roman sources," he mused.

"But is it possible for someone living in some Galilean hole to have had contact with the works of the philosophers? Does he even know Greek? And anyway, he presents the problems very differently, independently, and he resolves them differently."

"I never knew I had such a learned wife. You never cease to amaze me with your knowledge."

She blushed. Again she was unsure if he was making light or being serious. She paused, eyed him uncertainly, and then began lightly: "What else do I have to do but sit morning and evening waiting and pining for you, my lord and master, who wander the world and and pays only an occasional visit to your wife. I could gossip with the women slaves, of course, or embroider, or have your soldiers teach me how to play at dice, but somehow I prefer to read the philosophers. Besides, it's your own fault. You're the one who bought so many of their works during your peak years in Rome. You paid a fortune for them. Now I'm making sure it wasn't wasted, so I read."

"And well that you do. As a matter of fact, you might"— here he feigned seriousness—"you might write a comparative study entitled, 'The Teacher of Nazareth,' or no, 'Jesus of Nazareth and Socrates.' Or perhaps, 'Jesus of Nazareth and Plato.' Only try to make sure my name is included. Insert it in the title: 'Jesus of Nazareth Living in the Time of Pontius Pilate.' Or simply 'Under Pontius Pilate.' This way our name will enter history. So far there hasn't been much opportunity."

"Don't tease me. Tell me, what do you think they'll do with him?"

"I have no idea. I can venture a guess, that they'll forbid

him to teach and then release him. Maybe scourge him as punishment."

"And if he refuses to obey?"

"Then at least he'll promise to try—the scourge is very persuasive."

"And if he still doesn't agree?" she persisted. "Do you really think he can stop teaching? Do you think even for a moment that he'll agree to remain silent?"

Her questions nettled him, especially since he had to admit she was right: Jesus would not agree. Pilate was not quite sure how to answer her; he hadn't reflected that deeply on the situation yet.

Meanwhile, she went on: "Could Socrates stop teaching? No, he couldn't. He could only perish. It must be the same with our teacher. What a shame he doesn't write down what he teaches. And I'm not sure if any of his disciples do. I'm afraid all those values will be lost. After all, he's not just some prophet, as they call him, concerned with strictly religious affairs; he is a deep philosopher, who is concerned with basic human problems, individual and social."

"Why do you say this?" he asked.

"Because I fear they will put him to death."

Pilate gave a patronizing laugh. "Don't be childish. You can't kill a man unlawfully. Times have changed. We're in a legally governed state, not among barbarians. Of course, if the Jews were governing themselves, they would undoubtedly have knocked each other's brains out long ago. And they know it, too. After all, we're here because they invited us. They couldn't manage themselves by themselves. They were slaughtering each other, and if we hadn't entered Jerusalem, there might not be a single Jew left in the world today. Fortunately, they have Roman law now, and without it they cannot make the slightest move."

"You must defend him. So that human folly doesn't cost him his life. As in the case of Socrates."

Pilate had a distinct dislike for shouldering responsibility. Instinctively, he covered himself. "What have you got into your head? He has the people from the provinces behind him, and they have all been in Jerusalem for the last few days. He isn't as naive as you think. He came now, and not at any other time. And believe me, he'll leave along with them. He won't stay a day longer. And there isn't a man alive who would dare to kill him. Not one, not among the scribes, nor the Pharisees, nor even the priests. They arrested him, they'll question him, judge him, at most forbid him to teach, and tomorrow morning release him." He paused. "There's one other thing I have to tell you." He said it as if he had just now remembered, but in fact it had been in his mind from the start of their conversation. "He is due for at least one hearing with me." He didn't look at his wife when he spoke; he didn't want to see the fright rise in her face. He heard her muffled voice: "In relation to what?"

"In relation to his Kingdom of God."

"I was afraid of that." Her muted whisper irritated him even more.

"He may be very wise, he may be a philosopher like Plato and he may be as good an educator as Socrates. None of that concerns me. But if he starts playing politics, I'll destroy him."

"But you know his expression 'Kingdom of God' has a different, purely religious meaning."

"That's not entirely true. If you can prove to me that the Jews never established kingdoms, because 'that's not what they had in mind', and if you can prove to me that they never had any kings, then I'll take your word for it." He paused a moment, then asked, "And who among all the Jewish kings was the greatest?"

"Solomon perhaps."

"No. The greatest king was undoubtedly David."

"Possibly." She looked at him wide-eyed, not sure of his meaning or of what was coming next.

"And do you know"—he turned on her aggressively—"do you know what line our teacher from Nazareth is descended from?"

She didn't answer.

"Then write it down, so you'll have one more detail for his biography: he comes from the line of David."

A heavy silence fell between them. Pilate paced the room

with broad, heavy steps, watching his wife's stunned reaction with satisfaction. He wanted to leave her then for added impact, but he began to soften, to feel sorry for her. He went on mildly, "He can philosophize all he wants, and educate the people all he wants, but politics are my domain and that's what I'm here for. Palestine is part of the Roman Empire, and it will remain so for all time. If anyone dares raise his hand against that fact, I'll hang him on a cross, regardless of who he might be."

She said nothing. Pilate paced briskly then said, "I'm returning to the Praetorium. My presence is necessary there. I don't know what may happen."

"I understand," she said in a wooden voice. "It's a pity you can't stay. Then I wouldn't have to worry about you."

"Or about him. Isn't that right?"

She did not react to his irony. "I'm going to be very anxious," she said simply.

"Tomorrow, as soon as the matter is cleared up, I'll be home directly."

He tried to change the subject, ask about the children, their plans for the next few days, but their conversation became stiff, halfhearted. Finally he rose. He clasped his wife to him, then went out into the courtyard. His litter was waiting. The escort guards were burning torches. He got in without a word. He gestured with his hand to his wife standing in the door. She answered with a wave of her scarf and was still waving as he disappeared around the corner of the building.

The rhythmic swaying of the litter soothed him. He felt contented with himself. At times like these his thoughts turned to Rome, and he would be filled with feelings of contempt mixed with superiority: what did those petty Roman functionaries understand anyway? They believed that the only things of importance in the world happened between the Forum Romanum and the Aventine. Nothing else interested them. From the provinces they demanded only peace and quiet, Pax Romana. That was the phrase they repeated over and over like parrots. Pax Romana. All the occupied nations were expected to be deliriously happy by reason of being under Roman rule. They really believed that in Rome. And

they wanted everyone else to believe it too. All they did was
sit around in Rome and talk about Pax Romana. But just let
them get up on their horses and come and see the provinces.
Then they would see what **Pax Romana** really meant. They
would like it to be nice and quiet. They would like all the
peoples to work, to supply Rome with wheat for their cakes,
grapes for their wines, marble for their palaces. And slaves
for handing them everything. And gold for their wars. And
for everyone to think, speak, and act like a Roman. But the
problems that boiled beneath that lid of **Pax Romana**—that
did not interest them in the least. But he knew. He had to
know. He had to do everything possible to prevent that lid
from suddenly exploding into the air. He had to pacify and
appease; he had to know when to sympathize and when to
threaten; when to be generous and when to crucify. To keep
the peace, that was all that mattered. Rome could not care
less what it cost him in nerves, in effort, in money; how much
this Jesus affair was costing him. Who of those bureaucrats
would believe how much he had to pay out to those inform-
ants to keep him up-to-date on everything Jesus said and did.
As if that were not enough, he had to keep up with what the
priests and Pharisees and doctors of the law had to say about
everything Jesus said. But just let him relax his efforts, just
let him be remiss and let the situation blow up into an incident
of some kind. Then, naturally, it will be the Procurator's
fault, no one else's. Did anyone in Rome give a fig about the
problems and difficulties he had to contend with here? It was
supposed to be quiet and that was that. Whatever else happens, Pilate will be to blame. . . .

His thoughts and images began to recede, blur. Slowly, in
spite of himself, he succumbed to the gentle rocking of his
litter and dropped into the soothing sleep of a child lulled in
his cradle. When he awoke, the litter stood outside the Praetorium. He felt refreshed, as if he had slept the night through.
He jumped to the ground and returned to his rooms, but first
gave instructions for the centurion to report to him.

Striding across his room, he tried to focus on a plan of
action for the following day, but somehow he could not keep
his mind on it. He paced, disturbed . . . something gnawed

at the back of his mind. It took a moment for him to pinpoint the source of his agitation: it was the news from Rome that he had received before noon that day. He had tried to disregard it, laugh it off—he had even repeated the old joke about Tiberius and Sejanus—but he knew he was only deceiving himself. The words "Tiberius no longer trusts you" stuck in his mind like a splinter. And now this whole Jesus affair was pressing down upon him like so much dead weight. It was a load he could do without. Of one thing he could be certain: a very difficult day lay ahead of him. He tried to concentrate, to recall everything he knew about Jesus. So that he would not leave anything out, he tried to arrange all the facts about him in chronological order in his mind. He knew a great deal about him, if not everything. He had, after all, conscientiously followed his every move and activity, and almost every day had brought in fresh reports. In the last couple of years, Jesus had become the most prominent personality in all Palestine, and of course, Jerusalem. His name was on everyone's lips: Pharisees and Sadducees, the masses and the army, the Romans and the Jews. Every scrap of news about him spread with the speed of lightning to every corner, however remote.

He felt extremely agitated. He had not expected to be so disturbed by the news of Jesus' arrest. Yet he had to admit that his entire stay in Palestine was, in one way or another, linked to that man. He thought back to his first days in Jerusalem. Scenes and emotions flashed through his mind as if in a kaleidoscope: new faces, gestures, briefings, questions, puzzlement, anger, indignation.

First there was his arrival in Palestine: the mute sullen crowds, the sporadic shouts at him in a language he still did not understand, the columns of soldiers, which since that day still accompanied him everywhere he went, the cage of palace and Praetorium from which he could never venture alone. Now it returned, like the jab of a needle, the memory he had tried so hard to obliterate: the day in Rome when he had received the Emperor's notice. He had read it aloud to his companions grouped around the table at his summer residence just outside the city: Caesar wishes to inform him that, in recognition of his services and abilities, he was charging

him with the highly responsible office of Governor of con-
quered Jerusalem.

It had come as a staggering blow, a total disaster. He could
not imagine himself living away from Rome. Even now, the
mere thought of that day reawakened the waves of panic that
had swept over him then. He had gone completely to pieces,
even threatening to take his own life. In that one instant, his
life and plans had suddenly crumbled. Tiberius' message was
unmistakably clear to all of them, to himself and to his friends:
the Emperor had seen through them. Tiberius could not, or
would not, or was afraid to bring them to trial and sentence
them to death—perhaps because he had insufficient evidence
against them. So he bestowed distinguished posts on them at
the far corners of the earth. Palestine had fallen to him. How
had Caesar put it? "I am entrusting you with an extremely
important task in appointing you the Governor of Jerusalem.
I am sure you will not disappoint my trust in you. Depart as
quickly as possible, because you are greatly needed there."
To this day he wondered whether he should not have pulled
out the dagger he concealed under his toga and killed Tiberius
then and there. "I think," he sighed aloud to himself, "that
to the end of my life I'm going to regret that I did not murder
the tyrant. I would have been another Brutus. Though there
is really no comparison between Tiberius and Julius Caesar.
After all Caesar was a democrat. Tiberius is little more than
an eastern satrap." The others had consoled him when he
was leaving, that it was not the end but a beginning; they
would stay in touch; they would yet return to Rome at the
head of their legions to overthrow the tyranny and restore
freedom to the citizens. He did not believe it when they were
saying it, though he had wanted to—desperately.

Then his arrival in Jerusalem, where silence began to ring
in his ears. The silence of the provinces, where nothing was
happening, because the single place of importance to him in
the entire world was Rome. He thought he would go mad
from humiliation and loneliness. Then came the first contacts,
which he resisted at first. But the rhythm and whir of the
administrative machine gradually drew him into that odd
new world. He had to admit, it all began to absorb him,

slowly at first, then more and more deeply. But it was a dim world. The single bright spot in it, he discovered, was his wife. In Rome he had hardly even noticed her, she simply failed to awaken his interest. Here she turned out to be a loyal companion and confidante who, with her feminine solicitude and thoughtfulness, anticipated his needs and wishes and mitigated his difficulties in every way she could. One other individual he had discovered then was the centurion: a stocky, scowling man of few words, who fretted about the Praetorium as if it were his own home, and who knew soldiers the way a father knew his children. Pilate enjoyed talking with him; he liked his independent, logical way of thinking. The centurion knew Palestine and the Jewish nation better than anyone in the court—he had spent half his life here. He had a large number of trusted people in his service, and he spoke fluent Aramaic. He assisted him every step of the way, beginning with the first, elementary information necessary for survival in this country. Well he remembered. . . .

It must have been the second day, right after his arrival in Jerusalem. He decided he wanted to go into the city. And he probably would have gone alone, but at the last minute he ordered the centurion to accompany him. Instantly the centurion summoned an escort. "It's not necessary," he told him. "Don't call anyone, we'll go alone." The centurion adamantly opposed him. "We can't go any other way. And not on foot, either, but on horseback." "On horseback?" He was amazed. "For what? It's just a few steps." The centurion said, "It's easier to spot a flying spear from a horse." Then with a sad smile he added, "They have little love for us here."

No, this was not Rome where, in the Forum, among the strolling, chatting citizens, one might come upon Caesar. Here it was helmets, armour and horseback.

In time, the centurion became not only his official aide, but a man in whom he placed his trust. Even now, he still felt the other's discreet attention—and he still needed constant assistance. He had to admit to himself, in all honesty, that without the centurion he would hardly have been able to take one judicious step alone. Hardly a day passed when he still was not confronted with strange new situations, problems, delegations, appeals, demands, repeals—things that were still foreign to him and his Roman way of thinking. . . . Somebody levying charges against somebody else for reasons that to his mind were nonexistent, or at most so trite as not to warrant his time or attention. Then the old centurion would prudently explain and advise, yet in such a way that Pilate never once felt any officious intrusion on his part.

It certainly was a strange and different world. He liked to tell his visitors from Rome: "It's enough just to sniff the air to know instantly that one is not only in the East, but in Palestine." But it was no joking matter; he knew only too well how alien this world was. He had been here many years already but the longer he stayed, the less he seemed to understand.

Very early in his stay he had got a taste of that foreignness. It may have been the third day after his arrival in the city. He was awakened by a peculiar silence. The sun was already fairly high. Puzzled, he went to his window. Not a sound issued from the city. He was perplexed at first, then disturbed, finally frightened. He called his servant and asked what had happened. At first the girl failed to understand. "Why is it so quiet?" he asked her. She smiled. "Today is the Sabbath, a holy day," she replied.

The things he later heard about the laws governing the Sabbath seemed so incredible, so monstrous, that he simply refused to believe that in the era of Pax Romana, in the time of Virgil and Horace, such things could still exist. Every time he told his Roman friends about them, he liked to throw in his own ironic commentary. "You see, this is a vision of the future at which we, too, will arrive under the gracious rule of the divine Tiberius. All things done at a command, strictly according to the rules, including what time you must eat meals and exactly how much. And most important, what you are permitted to think about it, and not just that."

But he was curious. He had to find out why—where it came from, how to account for it. Even the centurion could not answer his questions. He persisted; it intrigued him. He felt that an answer to these questions would help him understand many other thorny issues. He remembered how he had waited with his questions. Until he finally came upon those who could best satisfy his curiosity: the Jewish superiors.

He could still see them: their studied gestures, their demeanors so full of self-esteem; that careful stroking of well-groomed beards, those lowered eyelids, those indulgent smiles, those significant silences. No, they would never let themselves be caught off guard. Not even when they knew nothing. Nor in the opposite case, when they knew everything but would say nothing. They would not give their answers immediately. They excused themselves, saying that there were others better qualified than they to answer, and more fluent in Greek. They asked if the scribes and Pharisees could be included in these discussions. Pilate remembered those next meetings well. He sensed how the attitude of the Jews had changed toward him—they must have begun to treat him as a potential proselyte, as they called it. And all he wanted was to gain some insight into things that were still incomprehensible to him.

They were not easy, those talks. Not just because they had to make tedious use of an interpreter—some of the Jews refused to speak Greek, though he knew very well that they understood him perfectly—but because of the difference in their mentalities. He simply could not fathom why he was unable to elicit a straightforward answer to a straightforward question; why every question was always unclear, and every answer even more vague; why "yes" was never "yes" and "no" was never "no". He was forced to block them, corner them with auxiliary questions, seal off all escape, before arriving at one unequivocal statement—which in the end, he had to formulate himself. They limited themselves to silence. Now and then they told him how close he was getting to the truth—but always with the attitude that it was they who were the sole possessors of truth. As if it were some kind of equipment in their homes. That was what irritated him most and provoked him to unreasonable aggressive outbursts. Later he regretted letting himself get carried away by his exasperation, because it simply made no sense. But the thing that wearied him most was their constant refuge in revelation, what they called Scripture, the Law, the Prophets. When all their counterarguments were ended, it was the last word. That, and one other—God.

The topic of his discussions with the Jews was the one over which he had spent many a night with his friends in Rome: the freedom of the individual in relation to human institutions, particularly the State. If he were ever to repeat some of the discussions he conducted here in Jerusalem to his Roman friends, they simply would not believe him.

He remembered how once, finally, after a round of acrobatic juggling of questions and answers, he finally managed to discover one thing: that the source of all those insane rules binding every Jew to wash his pots and hands before eating, or to limit the number of steps he could walk on the Sabbath, was love of God. At first he thought he had heard wrong. Or they had misunderstood him, or he them, or the interpreter had made a mistake in translation. "The whole Law and the Prophets are based upon this," they repeated. Therefore, out of love of God came the shunning of pagans in the streets, the scrupulous precautions to keep a pagan's shadow from falling on them, the avoidance of all contact with sinners, the stoning of adulteresses, they explained feverishly. And finally there was that last astounding assertion—and so he who fulfills all the laws, loves God. "And do you fulfill all the laws?" He surprised them with his question. They fell silent. "If so, then you must all be saints." He started to laugh. "Forgive me, but I imagined a saint differently." They were offended, and left in a huff. They stopped coming. Pilate regretted he had allowed such discussions. On the other hand, he was not sorry: thanks to them, he had met Joseph of Arimathea. He noticed at once how different he was from the others; he was conspicuous in the way he truly endeavored to meet him halfway, bring him concrete assistance. He had never expected to find common language with a Jew.

Then came a difficult period. News from his friends, dispersed by Tiberius over the whole of the Empire, trickled in less and less frequently. They were getting old or swallowed up in their work in their own remote corners. Communication slowly petered out, then died. In Rome he had practically no close friends left. He would not have much to return to there, was not even sure now if he would want to. Palestine, which might have been a mere stopping station along the road to a distinguished career, turned out to be the terminus. It drew him deeper and deeper into itself. Especially the contests with the Pharisees and Sadducees. He tried from a variety of angles to chew at them, get under their skin, but his efforts bounced right off them as if off a wall.

He felt sorry for the Jewish people. He came to know Jerusalem's broad streets and its dingy alleys; its wealthy stores and its squalid little market stalls; he knew rich men and paupers. And with every day he grew increasingly irritated by the sight of the temple, dominating, lording over the city like a monstrous living entity. The temple—the hub and focus of attention of every Jew, rich and poor. The temple, dripping with gold, and its servants, who preached love of God and neighbor while passing indifferently by the destitution of their own kin. His burgeoning hatred towards these people exploded at times into angry outbursts. That was what had happened in that wretched incident over the aqueducts. But it was then, after that incident, that he also found out exactly the kind of influence the priests and Pharisees had in Rome. Almost immediately a reprimand came from the Emperor. The other incident was far worse. The very thought made him ashamed: those Roman military insignias that were supposed to symbolize the beginning of a new order in this country. That was a stupid move on his part. Reproof from Rome came even more swiftly and was much more sharply worded. And then he began to feel like a man trammeled. His hatred for the priests and Pharisees swelled. But something inside him died. Because he believed he had meant well. And he was not allowed. If it's no, then it's no.

The centurion entered.

"Anything new?" Pilate asked him.

"Jesus has been taken before the Sanhedrin."

"Nothing else?"

"No."

"Is it quiet in the city?"

"Quiet. Just a lot of noise at Herod's palace."

The centurion left. Herod . . . the one who had put to death

Jesus' precursor, John the Baptist. He himself would not even have taken notice of the Baptist—just another one of those prophets preaching penance—were it not for his connection with Jesus. He could not remember the first time word of Jesus reached him, or what it was about; whether it was about some wedding in Cana in Galilee, where there had been a 'miracle' of water changing into wine, or some kind of 'multiplication of bread'. He could not remember. He paid it little attention, and 'miracles' like that later became more and more plentiful. They were just so much fodder for his jokes about the gullibility and backwardness of the Jews. But what really arrested his attention, the thing he genuinely stopped to listen to, and even now made him marvel, was the news that this master from Nazareth actually healed on the Sabbath. He was incredulous. He demanded confirmation, then set about checking the veracity of the reports. Subsequent accounts brought him even more details. Out of the deluge of rapturous reports and panegyrics he singled out facts that to him were more incredible even than multiplied loaves of bread or a walk across the surface of the sea. To him the real miracles were the teachings of this son of a carpenter, who preached that man was not made for the Sabbath but the Sabbath was made for man, who quietly explained the essence of the matter by using the simplest of illustrations to point out the senselessness of the Pharisaic laws: "And if your ox falls into a cistern, will you not hurry to pull it out on the Sabbath?"

Pilate had never expected that in a nation so rigidly bound by rules a man so free could appear, who could look through the eyes of a child at that jungle of laws and prohibitions and cast them off—as he put it—"the way you discard an old wineskin or an old cloak". And he did all these things using the same Law and the same Prophets that the Scribes invoked as their ultimate argument. He thought about it so many times, and always with the same degree of amazement. The conversation with his wife returned to him: how had Jesus managed to grasp the most essential problems relative to social life, and especially to the relationship between man and the institution? That was a problem over which the best minds of Greece and Rome had pondered. How had he arrived at the fact that a man is not made for the Sabbath, but the Sabbath for man? How had he, a Jew raised in Galilee and therefore in a purely Jewish environment, been able to rise up to such a statement of fact, that every institution—even the most sacred—was created by men? In other words, though a man living in a society must submit to the institution, conform to its laws, on the other hand, he must rise above them, must be free in relation to them, able to keep them at his command. How had he, a member of a nation that was taught from earliest childhood to be blindly obedient to the institution, seen so clearly that man cannot be a slave to it. And he was absolutely right, that was exactly true. Only that kind of a relationship guaranteed freedom and the personal freedom of the individual: it also made progress possible in a society. The instant a society recognizes an institution as inviolable, as sacred, it means the end of culture—ossification, stagnation. Pilate had to admit that Jesus, like very few others, including the philosophers, understood that man can only live his life based on the principles of change, continual change. Heraclitus had said it before him: "You cannot enter the same river twice." Jesus was not just another fanatic or utopian who rejected all institutions. He himself taught others to conform to them, but also to reject and modify them when there were sufficiently justifiable reasons, to create new institutions, to treat them as tools. That simple Jew, that carpenter from Nazareth, preached truths with his stories and parables and especially with his life, that only the greatest minds of Greece and Rome were capable of formulating—Plato and Aristotle. He proceeded in freedom and in truth like Socrates. And he achieved it all by such simple means that even those other minds could not have conceived of them. Pilate caught himself repeating exactly what his wife had tried to tell him earlier.

In the beginning, he had been suspicious of Jesus' teachings, they were so unbelievable. He thought he smelled a trick of some kind, though he was not really sure if it was a trick on the part of the Pharisees or the Sadducees, or if it was aimed against the Romans or against the priests. But that

impression was shortlived. He was quickly persuaded that
this man was acting independently, that no one was supporting him. In fact, it surprised him to see this sagacious young
teacher committing a serious tactical error in coming out
against all the governing Jewish groups at once. At the same
time he realized that the broad masses of people who listened
to Jesus had not yet caught on to the real point of his teachings. Excitement was still loud and strong over every new
miracle: talk of healings, raisings from the dead, unheard-of
hauls of fish, multiplication of bread, fell incessantly from
people's lips. Pilate shook out of sheer exasperation: when
would they finally come to understand that the point was not
in the miracles? Would someone finally understand him? And
who would be the first to grasp his meaning, the people or
the priests? Actually, it was an unnecessary question. He
knew the priests well enough to be certain that the events and
teachings would not escape their attention. For that matter,
Jesus never intended to mask himself—he even took as an
example the parable of the Samaritan who took it upon himself to care for the wounded Jew. The only problem was, who
among his listeners was able to see the subtlety of that story,
which was meant to demonstrate how the priests and Levites,
hurrying no doubt to the temple to render their "service to
God", failed to render service to the man in need.

He did not have long to wait for a reaction from the priests
and Pharisees. He began to observe their duels with Jesus.
Their strategy quickly became apparent—they tried to catch
him out on something that would not only completely discredit him before the populace, but present them with a case
for taking him to trial and sentencing him. Like the incident
with the adulteress, whom they brought to him to be judged
because she had been caught in the act of adultery and Moses
commanded them to stone such a sinner. When he first heard
the account, he felt sure Jesus had no way out of the situation.
Then the answer: "Who among you is without sin, let him
throw the first stone." It was not only a testimony to great
wisdom, but to courage as well. And it was no deft trick with
which he managed to dodge the trap set. It was a living
example of the thesis he emphasized in all his actions: free-

dom. After all, in the end the scribes felt that they were
without sin; they considered themselves just men because
they fulfilled all the laws. Therefore, they should have picked
up stones and hurled them at her. But not one of them dared
to do it. Had they perhaps understood that justice was more
than mere fulfillment of rules? Or had they refrained for some
other reason? Perhaps because of what he was writing there
in the sand. It was reported that they went up to him one by
one to read what he was writing.

How he envied Jesus then. It was what he had always
dreamed of—to give people freedom. That Nazarene preached
his, Pilate's, deepest belief, the thing he and his Roman
friends had considered their own deepest discovery. For that
matter, a discovery that was a continuation of Greek thought.
Freedom. The magic word.

When he once remarked to his wife that the truths Jesus
taught were far above the heads of simple fishermen and
farmers, she had disagreed. The form in which he delivered
his teachings, she said, enabled everyone to understand them.
Even then she was already pleading with him to protect Jesus
from impending danger. Jesus must himself have realized the
danger. Pilate sensed a certain haste, an urgency in his activities. As if he were afraid he might not have enough time to
say everything, do everything. He provoked, he made himself
a target, he focused attention on himself. Continuously he
shocked; he would not allow a moment's respite. And he must
have known he would die. He talked about it.

Day by day Pilate waited for news of his tragic death,
though he had to admit that Jesus was successfully stretching
the days of his life, ingeniously postponing his demise. He
won the masses over to himself. They were not only his
support but his defense as well, and in a situation in which
he controlled nearly the whole of the province, not even the
Pharisees could afford to have him murdered. Once it did
happen that word was brought to him of Jesus' death. At the
time he was in the middle of a meal with his wife. The
messenger arrived with the news: Jesus had been killed; he
had simply been stoned. His wife's reaction startled him: she
grew faint, rose from the table. He had not realized she had

felt so involved in the fate of this man. As it soon turned out, the news was a false alarm. Jesus had somehow managed to get away. But it was only a question of time; sooner or later it had to happen. For the moment it seemed that the attempt on his life would restrain him, cool his zeal. In the meantime, the exact opposite happened: he seemed to increase the tempo of his activities, intensify the sharpness of his attacks. Shortly afterwards came the words, repeated later throughout all Palestine: "Woe to you, Pharisees, hypocrites". Pilate had been completely taken aback. It was a formidable accusation.

Through it all, Pilate perceived the paradoxical nature of the situation. Ultimately the teachings of the Pharisees, scribes and priests were merely an example of how it was possible to interpret divine revelation falsely. But the use of that example could cost Jesus his life. Every new "Woe to you!" was one more syllable that would sign his own death sentence. The priests and Pharisees would forgive him nothing. Because they would either have to accept what he said and leave their high offices, or deny everything and try secretly to do away with him. "Whited sepulchers. . . .": Could anything be more apt?

The centurion came in. Whenever Pilate looked at him, he got the impression that his armor was too tight. "What's happening in the city?" he asked automatically.

"Jesus has been sentenced to death by the chief priest and the Sanhedrin."

Though he had long foreseen this eventuality, the centurion's words still stunned him. He had nurtured a hope that Jesus would somehow escape their verdict. There was a long pause. Finally he asked, "What do you think, what will they do next?"

The centurion thought a moment. When he spoke, his voice carried a distinctly nervous edge. "I think they will either kill him in secret—though that's highly unlikely, they would be afraid of risking the responsibility before his followers—or, if they want to pursue the matter through official channels, then sooner or later they'll come here."

"For what?" Pilate wanted to make him keep on talking.

"They'll accuse him before you and demand his arrest.

Then, when we have him in our prison, we'll be the ones fighting off the mobs trying to break him out."

"Nonsense. In order to turn him over to us, they have to charge him with something. As far as I recall, it has never been said that he killed anyone, or stole, or committed a dishonest act."

"And if they accuse him of rebellion against Rome?"

The question took him by surprise. He thought no one would ever stumble on the charge, which he considered to be his own original concept. He tried to throw the centurion off the track. "That's ridiculous. He never meddled in politics. I believe it was you who told me about his 'Give to Caesar what is Caesar's.' "

"Yes, but the possibility still exists. When he entered Jerusalem for the festival there were rumours that he was coming to take over and to liberate the city from the Romans."

"Yes, but he didn't take over, nor did he ever intend to." He tried to take the centurion unawares. "But I can see that you're very anxious about him."

"Yes. I have been for a long time," the other replied quietly.

"How do you know him?"

The centurion was silent for a moment. "Some time ago," he began softly, "my old and faithful servant, who works at my estate outside Capernaum, fell seriously ill. He is much more than a servant, he is my friend, almost like a father. He raised me." He spoke in short, simple sentences, pausing every few seconds as if he were seeing into the past. "His condition worsened. It was hopeless, he was dying. I did everything I could, but nothing helped. Then someone brought me word that Jesus was preaching in the town. I already knew about his cures, how he healed the sick. It was my last hope. I went to him. He was sitting on a rock. He looked very tired. There were so many people crowding around him, pressing on him that I could barely force my way through. When I reached him I simply made my request."

"How's that?" Pilate interrupted, amazed. "You wanted a Jew to enter your house, a pagan's house?"

"I wasn't thinking about anything except saving my friend."

"Then what? Tell me."

"He answered me without the slightest hesitation: 'Very well, I will come to you'. Then I saw his feet, they were sore and bleeding. His face was hot and covered with perspiration, and his lips were parched—it was a scorching day. I thought to myself, he won't make it there in time. Without knowing what I was saying, I cried out in despair: 'Just say the word, and the illness will depart from him.' Then he looked at me oddly and said simply, 'Go, your servant lives.' "

"And what did you do?"

"There was nothing else to do. I went back."

"Did you believe his word?"

"I suppose I did."

"Well, and then what?"

"On my way back, my people spotted me from a distance. They ran out to meet me, crying and shouting for joy that the sick man was well. I checked to see when his condition had changed, and it was exactly when he had said, 'your servant lives'."

"This is all very strange. But I see why you would like him set free."

After a pause, the centurion said, "Not just me".

"Who else?"

"A great many people. Certainly your wife, sir," he answered timidly.

Pilate felt mildly offended that the centurion had made bold to mention to his wife. But he asked quietly, "How do you know this?"

"She has spoken to me many times about him, asked me questions—what I knew, or if I had any new information."

"She's still afraid that one of these days the Pharisees will secretly kill him."

He crossed over to the window and watched the soldiers standing in the torchlight. "Ultimately," he began slowly, "it's not solely in my own interest that he should live. It is certainly also in the interest of Rome that the Pharisees do not remain the exclusive ruling power here. That is why we cannot commit any error that will permit them to accomplish their schemes through us." He paused and yawned. "I must go and get some sleep now. It's high time, it's almost morning."

He lay down but, despite the hour, sleep eluded him. The sentry's steps measured off the time. He lay awake a long time, trying to settle on a plan of action, when he suddenly remembered that Jesus came from Nazareth. He sat upright in his bed—why, that put him under Herod's jurisdiction. That was he would do. If they came to him he would simply send them to Herod. Let him judge Jesus. Won't he be surprised, he thought to himself, amused. Let him have the satisfaction of allowing him to judge one of his subjects in my city. And I will be rid of the whole affair.

Pilate was jarred out of a deep sleep by a manservant. He looked up, saw an alarmed face hanging over him. "They're here," the man said.

Pilate sat up with a start. "Who?"

"The priests with Jesus."

"Now? What time is it?"

"Five."

"In the afternoon?"

"No, morning."

"What do they want?"

"They want you to judge him."

"At this hour? Absolutely not! Tell them to get out, and as fast as possible."

The servant left. Pilate rubbed the sleep from his face and eyes. So they had decided to sentence Jesus to death through him after all. And so early, as early as they could possibly make it. While Jerusalem slept. No. Let them wait. He was not going to get up until eight.

The manservant appeared in the door again. "Sir, they won't go. They demand an immediate hearing. They say it is a matter of great importance and that if it leads to trouble they will denounce you to Rome. What shall we do?"

Pilate flinched. They were showing their teeth, he thought to himself. He said to the servant in a conciliatory tone of voice, "Oh, well, they could have said it was important in the first place. Very well, I will get up."

He dressed leisurely, dawdling deliberately to keep them waiting—it was a small satisfaction he always permitted himself with them. Unseen by them, he observed their group from behind a curtain. Not one familiar face among them. They stood on the terrace in a tight little pack, straining visibly to check their tongues, and only whispering among themselves in quick, urgent spurts. A short distance ahead of them stood Jesus. His soiled, wrinkled garments contrasted glaringly with the ceremonial robes of the priests. Pilate could not see his face; his head was bowed low on his chest. He appeared to be on the verge of exhaustion, scarcely able to keep his balance.

He would have made them wait there a while longer, but he felt sorry for the prisoner. He stepped out on the terrace and listened with a stony face and silence to their salutations and assurances of devotion and gratitude. Midway through them, he broke in with a brusque, "What is it you want?"

They pointed to Jesus. "We want you to judge him."

The centurion was right, Pilate thought to himself. Without so much as a glance in his direction, he retorted, "You have your law, judge him yourselves."

"He deserves death, but the Law prevents us from putting a man to death."

No, not even the centurion had anticipated this, he reflected. They have brought him here for me to kill him! I was supposed to commit their crime for them. With an effort at controlling his voice, he asked them, "What has he done?"

"He incites the people against paying taxes to Caesar."

Pilate snorted ironically. "And since when have the priests cared so much about the imperial treasury?"

Undeterred, they went on: "He has proclaimed himself the King of the Jews."

"Very well, let him come in," he snapped. "I will question him."

He inspected the prisoner now for the first time. Even had he known Jesus earlier, he would have hardly recognized him: his face was badly swollen and darkly bruised under the eyes;

blood, dripping from his nose and cut lips, formed black clots in his beard. What a beating they have given him, Pilate thought. He eyes swept over Jesus' mussed hair and torn, rumpled garments; he noticed traces of spittle on his clothing. And so, he mused ironically, this is what rebels against authority look like. In Rome they beat them like this, too. Except they probably do not spit. I might not have a chance to look like this, he thought bitterly.

"So, you are the King of the Jews?" he asked abruptly.

Pilate braced himself for a barrage of oaths and entreaties. There was a long silence. For a moment he thought the prisoner had not registered the question. He looked up to repeat it. His eyes met a steady gaze from under red-rimmed lids.

"Do you say this from yourself, or have others told it to you?"

The words were uttered with effort through split, puffy lips.

Suddenly Pilate heard his own voice excusing, justifying himself before the prisoner: "Am I a Jew? Your own nation and the chief priests have delivered you up to me. What have you done?" Instantly he regretted his words.

A barely audible whisper reached him: "My kingdom is not of this world. If my kingdom were of this world, my servants would certainly fight so that I should not be delivered to the Jews."

Pilate felt almost hurt by his reply. He spoke like a prisoner to a procurator—but he was on his side, he wanted to help him. He did not want that kind of answer. He repeated the question. "Are you a king, then?"

This time the answer was unmistakable: "You have said it."

He lost his patience; he was sorry he had asked the question to begin with. He stepped directly in front of Jesus and shouted angrily into his face. "Listen to me. You can't talk like that. I understand you but others don't understand you, especially those who want to see you dead." He exploded. "Why did you have to rail against them in the first place, with those 'whitened sepulchers', and those 'broods of vipers'? They're like that, I know, but why did you have to tell them

to their faces? Why did you continually provoke them? All
those healings on the Sabbath, those barbs against the temple,
and all that talk about mercy being more important than
their sacrifices. Where did it get you? You could be free now."

He stopped short, suddenly realizing how he was contra-
dicting himself. Denying the thing that only a short time ago
he had admitted as his, Jesus', greatest intellectual achieve-
ment. It was a good thing his wife was not there to hear him.

He started toward the door, when the same quiet voice
reached him again: "For this I was born and for this I came
into the world, that I should give testimony to the truth."

Pilate felt his anger suddenly leave him. Give testimony to
the truth, he repeated in his mind. It was what he had always
dreamed of doing. He drew up to Jesus and peered closely
into his face as if he were seeing him for the first time. He
must have a fever, he thought to himself. He can hardly stand
on his feet. That beaten face must hurt him a great deal.

He could not bring himself to look at Jesus that way much
longer. He fluttered his eyelids, then dropped his gaze. Suddenly he wanted very much to return to his own reality. He
looked down at his own manicured hands, he adjusted his
immaculate toga, then took another long look at Jesus. No,
he would not want to be in his place.

"What is truth?" he muttered, moving toward the door.
He did not want him here any longer. He disliked the company of losers. He went back out on the sunny terrace and
addressed the Jews curtly: "I find no guilt in him."

They burst into vociferous protests. "He walks around the
whole country from Galilee to Judea, stirring up the people,
proclaiming the coming of a new kingdom."

Pilate knew he should not ask anything more, nor even say
another word. He told himself: Do not get involved in a
debate with them, because you will lose. He felt he should
say simply, "I am releasing him". But he could not resist.
He asked casually, "Around Galilee, you say? Is he not by
chance a Galilean?"

"Yes . . . Galilean." They suddenly grew quiet, wary, they
sensed a catch.

"Ah, yes." He pretended surprise. "I hear that Herod is in

the city for the holy days. Jesus is his subject. Take him to Herod, let him judge him."

They did not move. They had not expected it; they could barely conceal their surprise. The furious whispering started again. Pilate watched them with a sneer. How satisfying to hear their nervous murmurings. Finally they took flight like a flock of flushed sparrows, very angrily shoving Jesus along in front of them.

From his window, Pilate could see large numbers of people gathering on the square outside the Praetorium. They formed into small groups and stood talking and gesticulating in the direction of the palace. They must be Jesus' followers, Pilate thought to himself. They think Jesus is here.

He summoned the centurion. "Well, we're rid of the trouble," he said to him. "I sent them to Herod."

"That's very bad, sir," the centurion said in a clipped tone of voice.

Pilate was offended by his tone. "Why do you say it's bad?"

"Forgive me, but after questioning him you said, 'I find no guilt in him.' Then you should have ordered him released. But you sent him away."

"To give Herod a treat," he laughed.

"I'm not so sure Herod will be inclined to judge him. If he did so, he would gain the support of the priests and Pharisees, but turn the population against him."

"That's exactly why I sent them to Herod. He won't condemn Jesus to death. He made one stupid mistake like that with that Baptist, and anyway, he was drunk at the time. He won't repeat the mistake. He'll let him go."

"I certainly hope it happens that way," the centurion sighed.

"You always have doubts of one kind or other," Pilate said. He returned to the window. The square was slowly filling with throngs of people. "Look how many of them have massed out there. They think I'm holding Jesus."

The centurion scanned the square uneasily. People were still streaming in. "I don't understand it," he said. "They should know by now that Jesus is with Herod."

"One way or the other, the matter is settled. Now I can have breakfast in peace. I haven't eaten a thing all morning."

Breakfast was a protracted affair; he liked to linger over his meals. Next he received his morning reports. Nothing out of the ordinary. He had already satisfied himself that it would be a day like any other when a messenger hurried in with word that the priests were waiting with Jesus out on the terrace. A fresh wave of alarm swept over him. "What do they want?"

"Herod has sent the prisoner back to you. He says that though Jesus is one of his subjects, this is the city of Jerusalem, and he does not wish to intrude in your sphere of jurisdiction."

There seemed little else for him to do but convey his appreciation to Herod for so magnanimous a gesture and assure him of his sincerest regards and friendship. "Write it very ornately," he instructed his scribe. "Then I'll sign it."

As he passed into the hearing room, he was struck by the uproar coming from outside the Praetorium. He went to the window. The square was crammed with a sea of dark and angry faces; he had never before seen such a crowd on the square. Just as the centurion had predicted—the mob was massing outside to fight for its master. Suddenly an idea flashed through his mind. He summoned the jailer. "Whom do you have in the prisons under sentence of death?" he asked him.

"There a few of them. Of the Jews, Barabbas and Didymus."

"Barabbas the bandit, is that right?"

"Yes."

"Good."

He was going to surprise them. He crossed to the windows that opened on to the terrace. Jesus was standing off to one side in an odd white robe that hung about him crookedly. Where did that come from? he wondered. Did they try to make a buffoon of him over at Herod's? Jesus seemed to have reached the limit of his strength.

Pilate ordered criers posted at intervals around the square, then he called in the interpreter. He decided he was going to pay off all the old scores. He would have his fun, he was going to show them. He stepped outside, sat down in his chair without a word, and listened icily to the priests' complaints. When they were through he addressed them, without any prefatory remarks, in short, concise phrases, so the interpreter would have time enough to translate and the criers time enough to relay it to the crowd: "You have turned this man over to me as one who perverts the people. And behold I, having examined him, find no guilt in him of the things of which you accuse him. No, nor Herod either. Because I sent him to him, and behold nothing worthy of death has been proved to him." He paused, then went on: "But you have a custom at the Passover, in which as a sign of Rome's benevolence and generosity toward the Jewish nation, one Jewish prisoner may be released."

Silence cut like a scythe across the square. Pilate noted with satisfaction that his words had taken them by surprise.

"Whom do you want that I should release?" he cried out. "Barabbas or Jesus, whom they call the Christ?"

The silence deepened. So there would be no doubt in their minds as to his meaning, he added, "Do you will that I release to you the King of the Jews?"

Suddenly a solitary voice sounded shrilly over the hushed square: "Barabbas!"

Instantly the throng took up the name like a political slogan, and in a moment the whole square reverberated with the deafening cry, "Ba-rab-bas!"

It struck Pilate like a blow. He felt as if he were suffocating, choking. He shut his eyes. The clamor only intensified.

Now he understood that he had fallen into a trap of his own making, laid by his own vanity. And there was no way out. He could not act against the people's will. He began to shriek hysterically at them in an attempt to drown out the roar of the mob. Slowly the noise subsided.

"What will you, then, that I do to the King of the Jews?" he shouted.

Again a lone voice cried out in the confused stillness: "Crucify him!" And after it, like a roll of thundering echoes, the throng seized upon the words and began to chant: "Cru-ci-fy him! Cru-ci-fy him!"

That was the second blow. How was this possible? The people demanding the death of their master? The same people who followed him, who listened to his sermons, who were healed by him? The same people who only a few days earlier had wildly welcomed him into Jerusalem were now screaming for his execution? How could that be? For what? Why did they want his death? He didn't understand. The mob bellowed in unison, working itself into a frenzy.

A soldier came up from behind with a scroll in his hand. "A message from your wife, sir."

He took the scroll and returned with the soldier to the Praetorium. "Summon the centurion," he barked.

Roughly, impatiently, he unraveled the scroll and read. His eyes sped over the contents, but without really focusing on the words. The letters seemed to slip away over the edges before his eyes; he could not concentrate on the message. He started again, from the beginning, slowly. "She wants me to release him," he muttered aloud to himself. "As if it were up to me," he added angrily.

The centurion entered, his face inscrutable as always, though Pilate thought he could detect a strained, tightened look. He fairly pounced on him. "Have they gone mad?! What's happening? Have you gone mad?! You say Jerusalem is packed with his followers! This is insanity. Do you hear what they're screaming out there? They're demanding his death!"

The centurion was silent a moment, then very deliberately he said, "You should have dismissed them altogether, at the very start, and not sent them to Herod."

"Should have, should have, I'm not asking what I should have done, but what I should do now."

The centurion said nothing.

Pilate felt his skin prickle with cold. He fell heavily against the wall. "Yes, I made a foolish mistake." The mob howled outside without respite.

An idea raced to his mind. It was desperate, frantic, but maybe the last thing, the only thing he could do: scourge him. If they saw him whipped, bleeding, they would have a change of heart. If they saw what their madness had driven them to. . . .

He returned to the terrace, signaled that he wished to speak. An expectant hush dropped over the square. His steady voice belied the fear that was welling inside him. He said, "I find no cause of death in him." He pointed to Jesus. "Therefore, I will chastise him and let him go." Too late he realized the contradiction in his words.

The criers had not yet finished relaying his words around the square when a tumultuous uproar broke loose from the crowd. This was no longer chanting, but frenzied shrieking of "Crucify him!" which detonated into one hideous wail. Pilate rose and barked the command: "Scourge him."

He left the terrace shaken. He half hoped that the rabble would attempt to storm the palace, then he could give his men the order to rout them. But they were just as aware as he was, and they kept their places and screamed. Let them scream themselves out, he raved to himself. Let the sun work on them a while, maybe they'll disperse. But he knew that they wouldn't.

The centurion returned, barely holding back his anger. "Why did you order him scourged, sir? For what? You know he is innocent!"

Pilate exploded. "Because I'm trying to save him! Don't you see what's happening? Do you want it to end in a massacre? This is our last try, to play to their pity. When they see him scourged, maybe they'll back down. Why, he's their teacher! And if they don't stop, then that's it, it's finished. After he is whipped, bring Jesus to me. Maybe we should wait a bit longer? Maybe they'll begin to disperse. Take your time, don't hurry. We have time now. Let the sun bake them a while."

He paced the floor nervously. Finally he halted at the window and scanned the mob. For the first time he noticed large numbers of priests scattered among the crowd, and directly below his windows a whole assembly of them stood clustered tightly together. That must be the core of command, he thought. It must be where the first cry of "Crucify him!"

had originated. "Go," he told the centurion. "There's no purpose in waiting." They would play out the comedy to the end. Maybe, just maybe it might succeed. . . .

He emerged on the hot terrace. At the sight of him, the roar in the square rose in a crescendo. "Bring the prisoner here," he commanded one of the soldiers.

The man who staggered toward him on the stairs now had no relation to the one he had questioned earlier this morning. This was a frightful mass of blood. His face was one dark clot of blood, down which fresh red drops trickled from under a plaited crown of thorny stems crammed down on his head. Pilate could barely bring himself to look at him. He strode up to Jesus, seized him by the shoulder and pushed him toward the balustrade. With a dramatic flourish, he pronounced three words to the expectant crowd, words with which he indicated each and every one of them in the square: "Behold the man."

An ember of hope still smoldered inside him—that they would be moved to pity at the sight. But again he had miscalculated. The howl of the priests reached his ears: "Crucify him!"

Like an echo, the mob answered, "Cru-ci-fy him!"

Pilate was beside himself with fury. "Why? What evil has he done?" he shouted. But the torrent from the square drowned him out.

He rose, and as he stalked toward the Praetorium, he flung at the priests, "Then you take him and crucify him, because I find no fault in him."

"We have a Law, and according to the Law he ought to die, because he made himself the son of God."

The words reached him at the entrance to the Praetorium. This began to exceed the limits of sanity. He felt the ground sliding under his feet. He ordered Jesus brought to him inside. The mingled odors of blood and perspiration followed him in.

"Where are you from?" he demanded. Jesus was silent. "You do not speak to me? Don't you know that I have the power to crucify you, and I have the power to release you?"

He saw the swollen lips move; he heard the barely distinguishable words: "You would not have any power over me were it not given to you from above. Therefore, he who delivered me to you has the greater sin."

Pilate could not help feeling impressed by his calm. The roar from the square filled the room. From time to time, a voice bellowed above the rest with a curse, an oath, a threat. He could feel his rage and resistance mounting at the sound— against the pressure of the mob, against his own helplessness, against being cornered this way. Now he knew what he would do: he would release Jesus in spite of the priests and the crazed rabble. He started toward the door, and at that moment a soldier entered. "Annas and Caiaphas wish to speak with you, sir."

"Let them come in."

They probably want to help me make up my mind, he thought wryly. But they are badly mistaken.

They came in bowing and speaking. At first, as usual, Pilate could not understand what they were getting at. But he was used to that: lengthy sentences that said nothing, that probed and marked off the terrain, that prepared the way for them to strike. He knew their methods well. But today he was not amused as he usually was. Finally it began to dawn on him: they were threatening him. More than that. They were bringing their influence in Rome out into the open. Though he had long been aware of it, there had always been a guarded web of silence around the subject. Now they were flaunting their power. His anger quickened, but he refused to be provoked. He listened, he would say nothing. His curiosity was piqued: how far would they go today? They were speaking bluntly: they would inform Caesar about this incident. Directly to his face they were unfolding their plan of revenge. They put it very tidily: "If you release this man, then you are not a friend of Caesar. Whoever makes himself a king opposes Caesar."

This was something novel, unexpected. He never thought they would go to such lengths, to threaten so openly, so boldly. His first impulse was to revile them and throw them out. But he restrained the impulse. He suddenly realized that they were in dead earnest; they were seriously prepared to destroy him in order to push through their plan. Only now did he fully understand just how badly they wanted Jesus dead. Then he remembered Tiberius, with his piercing, suspicious little eyes. And doomed Sejanus, and all his friends who had to die. Just let them denounce him to Rome, that he had released a rebel, the King of the Jews . . . and they would do it, there was no doubt about that. Fear swept him like fingers of ice. He had not realized that they hated Jesus to this degree. He could almost feel the fate of his friends on his own skin. So little was needed for a messenger from Rome to arrive with an order to appear before the Emperor and a command to give up his Governor's post. In that one instant, every vestige of tension fell away. He felt suddenly cold and indifferent. He admitted: the shot was right on target. Yet perhaps it was better that it had come now, rather than later, when it would be too late. He shrugged. Was he going to risk his future, his life, the life of his wife for one Jew? If they wanted his death so badly, they could help themselves.

He returned to the terrace. Without a glance in the direction of Jesus, he seated himself on the judgment seat. Leaning against the arms of the chair, he felt a stickiness in his right palm. He looked; it was covered with blood. He was perplexed—blood? From where? Then he remembered. Of course, Jesus's shoulder had been bleeding. He ordered water brought to him. He could almost see the silence settling over the mob. He stared out at the priests, at the dense sea of heads and felt a tide of hatred surge inside him at the sight of them. "I'm not through playing with you yet," he muttered under his breath. Thrusting his arm at Jesus, he announced, "Behold your King".

The throng bellowed back at him: "Away with him. Crucify him!"

He kept them waiting a long moment in suspense. "Shall I crucify your King?" he said finally.

"We have no king but Caesar."

Again he made them wait. Then, with an offhanded flick of his wrist, he tossed the order to the soldiers: "Crucify him."

He rinsed his hands in a stream of water that a servant poured. As he washed them, he turned in the direction of the priests and said, "I am innocent of the blood of this just man. This is your affair."

A voice in the crowd screamed back at him: "His blood be upon us and upon our children!" The crowd took it up like a chant.

And that was the end. He withdrew into the Praetorium amid a deafening chorus of, "His blood be upon us and upon our children!"

He thought he would vomit out of disgust. He rested a moment in the Praetorium, then called for a scribe. He dictated a sign in Latin, Greek, and Hebrew: "Jesus of Nazareth, the King of the Jews."

"Have them carry it along the way," he told him, "and then have them affix it to the cross."

After this last order, he retired to his chambers—only to be summoned before the palace again minutes later. One of the priests wished to speak to him about an urgent matter.

It was one of Caiaphas's closest advisers, with the request, in the name of the High Priest, that the text of the sign be immediately changed.

"It should be written, 'He who said I am the King of the Jews.' After all, he was not the King of the Jews, no one considered him as such, only he called himself that."

Pilate listened coldly to his protestations. He said curtly, "What I have written, I have written." He whirled around and stalked out. One more small, futile revenge accomplished. He returned exhausted to his chambers and lay down. A long time he lay in the cool and quiet of the room, with the curtains tightly drawn, until he finally fell asleep.

It was the rumblings of a storm that finally roused him. He gave a start—the room was in almost total darkness. He pushed aside the curtains: low coal-black clouds hung over all of Jerusalem. He passed into the courtyard. Large heavy drops of rain began to fall. Quick flashes of lightning lit the sky; thunder crackled in the air. In the cool wet rain he felt as if all his humiliation, all his weakness—everything he had been subjected to—were suddenly being rinsed from him.

Late in the afternoon, Joseph of Arimathea came to him.

Pilate was startled to see how shrunken and gray and haggard he looked. He did not wish to show any surprise; he greeted him simply with the words, "I haven't seen you for a long time".

Joseph appeared not to have heard. "I have come to you with a request. Grant me the favor of letting me bury the body of the teacher from Nazareth."

"Is he dead already?"

"Yes. He is dead. Just a few moments ago."

"Why do you want to bury him? Are you one of his followers?"

"His friend."

"I didn't expect it."

"He has many friends."

"Oh?" he turned on him furiously. "Then where were you when everyone was shouting, 'Crucify him!'?" It was the last of his anger.

Joseph hung his head. "I knew nothing about it," he said in his low melodious voice. "Even now, the people of Jerusalem don't really know what has happened. I learned about Jesus' arrest in the Garden of Olives in Gethsemane very early in the morning from one of his disciples. I dressed immediately and went to find him. I discovered that, although I am a member of the Sanhedrin, I had been overlooked—I was not informed about the special meeting of the Sanhedrin at which he was tried. . . . They knew I was one of his followers. I couldn't get hold of any information; no one knew anything anywhere. Until finally, by chance, I learned that Jesus was here with you, that he had already been sentenced to death by the Sanhedrin. I tried to come. Do you know that I was prevented from getting to you? Anyway, it was too late by then. They had already led him away to be crucified. I didn't see him, there were so many soldiers and Pharisees and priests around the condemned men."

"Very well. Take him, bury him," Pilate said after a pause. He turned away to signify that the meeting was at an end and strode over to the window. He stared at the drenched courtyard steaming and drying in the hot afternoon sun. A guard's voice shook him out of his reverie. "A Jewish delegation has arrived."

Them again. What more did they want? "What do they want?" he called out.

"They ask you to agree that the condemned men be finished off quickly and taken down from the crosses because of tomorrow's Sabbath."

With a nod of his head Pilate gave his permission. When they had departed, he ordered the centurion found. He wanted to speak with him. But he was nowhere around. Obviously avoiding me, Pilate thought to himself. Finally, late in the evening, he caught sight of the centurion crossing the courtyard. He called him over. He approached slowly, with visible reluctance.

"How was it with his death, tell me?" Pilate questioned him. "It's strange that he died so quickly."

The centurion averted his eyes. "He was very tired," he began in a muted voice. "He couldn't even carry the cross. At the very beginning of the march, he fell under the weight of it."

"So what did you do?"

"I had some villager carry it for him. But he was very faint, I thought he would surely die along the way. He reached the top of the hill completely exhausted. I never expected him to live another six hours on the cross. We crucified him at three, and he died around nine. But the last three hours were really a matter of slow dying."

"Around nine," Pilate repeated. "That was about the time the storm passed over Jerusalem."

"Yes."

"Did you break his bones?"

"No. When the order came from you to finish them off, he was already dead, so one of the soldiers only pierced his side. Then they buried him in a sepulcher nearby."

"Yes, I know," he interrupted him.

Throughout that night Pilate had all the garrisons kept in a state of readiness. He himself did not even bother to undress and only once or twice during the night did he doze fitfully. He insisted on being kept informed about the situation in the

city. As the hours slipped by, he grew increasingly convinced
that the expected threat of rioting stemming from Jesus' death
was illusory. The city was peaceful. Not everyone knew yet,
not everyone believed yet. Some odd and distorted rumors
had spread, but this was hardly the atmosphere that produced
disturbances.

On the Sabbath, under pretext of inspecting the garrisons,
Pilate rode the length and breadth of the city several times.
The streets were bustling with pilgrims, as they did every
year at this time: a colorful and often exotic assortment of
fishermen, shepherds, farmers, petty merchants from Galilee,
Judea, and Asia Minor. He watched them with contempt and
a burning rage. For their passivity, and for his own weakness.
He was struck by how quiet the crowds were in the streets.
No, it was not his imagination; he had never seen such a
restrained atmosphere during the festival days. They already
knew, he thought. Every year he rode the streets with a
strong, well-armed escort, prepared against assault by visiting
outsiders who were always hostile towards the Romans. But
this year, he could discern no sign of antagonism. People
quickly gave way at the sight of the cavalcade. There were
none of he usual catcalls, oaths, abuses or rock throwing. He
sensed that their restraint stemmed not simply from fear, but
actual horror at what they had perpetrated, all of them, he
and they both.

That evening he received word that some priests were back,
insisting that they had to confer with him. He was surprised—
such a holy day, and they decided on a meeting with a pagan?
Surely this was without precedent? It had to be something
extraordinarily important. He went out to them. They looked
worried.

"Excellency, we have remembered what the seducer of the
people said while he was still alive; that after three days he
would rise again. Command, therefore, that the sepulcher be
guarded until the third day. Then his disciples will be unable
to come and steal him away and spread the word among the
people that he has risen from the dead. Because then the last
error will be worse than the first."

Pilate detected a different tone of voice in their petition.

Almost as if they were confiding in him. He smiled to himself. So he had become their accomplice. They were treating him like one of their own. Revulsion shook him. He looked at them. Beneath the haughty veneer and seeming indifference, they were nervous. Now they realized the mistake they had made: they had not foreseen Joseph's request. They had not counted on Jesus' body being buried in a separate tomb.

He refused to be drawn by their familiar tone. "You may have guards," he said tartly. "Go and guard it as you know how."

He ate no supper that evening and went to sleep early. But it hardly resembled sleep. It was a tossing state of nightmares and hallucinations. He thought he heard the crowd roaring again. He thought he saw Jesus standing before him again in the empty room of the Praetorium—that horrible, battered face, that crushed, broken figure. He dozed, woke, dozed again, consciousness mingling with dreams.

He sat up with a start. It was nearly dawn. He thought he heard the rapid whack of heavyshod sandals, as if soldiers were running urgently around the empty square. He got up quickly. It was no dream, it was real. He could hear shouting, running footsteps. He threw on his tunic and ran out. A group of his soldiers stood huddled together—they were without helmets or shields or spears, their faces white in the twilight, their eyes wide and staring. Palace guards flocked and crowded around them.

"What has happened?" Pilate called out to them.

The soldiers turned blank faces to him and said nothing.

JUDAS

He had taken part in a number of conspiracies and revolts—
and in their crushing defeats as well. He had barely escaped
crucifixion during one of the uprisings against Rome. Then
zeal slowly gave way to disillusionment: he began to see
through the intrigues of those who regarded themselves as the
leaders of the nation; he saw how they trafficked in human
blood. So Judas Iscariot—spirited, hot-headed, impatient—
withdrew into himself, grew sullen and embittered. He tended
a small shop on the edge of the town, where he sold caraway,
pepper, and aniseed—as contemptuous of himself as he was
of his customers.

Then, when he had become resigned to the idea that
nothing in his life would ever change again, news reached
him of a new prophet, Jesus of Nazareth, who was travelling
around Palestine, teaching. He heard about miracles and
verbal skirmishes with the Pharisees and Sadducees. But he
was not going to get excited at the news, not this time. He
simply did not believe in prophets any more. He had seen too
many for his liking. Alive and crucified. He was not going to
make the same mistake again. But the news kept pouring in,
gathering strength like a wave, growing all the time in detail
and excitement. Until the day he heard that Jesus was coming
to his town. He could not help himself, then; in spite of all
his resolutions, he went. After all, Jesus was going to be in
the area anyway. Judas looked, heard, and stayed. And he
believed. Like a madman he believed, just as in his younger
days. But with one difference: now he knew about people;
experience made him a better judge of character. He stayed
because he was convinced that Palestine had never seen a

man quite like this one. And from that day on, by day and
by night, he followed at Jesus' side.

They were great days! Huge crowds, continual meetings,
discussions, assemblies, speeches, sermons stretching into
hours. Days full of the poor, the sick, the unfortunate; full of
lepers and paralytics and men possessed. They were days
filled with incidents bordering on the incredible, filled with
moments when he could not believe what his eyes were telling
him, when he questioned his own sanity, or wondered aloud
if it was all just a dream. Before his very eyes, scales fell from
the bodies of lepers and sores closed over; paralytics flexed
their limbs and walked; the sick stood up from their pallets.
He lived in a constant state of exaltation. And not only he.
Everyone—from the clamoring masses who flocked to Jesus,
cried out to him, knelt to him and begged from him, to the
witnesses who watched and shook their heads in disbelief—
everyone succumbed to the mass euphoria. And every day
bore out Judas's conviction anew, that this time he had not
been mistaken—he was right to have picked Jesus.

With his closest followers he travelled through Galilee,
Samaria, Judea. They slept in the homes of people only too
happy to lodge them, or under the open sky; they ate in
abundance at the tables of wealthy benefactors, or they simply
went hungry; they travelled the country on the wave of the
fame of the worker of miracles, or they were cast out and
reviled for the works of Beelzebub, prince of hell.

Within Jesus' little group of followers Judas proved very
useful. Somebody had to manage the purse and make sure
there was enough food to eat the next day. He accepted and
kept account of all the offerings, large and small, from friends,
benefactors, and strangers wishing, to help Jesus; and he
dispensed these monies as well: he bought their food, he paid
for their lodgings, and he distributed alms to the poor.

But as the months passed and the initial shock and novelty
wore off, Judas began to wonder what was it all leading to?
What did Jesus want to achieve? He had placed Jesus' activities in the context of his own aspirations: political. For that
matter they all did, all the other eleven who made up Jesus'
company of guards. For example, once he heard the mother

of the sons of Zebedee come up to the master and say to him: "Command, that these two sons of mine may sit one at your right hand and the other at your left hand in your kingdom." Then another time he listened, considerably surprised, to his companions arguing among themselves about who was going to be the most important in the kingdom. When he considered his own future, he did not wonder about whether he would be on the right side or the left side of Jesus, like the sons of Zebedee. He was already well placed. He was in charge of the purse; in the future he would be overseer of the treasury in Jesus' kingdom.

Judas had little regard for his companions. At times he thought them downright ignorant. They understood very little of what was happening, and he never bothered to discuss with them matters that he felt went over their heads. He kept to himself, off to the side; in their close-knit little group, he was the cat that walked by himself. Slowly, all his old dreams of a reconstructed powerful Israel, long since extinguished, sparked alive again. He watched Jesus' activities with considerable satisfaction. For the first time in his life, he felt he had met a man genuinely concerned with the good of the nation and not just with his own; an uncompromising critic of all evil, no matter who the perpetrator; a prophet who sought to reestablish the true essence of the Covenant—well did he remember Jesus' words: "I come not to destroy the Law and the Prophets, but to fulfill"; a prophet who urged an end to the formalism of the Law, the soulless rituals and sacrifices, who demanded true fidelity to God through a life of justice. In Jesus he saw a father to the nation, one who understood its weaknesses, faults and sorespots—and who recognized their source in its very leaders: the Pharisees and Sadducees, from among whom most of the priests were recruited. Jesus was highly critical of the Sadducees' lax attitude toward the traditions of the Law and the prophets; nevertheless his main target was the Pharisees who, through their influence with the broad masses of people, strongly affected their level of morality and religion. It infuriated the master to see the hypocrisy of the scribes: their attention to forms and appearances, the pains they took to avoid contact with anyone they suspected of being a sinner, their observance of the minutiae of the Law and rituals, while they neglected the real essence of the Law of Moses, which was justice and love. And how pure and exemplary and immune they were. Judas was delighted to see how the greater the number of people Jesus attracted, the more boldly he spoke out against the Pharisees: on the one hand he strongly exhorted his listeners to heed their teachings, on the other, he warned them against the demoralizing influence of the Pharisees' own example—the contrast between what they practised and what they preached.

Nothing escaped the master's attention; every detail he observed in life found its way into his teachings: the Pharisee they came across distributing alms at an intersection of streets; the Pharisee with his face streaked with dirt, and hair tousled and uncombed as a sign that he was doing penance; the Pharisee they saw standing vainly in the center at the temple; the Pharisee at a feast who rushed to occupy the first place at the table; the Pharisee who felt insulted because he was not addressed as Rabbi—all of them returned later in Jesus' parables, admonitions, and teachings.

Judas understood, as few could, what it meant to attack the Pharisees and Sadducees. To anyone who followed politics it was obvious that these groups, which held sway over the Jewish nation, were not going to stand idly by and watch a new, hostile power rise up alongside of them: Jesus of Nazareth with his disciples and the masses of people advancing behind him. He had to give Jesus credit for foresight—that he dared to speak out against them only after he had gained wide popular support among the masses.

At first the Pharisees adopted a wait-and-see policy. They did not know what Jesus' attitude towards them would be. In time, they realized that he was their most menacing opponent, who could in no way be compared to their old adversaries, the Sadducees. One thing they could not deny—he certainly knew the Scriptures. And they had to admit he was an extraordinary teacher. His parables conveyed perfectly what he wanted to say; he operated brilliantly with metaphors and allegories; he constructed graceful, easy-to-remember sayings in verse. But most important, he was a prophet of the people. He swept up and carried along the insatiable masses of the common people—the crowd. And herein lay his power—and the threat to the Pharisees. Not just to them, but to the whole of the Law and the Prophets. In his teachings they read a desecration of all the things they held sacred, a violation of the traditional truths of the chosen nation. Who was he to speak out against the nation's fathers, to consider himself greater than Moses? Who did not keep the holy day? Who scoffed at the teachers and priests? Where did he intend to lead the nation? What motives did he conceal?

Judas knew it was only a matter of time before the Sadducees recognized Jesus as their enemy as well. At first they enjoyed his attacks on the Pharisees—until they themselves came under attack precisely for falsely teaching the Scriptures. And that was how these two hostile groups, Pharisees and Sadducees, incessantly quarrelling and at odds with each other reached an understanding, joined forces and moved forward to fight. They hit hard—and Judas had not foreseen this—precisely where Jesus had gained his greatest successes: in the opinion of the crowd. They were unscrupulous. The indictment, "He has a devil," was let loose among the people. "He heals with the power of Satan, and with the power of Satan he casts out demons." Later other charges were circulated against him: he associates with sinners, prostitutes, drunks and publicans—he keeps the kind of company he himself comes from; he does not keep the Law of Moses; he does not wash his hands or his cups and dishes before eating; he does not keep the Sabbath: he heals on the Sabbath.

The Pharisees' slander drew a sharp reaction from Jesus. Judas never forgot the first time Jesus flung words of condemnation right into their faces: "Woe to you!" It came as a tremendous shock, to him and to the whole gathering there at the time. They froze; the air almost crackled from the stunned silence. "Woe to you, scribes and Pharisees, hypocrites, because you devour the houses of widows under the pretense of long prayers. For this you will receive the greater judgment. Woe to you, because you tithe mint, and aniseed, and cumin, and have neglected the weightier things of the

Law; judgment and mercy and faith. These things you should have done, and not leave the other undone. Blind guides, who strain out a gnat and swallow a camel. Woe to you, because you clean the outside of the cup and the dish, but within you are full of rapine and uncleanliness." After that, every time he heard Jesus return to that tone of voice, he caught himself glancing around in fright in case they were coming to seize the master. No one had ever dared to talk like that until now. "Serpents, generation of vipers, how ill you flee from the judgment of hell."

Judas knew, as did others, that the Pharisees would never sit back and ignore that kind of abuse. Sooner or later they would take their revenge. Outwardly they behaved as if they had not heard, or as if the indictments were directed at someone else, not at them. They made no response to the charges. Instead, they started to put questions more and more frequently to the master—shrewd, crafty questions, to which there were no answers, questions designed to compromise Jesus, make him lose face. Judas was terrified. Once, for example, they brought an adulteress to him and said, "Moses in the Law commanded us to stone such a one. What do you say?" Tirelessly, vigilantly, they counted on his finally stumbling, missing an answer, or wording it wrong and thereby inciting an angry outcry and surge of opposition. Then all they would have to do was use it against him, follow along with the "scandalized" throng, inflame their feelings, and provoke them into taking the law—mob law—into their own hands. And it actually did happen that way. He shuddered to think of it. Only afterward did he realize just how well planned it had been. While his and the other disciples' attention was being distracted, Jesus was dragged out of the town and nearly pushed off a cliff. Judas remembered his insane fear for the master's life, and how helpless he had felt—he thought it was the end for sure. How, in what manner Jesus managed to save himself at the last minute—Judas was never able to figure out. Then there was a second time—he was not there when it happened, but someone told him about the incident afterwards—when the mob picked up rocks to hurl at Jesus. Again an unusual piece of luck, or the extraordinary help of God, or both, saved him. That last attempt on his life demonstrated just how perilous the situation was. The Pharisees were not going to give up; they would keep on trying until they finally got rid of this new teacher. Judas understood this better than any of the other eleven disciples. They were hardly aware of any danger at all; but he saw it clearly. He could not shake off a feeling of events tightening around them. It was getting more and more difficult for them to move about; the disputes were becoming increasingly bitter; and the men who came to trap him with their tricky questions gave them to understand very clearly that they were playing for the highest stakes—the life of Jesus. Sooner or later something had to happen. Something decisive. But he did not know exactly when or how. He believed wholly in Jesus, in his wisdom and his strength. Jesus would certainly make no mistakes; he knew when to withdraw, and when, at the most opportune, best-timed moment, to seize power.

Judas often wondered what the Romans would do, how they would react to a situation in which Jesus took command of the nation. Their response was important. In the end, everything really depended on them. The way he saw things, he was fairly sure that the Romans, more precisely the Procurator, would not react at all. Most likely Pilate would secretly be satisfied and take the opportunity of getting rid of Herod. Herod had been a nuisance long enough: he had too many friends at old Tiberius' court, and the Procurator would be delighted to have someone else in his place, just so long as the new man proved loyal to him and to the Emperor.

But the one great unknown was still Jerusalem: a city in the hands of the Pharisees and Sadducees, scribes and priests, parties at odds and at war among themselves, groups which, while mutually hostile, shared a common prejudice against everyone and everything from the provinces, especially from Galilee, not to mention Nazareth with its poor reputation. At all costs, Jesus had to win over Jerusalem. This city alone would decide his triumph or defeat.

Then something happened that Judas had not imagined even in his wildest dreams. A masterstroke, Jesus' best-aimed move of his entire career. It began when Lazarus took ill—a man to whom Jesus was very close, and at whose house he often stayed with his disciples. Jesus learned about his friend's illness while he was still far outside Jerusalem. One of Lazarus' sisters asked him to come and heal her brother. By the time Jesus arrived, Lazarus was dead and his body already entombed for several days. Mary, his sister, told Jesus when she ran out to meet him.

She led everyone to a tomb in an immense garden. Judas had never seen Jesus so moved. He stood against the tomb and wept for his friend. Then—and Judas remembered every detail perfectly—he straightened up, and to the astonishment of the crowd, and in spite of their protests that it was, after all, the fourth day Lazarus was in his grave, he commanded them to remove the stone. He leaned over the entrance and loudly called out: "Lazarus, come forth". He said it so suddenly and unexpectedly that reaction was slow in coming. It came after the crowd saw a figure hobbling out in a shroud and bandages. Judas thought he was inured to the shock they produced. He had seen plenty of miracles. But this one was absolutely staggering. He stood rooted to the ground like the rest. The screams of the women finally brought him to his senses. Still no one dared approach the white cocoonlike figure standing in the entrance to the tomb, until Jesus finally told them to go and unbind him. They pulled the shroud off his head. Lazarus blinked his eyes a few moments in the blinding sunlight. He looked around, confused by the staring throngs gathered about him, around the tomb. He looked down at himself, at the bandages they were unraveling from his body. The truth slowly began to dawn on him, and then he threw himself into Jesus' arms.

Unlike the others around Jesus, Judas saw the raising of Lazarus as part of the master's political strategy. This miracle was the key event. Precisely because Bethany lay just outside Jerusalem, and because Lazarus was so well-known, large numbers of people had taken part in his funeral. News of his raising from the dead spread like fire around the city. Friends, acquaintances, strangers, whole columns of sightseers—all came in droves to Bethany to look him over, touch him, examine his tomb, gossip, point, exchange opinions. Jesus' popularity hit high point. The Pharisees and Sadducees suddenly recognized the danger they were in. Minute by minute they expected the worst to happen: an overthrow; Jesus would seize control. They lost their heads. At one point (at least that was the rumor Judas heard) they decided to kill Lazarus to stop the crowds from streaming towards Bethany. Hour by hour tension mounted. It was so taut that it was almost audible. And that was when Jesus announced his entry into Jerusalem.

This was the moment Judas had been waiting for—the battle cry to move forward into crucial combat. A brilliant move: the residents of Jerusalem still under the impact of Lazarus' raising; the city swelling with pilgrims come for the Passover, pouring in from every province, the great majority of them followers of Jesus. The word went out: he's coming! Throngs flocked to greet him; people threw off their coats, spread them over the road for him; a thicket of palm branches whipped up a furious wind, a jubilant wind; they swept in laughing, singing procession to the city: "Hosanna to the son of David".

Judas could not believe his eyes. He alternately wept, laughed, shouted, sang along with the others; he moved in a daze, waving the palm that someone thrust wildly into his hand. This was the crowning moment of his dreams! Wait . . . some Pharisees weaving through the crowds . . . silencing the people, threatening them. Suddenly the voice of Jesus—he must have seen them: "If they should be silent, these stones would cry out." That means he accepts the people's exultant reaction! But the tumult, the fever only reminded him more vividly of the danger. Suddenly he understood: they had no exit from this city; Jesus would either win power or die.

The throng was at the temple. This was it, this was the long-awaited moment. Those most important words would be delivered. Now, in the temple, Jesus would proclaim himself the son of David, to whom all power over the chosen nation belonged. He waited, breathless, expectant. . . . What's this? Jesus, entering the temple . . . starting to preach to the people the way he always does, as if he does not know what everyone is waiting for, as if he does not realize the opportunity he is wasting. . . . What is he doing now? Throwing the merchants out of the temple? What is he doing that for? Just needlessly enlarging the numbers of his enemies.

His hopes . . . tottering at the brink, about to crash. Why was he pulling out at the last minute? This was inexcusable. No, not a word about the real issue. Jesus . . . leaving the temple . . . leaving for Bethany for the night. That means he knows they're lying in wait for him. . . . Why doesn't he strike the final blow? Is he afraid? Did his courage fail him at the decisive moment? Has he stopped believing in himself? An opportunity like this to take over the city may never repeat itself. Doesn't he realize this is his last chance? They'll kill him the first opportunity they get, right after the festival days, as soon as the pilgrims from the provinces on whom he was counting for support leave. No, only they can sweep Jesus to the throne, this crushing mass of people in Jerusalem now and still pouring in. If he lacks the courage to go ahead, then let them take the initiative. But they have to be stirred into action. How?

And that was when he got wind of the news being passed around the city by the priests: a sizable reward for information about where Jesus spends the night. Much later, Judas had to admit that the prospect of a reward had figured, if not greatly, then at least to some extent in his making his decision. In the company of Jesus and the Twelve, he always keenly felt the absence of his own money. In their community, everything was shared, especially money. Of course, he assured himself, he would turn the money over to the common purse if the need arose, but the idea of having and spending his own money had its own special appeal. Of course he knew very well that the report of a reward was just one more attempt by the priests to scare the populace—they certainly did not believe such a man would come forward. Only someone close to Jesus would possess that kind of information. But the announcement suggested an unexpected solution to the problem. It came in a flash: he could report to the chief priests as one anxious to claim the reward, and in so doing, give them the chance to apprehend Jesus. The people were sure to rise up and wrench him out of their clutches, and then proclaim him king. But he would have to do it before or at the very latest during the holy days, while the outsiders were still swelling the city. Judas was no coward, but the very thought seemed so breakneck that it made him shiver. He shook off the idea—it was the devil's urging.

Turn his best friend over to his enemies? But the more he searched for an alternative to saving Jesus, the more his mind returned to the same plan, and the more rational it appeared. The role of traitor gained him one other advantage: it was a source of information. The thing that always bothered him most was not knowing, being in the dark about his opponents' plans. But in an arrangement like this, with him in the position of informer, he would be kept abreast of the priests' and the Pharisees' intentions. More important, he would know exactly when they planned to arrest Jesus, and he would have every right to ask in advance. His success would depend on absolute secrecy; he could not divulge his intentions to anyone. Full responsibility would rest on his own conscience. The Pharisees were cunning. He would have to put on a good act, pretend to be a traitor, give the impression of being a weak-hearted coward, the rat abandoning the sinking ship and as long as he was getting out, making a little money in the process.

He went to the temple. He located a priest he had met some time back and said to him, "Get me in touch with the High Priest. If possible, I would like him to see me today."

The priest returned before noon with the news that Caiaphas would be waiting for him that evening.

In the temple that evening, Judas tried to act as coolly as possible, although he could feel his heart pounding wildly in his chest and his palms were hot and clammy. He had never been in this part of the temple before, reserved for priests only. People outside told fantastic stories about its size and opulence. Yes, now he could see for himself: the halls were certainly very large and high, but probably a bit too dark and empty. Caiaphas kept him waiting a long time. Whispering priests glided past, throwing him curious, surprised looks.

Now and then a servant or Levite passed by without a sound. Slowly his nerves settled.

Finally Caiaphas came in. He did not actually walk in, he almost trotted in. Always in such a hurry, Judas thought. He saluted him with a greeting befitting the dignity and office of the highest priest and servant of the altar, but before he could finish his salutation, Caiaphas interrupted with a curt, 'Well, what is it you want?''

Very deliberately he articulated the sentence he had rehearsed in his mind a hundred times: "What will you give me if I turn him over to you?"

Judas watched with satisfaction the lightning impact his words made on Caiaphas. The High Priest blinked his eyes in disbelieving succession, started to say something but the sound caught in his throat, then finally stammered, "Wait here a moment. I'll ask Annas to come." He turned to hurry from the room.

"There's one condition. This has to remain strictly between us. No one else must know about it."

Caiaphas eagerly nodded agreement. "Of course, of course, I'll tell only Annas about it."

Judas waited longer for Annas than he had for Caiaphas. Finally he entered with an old man's unsteady gait—small, thin, shortsighted, possibly hard of hearing. The conversation with him was briefer even than with Caiaphas. Judas's immediate impression was that he was dealing with a cold calculator who would not give an inch more than he had to, who would squeeze as much as he could from a bargain—and that the people were quite right when they said there were really two High Priests, or in the end, actually only one: Annas. It was he who governed.

Meanwhile, Jerusalem bulged with pilgrims. Jesus and his disciples were constantly running into people they had met in their travels around Palestine. It was getting difficult for Jesus even to walk out on the street without creating a sensation. Each time his appearance drew a crowd. Within seconds he would find himself hemmed in by all kinds of people—begging him for something, reminding him about something, thanking him for something, cheering him, showering him with gifts, trying to find out when and where he would be speaking next, inviting him to their homes. He could not possibly meet all their demands and wishes and invitations himself, so, often, he sent his disciples, singly and in pairs, among the crowds.

Judas, like the others, was sent to various meetings, discussions, and lectures in smaller and larger groups; he, too, did his share of explaining, clarifying, defending against charges, denying gossip and slander, describing and reiterating miracles he had seen with his own eyes. Not until the evening meal did the disciples all meet with Jesus at prearranged places, which were now kept in utmost secrecy. It was then that they reported important developments, sought advice, heard their instructions, asked his intervention in one thing or another. It was exactly the way it had always been. Judas would then keep telling himself: I did not take the money, and the fact that I promised them means about as much as if they had promised me they would destroy the temple for thirty silver pieces. He watched hopefully for some kind of change in Jesus' activities, a sign, anything that would signify the start of maneuvers aimed at his taking over power. But to no avail. He could hardly tell whether Jesus was aware of the ever-growing danger, or if he even noticed the ring of ambush slowly tightening around him. At least he was sufficiently aware to leave Jerusalem for the night; now he slept primarily in Bethany, or somewhere on the Mount of Olives.

A man came to Judas a few times from the chief priests, and asked him a lot of questions about Jesus: what was he doing, with whom did he meet, what did he talk about? Judas answered reluctantly and cautiously; anyway, he was not all that well informed. In fact his interrogator seemed to know far more. Whenever Judas tried to turn the conversation around or ask him questions—such as, what was happening at the temple?—the priest either gave an evasive answer or said nothing at all.

Then on Wednesday morning the same priest came to him, in a considerable hurry. He was very brief: "It's tomorrow. Let us know tomorrow evening where Jesus will be spending the night. We'll be waiting for you at the temple, you'll get

the money then. Now if something happens and you don't
show up, just remember, we'll catch him anyway. Even if he
flees Jerusalem. Of course, if you come it will make things
that much easier for us, and you'll earn yourself some money.
Only no tricks," he warned. "Remember. We have long
arms."

Judas felt his heart pounding. Before he could answer the
man had already turned and gone. He suffered acutely that
whole day; he could not bear the weight of such a secret. A
thousand ideas stormed his head. Should he tell Jesus about
his plan? Then what if he runs off? No, not for fear of im-
prisonment, but for fear that the people really would declare
him king. Then his whole plan would fall through; the last
chance to save him would be squandered. Should he tell the
rest of the disciples? They would not understand. Or maybe
he should just tell Peter? If there was anyone he would rather
confide in, it was Mary—Lazarus' sister. There was one other
thing he could do: simply not go. The priest had said they
would get him anyway, even without him. But he was not
happy about letting the money slip out of his hands. Rather
a waste.

On Thursday morning, Jesus unexpectedly announced that
they would hold the Passover meal that evening. Judas gave
a start—was it a coincidence, or had he heard about the
priests' decision? The other disciples seemed surprised that
Jesus wanted to eat the supper two days in advance of Passover but, after all, they were accustomed to strange things
happening when they were with the master. None of them
appeared to know where they would meet for the feast. Judas
tried to find out, inquiring cautiously among them—either
they truly did not know, or they were concealing it from him.
Finally he decided that Jesus was keeping the location to
himself.

Before noon, the master summoned Peter and John. Judas
thought it might have to do with the evening's celebration, so
he followed them unobtrusively. He was right: he overheard
Jesus telling them to head into the city to prepare the supper.
He strained to catch the name or location of the house. That
would be extremely valuable; he could tell the priests at once,

and he would not have to leave for the temple in the evening. The fact was, he could not imagine how he could get up during the Passover supper and run off to the temple; he was not sure he would even have the time. Unfortunately, Jesus lowered his voice at that moment. Perhaps he noticed him hovering nearby . . . or maybe it was just a reflex action. He could hear him say something about a man who would be waiting for them at the city gates, and that he would be carrying . . . a pitcher of water? No, he must have heard wrong, who ever saw a man carrying a pitcher of water. Now he was sure that Jesus was giving them the prearranged password. Even repeating it to them a few times, but so quietly that he could not make it out. Jesus finished. Now there was only one thing left for him to do: follow Peter and John and find out where they were headed. Everything depended on whether or not he could manage to stay out of sight.

When the two started for the city, Judas waited a few moments, then very casually began to saunter along after them. As he was moving away from the others, he heard a voice call out to him that sent a chill down his spine: "Judas".

Jesus was calling him. Judas froze in his tracks, turned around. Jesus was motioning him to approach. He went over, trying to look natural, at ease. Jesus started to say something about wanting him to stay there with him because he was going to need him badly. Later it turned out that he was not so badly needed after all. But the chance to follow the other two was gone. He still had not discovered the location of their supper.

Later that evening, the Twelve gathered at a prearranged spot. From there Peter led them to the meeting with Jesus. The house was at the very edge of the city in a quiet area. An entrance through an inconspicuous little building, then a courtyard, finally a gate leading to the main residence . . . wide stairs to the second floor . . . the floor of the dining room—Judas made a mental note of every detail; in a short while he would be coming back this way with the temple guards, though it would be worse then, completely dark. Now he knew what he needed to know. He would have liked to have slipped away to the temple then and there to inform the priests and lead them back. But he could not see how that would be possible. His mind raced to find a pretext for getting away, but he could not think of anything to justify his leaving.

A large clean hall was festively prepared. Jesus was already there waiting for them, looking very solemn and very ceremonious. He wore an apron around his waist. As they filed in, he picked up a bowl of water, walked up to Peter, and stooped like a servant at his feet to wash them. The others sucked in their breaths in astonishment. Peter moved like lightning. He pulled Jesus to his feet. "Lord, you wish to wash my feet?! Never!"

Jesus looked him steadily in the eyes. Very quietly he said, "If you do not agree to this, then you will have no part with me."

Peter dropped his arms. He practically shouted: "If so, then not only my feet, but also my hands and my head!"

In the hushed room, Jesus came up to each one in turn, knelt to remove his sandals, then washed his feet soiled with the dust of the street, and wiped them dry with a towel.

Judas waited tensely for his turn, thinking to himself: Does he know about me or not, and if he does, will he betray himself with some sign or gesture? But Jesus knelt at Judas' feet and washed them just as he had the others'.

When they had settled in their places around the table, Jesus spoke to them. "You call me Master and Lord, and you say well, for so I am. If then I, being your Lord and Master, have washed your feet, you also should wash one another's feet. I have given you an example, that as I have done to you, so you should also do."

They commenced the supper in the normal fashion, with prayers. Nothing seemed to indicate that it was going to be different from any other, everything proceeding as usual. Then, just when Judas was feeling reassured that nothing out of the ordinary was going to happen, Jesus said very quietly, without raising his head, "One of you will betray me."

Silence fell like a hammer blow on the room. Judas stiffened. So he knew after all. They'll kill me right here, he thought in panic. His first impulse was to bolt out of the room. He strained with every muscle to hold himself down. There was a spark of hope—it was possible he didn't know who it was. Peter's voice boomed. "Is it I, master?"

Instantly a flood of questions broke loose from the other disciples. They pushed past each other to get to Jesus. Judas knew he could not just sit there doing nothing without giving himself away, and he still was not sure if Jesus knew it was he, so he got up and asked along with the others, "Is it I, Lord?". Above all the clamor, Judas was stunned to hear the reply directed back at him: "Yes, it is you."

He returned to his place, shaken. So Jesus knew, and he called it betrayal. But he still could not divulge his plan to them, not even to him. He felt hurt and angry with Jesus: he should understand, he should trust him, after all, it was his welfare he was concerned with. He could feel his hands trembling, a painful tightening around his throat, perspiration beading on his brow. He was not going to be able to stand this tension much longer. . . . Someone handed him a piece of bread dipped in wine. . . . Jesus . . . talking to him out loud, everyone listening . . . "What you have to do, go and do quickly."

He looked around. None of the other disciples looked surprised by the command; they must have thought he had received prior instructions for a task, and now the master was simply reminding him to go and do it. Judas leaped up and bolted out of the hall.

Outside, the night seemed blacker than usual, coming as he had from a brightly lit room. He lost his bearings in the dark, started to follow a lane that led away from the city. It took him several minutes to realize his mistake. The time lost unnerved him. He broke into a run, only to stop a moment later, afraid of stumbling and breaking a leg. Finally, against a strip of moonlit sky visible between the narrow streets he saw the massive silhouette of the temple. The sight calmed him. He slowed his pace to catch his breath, collect himself, put the mask in place for the priests. Still his heart thumped unmercifully. The temple walls loomed ahead. He hurried into the darkened gallery. There was no one there—where were they? Had they already gone? But where? Was there some mistake? Had he misunderstood his instructions? In a panic, he tried to recall the conversation with the messenger-priests. No, there was no mistake, it was definitely set for Thursday. He came out on to Solomon's portico, awash in pale moonlight. Torchlight flashed among the pillars; men were moving about there. He breathed a sigh of relief. He darted among them, scanning their illumined faces for a familiar one. Not a priest in sight. All these men looked like temple guards. He searched around for someone who might be waiting for him. They all appeared to be waiting. Some sat propped against the pillars, while others stood around in idle groups or paced the ambulatory aimlessly, up and down. Finally he accosted one of them who was standing off by himself; he asked him where the priests were.

"They're holding a council right now," the man answered.

"But I have to talk to one of them immediately," Judas fairly shouted, agitated.

"Well, you won't talk to them 'immediately'," the guard laughed, "because no one is allowed in there. Wait a moment. Nothing's going to happen. Don't worry, the temple is eternal."

Judas moved away, nettled. Why were they not here? They were supposed to be waiting for him. Everything was supposed to be ready. They were to leave at once. The minutes dragged. He reassured himself: there was nothing to fear, they would make it on time. Jesus and the others had only just begun the supper. They would still only be about halfway through. They would certainly not be rushing through the meal, and they still had the second and third cups ahead of them. Then they would probably want to rest a while. Only one thing worried him: what if Jesus knew, not only about his contact with the priests, but also about the trap set for tonight? He glanced around impatiently. He just could not stand around idly, he had to do something. If Jesus had somehow found out, that would radically alter the situation, and their plans. He had to let the chief priests know. He started toward one of the entrances, when the man he had spoken to—and who apparently had been observing him the whole time—called out: "They're coming out now."

Judas could not see anyone.

"Over there." The man pointed.

A stream of dark figures spilled out through another gate, not the one Judas was heading toward. He positioned himself so that his face would be fully lit and recognizable in the moonlight. The priests dispersed into groups of twos and threes, passing all around him, murmuring absorbedly among themselves. An occasional low burst of laughter bounced and echoed off the walls. No one paid him the slightest attention. He tried to shrug off his nervousness. After all, they were the ones who should be anxious about his helping them, and not the other way around. He was the seller with the goods, and they should know they were getting a good deal. They should be worrying about him. If he looked too anxious he would spoil the whole plan.

A lone figure hurried toward him. He recognized the messenger-priest. He greeted him, then, trying to sound nonchalant said, "Has anything been changed?"

"No, nothing. What could change? A man's word is his word."

"Then why aren't we going yet?"

"We'll be going right away. I'll just ask Caiaphas and the elders."

"What do you mean 'ask'? What does 'ask' mean? Didn't you tell them about our agreement?"

"Yes, yes, of course I told them, but—"

"But what?" he demanded. He was losing his patience.

"But . . . well, I'll tell you honestly, Caiaphas doesn't believe you."

"He didn't believe I would come today?"

"That's right, imagine, he didn't believe it."

"Is that supposed to mean that he doesn't want my help?" He was practically insulted.

"Did I say he doesn't want it? Of course he does, he wants it. Just wait here for a moment." He left.

Judas was alone. The tension had dropped from him. So they didn't believe him. Did they know something? But what could they possibly know? From whom? It was a good thing he hadn't told his plans to anyone. If they knew what he was planning, he would not leave here alive. No, they couldn't find any fault with him. As long as he played his part well. After several minutes delay, the priest returned.

"We can go now. Caiaphas is agreed. At least for now."

"What do you mean, 'for now'?"

"He's still not sure about you. But he will be sure when you deliver Jesus to him."

"Is that only up to me? It's up to you too."

"You don't have to worry about us."

"I don't? How long have I been waiting here? Everything was supposed to be prepared and now I find that nothing is. Am I supposed to know if we'll even find Jesus there with his disciples now? What do you think, that I told him to wait for us until we got there?"

"Why are you shouting like that? Keep your voice down. The guards will be ready in a moment. Don't get excited."

The men were slowly extinguishing their torches and forming ranks.

"Why shouldn't I get excited?! How can I not get excited when he already knows!"

The priest grabbed his arm. "What does he know? How does he know?"

"He knows. How—I don't know. But he knows that I'm in touch with you. He gave me to understand that just a few minutes ago."

The priest eased his grip on his arm. "You don't mean to tell me that he knows about tonight?"

"Did I say that? I didn't say that. I just said that he knows that I am meeting with you and that I'm planning an attempt on his life with you."

"How do you know this?" the priest pumped him.

Judas answered reluctantly. "He said, 'One of you will betray me.' And when I asked if it was me, he said yes."

"In front of all of them?"

"No one heard." He wanted to change the subject. "Are you sure there are enough men?" he asked, glancing around.

"This is what's left. All the others have gone to surround the city."

"So you don't believe me?"

"We don't believe anyone." Then he added, "Not even ourselves."

He pulled Judas to the head of the column. They moved forward. The deeper they went into the city, the faster they sped. Privately, Judas had to concede that the party of men, though they had impressed him poorly at first was, after all, quite imposing. No noise, no shouted orders; they moved like cats. Judas stopped talking to the priest. He concentrated his attention on not losing his way. The last thing he wanted was to make a fool of himself by getting them all lost. Several times at a crossroads he was not sure if he had taken the correct turning, but each time—after he had sweated himself into a panic—he found it was the right street after all. Finally there was a familiar lane, a cross street, then a wall, a corner. There was the entrance gate. He stopped. "This is it." His heart pounded.

The priest looked around. "Where are they?" he asked.

"In the house behind the courtyard, on the second floor."

"What is the layout there?"

"Stairs going to the top. Two doors in the entrance hall, one leading into the room where Jesus is, the other opposite, opening into the owner's house."

"Good. You come first with me and Malchus and a few of our men. The rest will block the gate. Do you know if there's an exit into another street?"

"No, there is none. I checked. Of course, there may be a concealed passage."

"What about windows?"

"Only on one side—they open on to the courtyard."

Judas noticed an enormous man listening to their whispered conversation. He must be the group leader, he thought, the man called Malchus. The priest turned to him and said, "Did you understand? Do you know what you're supposed to do?" The giant nodded his huge head.

"Let's go," the priest said a little louder. "Judas will lead the way."

Judas moved in front of the others. He pushed open the gate, looked around: the courtyard was deserted. He stared up at the dining-room windows, aflame with light. A sigh of

relief escaped him: they were still there. They ran on their
toes across the open courtyard to the entrance, then up the
flight of stairs. Judas could hear his own heavy breathing and
that of his companions once they had reached the landing. A
moment of concentration before breaking in . . . only why was
it so quiet? Were they praying, or had they fallen asleep? He
made a short running leap and threw his weight against the
door. It flew open. He staggered across the floor with the
momentum. Malchus and his men burst in behind him. He
looked around. The hall was empty. The tables were strewn
with cups and wineskins and scraps of left-over food. Before
he could recover from his astonishment, a hand tightened
around the scruff of his neck. The giant Malchus swung him
around bodily. Still gripping him by the back of the neck
with an iron hand, he grasped him by the throat with his
other hand and lifted him off his feet like a sack of feathers
to the level of his own face. "Where are they?" he demanded.

Judas tried to speak but only a gurgling sound came out of
his throat—the giant's hand choked off the air to his wind-
pipe. Red patches sparkled before his eyes. He felt himself
losing consciousness. A single thought screamed through his
mind—he's going to kill me! Then he blacked out. The next
thing he knew, he was on his feet again. His legs buckled, he
sank gasping to his knees. He heard the priest, trying to calm
Malchus, explain something to him, but his head buzzed and
he could not understand the words. A second time he felt a
mighty hand clamp around his neck. Now he was a dead
man, he thought. But Malchus only yanked him to his feet
and slapped him lightly across the face a few times to revive
him. He wasn't going to kill him after all. He heard Malchus
ask someone to pass one of the wineskins. A moment later
wine splashed over his mouth, face, eyes, and down his beard
and throat on to his clothing. He started to choke and gag,
but the wine brought him to his senses. He focused on the
room. The guards had turned away and were concentrating
their attention on someone else. For a moment, Judas couldn't
think who it might be; then he remembered having seen the
man out of the corner of his eye, cleaning the tables when he
had rushed into the room. One of the house servants, he

thought. Now they were interrogating him. "Where are they?" Malchus demanded. He must have employed the same persuasive methods on the servant that he had employed on Judas only moments before, because the man was bleeding profusely from nose and mouth.

Judas watched the scene with indifference, still panting for breath. The man being questioned stared around at them, terror-stricken, stammering out his answers and sniffing every few seconds trying to stop the blood running from his nose. He told them: they were here, they ate, they left; they may have been in a hurry, because they did not wish to be served the fourth cup; where they went, he did not know. In tears, he pleaded: he was only a servant, why should anyone tell him anything? He had no say in this house, he was only there to clean the tables.

As if he hadn't heard a word of the man's pleas, as if he were stone-deaf, Malchus repeated his question in an even, deadly tone: "Where are they? Tell me, or you will die."

At that moment a figure appeared in the door attired in rich elegant robes—the master of the house. He glanced quickly around the room. "What is happening here?" he asked. His voice carried the self-assured tone of authority.

Judas caught the sudden flustered look on the priest's face. He saw him smile weakly and make a vague motion as if to explain. Seeing the priest's reaction, Malchus quickly released the servant.

"Who injured my servant?" the man in the door asked, in the same level voice.

The priest waved his hands in another apologetic gesture. No one answered. The hushed room vibrated with the shrill chirping of crickets from beyond the open windows. Finally the master of the house pointed to the priest. "You stay. The rest of you get out." It was said in the same self-assured tone of voice. He stepped away from the door. The company edged out into the hall, then down the stairs.

Judas clung to the wall for support on the way down. The loss of consciousness, though momentary, had considerably weakened him. His neck hurt. They joined the men waiting expectantly outside. Judas leaned back against the side of the house. His legs wobbled precariously. He slid down along the wall to the ground and crouched in a heap. Moments later the priest emerged. As if nothing at all had transpired upstairs, he announced loudly: "The master of the house doesn't know where they could have gone. But our friend Judas here will certainly answer that question." He pulled him up by his clothing. "Now, where could the teacher of Nazareth have gone; what do you think, Judas?"

Judas blanched. He tried to think straight, calmly, but all he could recall was the attack on him upstairs. He tried to shrug. He had to salvage the remains of his dignity. In as natural a voice as he could muster, he said, "How would I know where he went? All I can tell you is that Jesus usually spends the night in Bethany at the house of Lazarus—at least that's what he has done for the last few days. That I can tell you for certain. But at other times he stays in a variety of places, even in the house of Joseph of Arimathea."

"Try, Judas, to remember where those other places were?"

The priest's affected reasonableness and the exaggerated repetition of his name grated his nerves. But he pretended not to notice. Trying to appear normal he said, "Sometimes he stays the whole night in prayer in the Garden of Olives behind the Cedron." The words "at prayer" stabbed at his heart like a dagger.

"And where else?" the priest asked relentlessly.

"No, nowhere else, I should think."

"Now, if Jesus went to Joseph of Arimathea," the priest mused aloud, "then he's already in our grasp. His house is also surrounded. If he headed for Bethany, then we have already caught him, or we will shortly, because all the gates are covered. But we all know he is slyer than a fox and he could have managed to slip past. With all the pilgrims and the gates open all night during the festival days, that is possible."

Judas realized in a flash that the priest had just revealed information that had been kept secret.

"But the information our friend Judas has given us—the garden behind the Cedron—this is valuable and worth checking."

The successive "our friend Judas" rang in his ears like a jeer.

"I propose," the priest went on, "that we divide into two groups. The first group, under your command"—he pointed to one of the guards—"will set out for Bethany. Pick the fastest runners and go as quickly as you know how. The second group will come with me and Malchus. We'll go to the garden behind the Cedron."

For a second time Judas was forced to admire the guards' proficiency. The first group was formed and on its way out of the courtyard within seconds. As soon as they had gone, Judas felt the priest's hand on his shoulder. "And now you lead the way to the garden. Let's go. Oh, one other thing: so there's no mistake or mix-up, you will walk up to the teacher and kiss him in greeting, just to make sure we do not mistake someone else for him in the dark. And remember, no tricks. If you betray us, you will die. Instantly. No trial."

He led them like a hound leads hunters in hot pursuit of a quarry. But he was a hound on a leash, with the priest holding him on one side, and Malchus on the other.

They descended in the direction of the Cedron. The night air magnified the shuffling of their footsteps and the occasional clanging of weapons against the stones. They reached the edge of the city. Just a few more small dark houses, then the rocky slope of a hill with a dried riverbed at its base. They halted at the bank. The order was given to put out the torches. They started to break up into groups. One section would circle the garden from the left, the other from the right. Judas' group, under the priest's command, headed directly toward the gate.

The torches proved to be unnecessary: the moon shone almost too brightly. They approached by way of the riverbed, which wound its way up the gentle slope of Gethsemane, covered with low grass and scattered brush. A wall of olive trees rose darkly behind them. Suddenly the startled whisper: "Look! They're sleeping!"

They halted. Judas moved to the front. Just in front of the entrance to the garden, plainly visible in the silvery light, the disciples lay, fast asleep. Breathless, Judas counted—eight of them. Where were the rest? The priest hurried up to him. "What do you make of that?" he whispered.

"I have no idea what it means. There should be eleven of them."

"Where is Jesus?"

"He must be in the garden, praying. Only I don't know where the other three are. The master must have left these here to guard the gate and entered the garden with the others."

"Well, we'll take these."

The priest moved to the rear. Whispering spread through the party. Crouching low, almost crawling, they formed a wide arc and closed in around the sleeping men. Moments before they sprang, one of the disciples awoke, saw them and tried to raise the alarm, but he was instantly smothered by a wave of men. It was all over very swiftly—shouts and cries stifled, mouths quickly gagged, arms twisted, tied with ropes. Much more swiftly than Judas had anticipated.

"Quickly now, we're going in. Torches!"

Torches were hurriedly lit. A long whistle sounded—the signal for the surrounding groups. Warmed by the fight, flushed with easy victory, the men rushed into the garden. They crept among the low olive trees, holding their torches near the ground. Like an animal chase, Judas thought. He caught the fever of the hunt. He plunged into a small clearing flooded with moonlight. Suddenly he saw four figures standing under the cover of the trees, poised as if they were waiting for his party to approach. The priest, who had followed at his heels, shouted to him, "Now! Begin!"

With fast, determined steps, Judas crossed the open space. He recognized Jesus standing with Peter, John, and James. He could feel the terrified stares of the disciples.

"Judas, what . . . what are you doing?" one of them stammered.

Judas ignored him. He embraced Jesus and kissed him. "Hail, Rabbi!"

In the dark he caught the faint gleam of Jesus' eyes resting quietly on his; he winced at the aggrieved voice: "Judas, do you betray the Son of Man with a kiss?"

The guards, who had followed at a distance, now sprang forward. Peter moved quickly. He leaped in front of Jesus, trying to block him with his own huge body. Judas saw Malchus rush up to them with a spear in his hand. Peter tore out his sword and struck ferociously at him. Malchus recoiled, lowering his head to avert the blow. The sword slid along his helmet and looked as though it may well have hewn away the giant's shoulder, had it not been for his heavy brassard.

"Peter, put up your sword!" It was Jesus rebuking him. The men stopped in their tracks and stared at him.

"Whom do you seek?" he asked severely.

A long uncertain pause, then a hoarse voice: "Jesus of Nazareth."

"I am he. If therefore you seek me, let these disciples go their way." He turned abruptly to the chief priests standing to one side of the detachment of guards and addressed them: "You came out as if for a thief with swords and clubs. When I was with you daily in the temple, you didn't raise your hands against me." Still speaking, he moved into their midst. The posse of men swooped around him and, spurred on by the shouts of the chief priests, began to move quickly in the direction of the gate. Stunned, dazed by the capture, Judas scarcely noticed someone pressing something into his hand. His palm closed around it mechanically. A few minutes later he noticed he was holding a pouch of money. He secured it under the rope around his waist; he tightened it around him. Now he felt a little better—at least the next item on his agenda was taken care of. With any luck everything else would go as smoothly. For several minutes he followed the receding group, then suddenly he stopped short: the thing he had wanted most to happen had happened.

Gradually the garden emptied; the cool night stillness fell over it. Overhead the black sky was almost bright behind a myriad of stars. He felt suddenly drained of all his strength. His shoulders sagged, his legs shook with fatigue. He had to wait for a while, rest, let the others move away a little farther. He sat down on the ground and tried to collect his thoughts: everything now depended on good and fast communication. But there was time enough for that. Tomorrow they would be getting ready for the trial; the earliest they could convene would be on the first day after the Sabbath. In the meantime, by tomorrow afternoon at the very latest, the people would declare Jesus king.

He listened to the retreating echoes of the company clattering down the dry gully of the Cedron. A few more minutes . . . let them enter the city. Finally he rose and very slowly descended the hill—he was afraid of running into stragglers from the group of chief priests. Only after he slipped into an alley did he finally feel safe. Which way? He lost his bearings—the moon rarely penetrated the narrow little lanes. He blundered blindly among the streets, groping as if he were closed in a labyrinth. It infuriated him. He did not wish to talk to anyone, or ask directions, but anyway, there was no one to ask. In the dark he repeatedly tripped over the inert forms of pilgrims sleeping against the sides of buildings. Finally he stumbled on to the street where the disciples kept their quarters, but the darkened windows worried him: they should have returned by now. Perhaps they were sitting in the dark. He went in, lit a few oil lamps. Empty. Uneasiness made him queasy. But no, one of them would have to come back. He needed only to wait a few more minutes. He waited. Not a sound in the street. What if no one came? What then? He hardly knew anyone in Jerusalem. Feverishly he picked his brain for names, people he might know in the city. There was Joseph of Arimathea. But how to get there? Gamaliel. He did not know the way there either. Nicodemus. Yes, he could go to him. It was quite a long way but he could find it. However, maybe it was best to stay here and wait after all. They would have to come eventually. They weren't going to sleep outside now. A frightening thought occurred to him: what if they were afraid that the priests might be setting a trap for them here in their quarters—to arrest them, throw them into prison with Jesus? In that case, it would be better to put out the lights. He blew out the lamps and waited in the dark. The minutes dragged by interminably. Then . . . footsteps. Cautious, stealthy footsteps . . . someone creeping toward their room. They paused. One of the disciples or one of the priests—how good not to have to fear either one. Now the

stairs . . . the curtain moved gingerly. Judas saw a dark silhouette in the scant moonlight. One of us, he thought. Might
be Thomas. He waited for him to light the lamps. Yes, it was
Thomas.

The disciple held up a lamp and surveyed the room timidly.
He spotted Judas. With a startled cry, he sprang toward the
door. Judas was quicker; he reached it first, barred the
opening.

"Don't you recognize me?" he cried. "It's me, Judas!"

Thomas cowered, his arm crooked in front of his face as if
he were warding off a blow. "Judas . . .," he stammered.

"Where are the others?"

Thomas glanced apprehensively around the room without
answering.

What a coward, Judas thought to himself. "No, there's no
one here," he reassured him. "They released you, didn't
they?"

A fresh wave of fear rose in Thomas's face. He began to
edge toward the door. Judas held him back with both arms.
"Wait," he said in a kindly voice. "I have to explain everything to you."

"Explain?" Thomas repeated.

"Yes, explain. You see, my plan is this: since Jesus doesn't
want or is afraid to take over leadership of the Jewish nation,
then the Jewish nation will itself have to proclaim him king.
But that will only be possible when the people see that he's
been arrested by the chief priests."

Now, hearing himself talking aloud, his words, his arguments suddenly sounded hollow, empty. For the first time he
felt unsure of what he was trying to make Thomas believe.
He kept on talking, uttering the words, but his mouth felt as
though it were full of straw. He listened to himself: would his
words finally ring true, would he succeed in firing not just
Thomas's enthusiasm but his own. His voice seemed to come
from another room. ". . . . The conditions are ideal right now
. . . Jerusalem full of pilgrims who know us, whom Jesus
taught and healed and fed. . . . After the festival days . . . no
one left to defend Jesus when the priests move against him
. . . they will surely move against him. . . ."

He thought he would never finish. He recited it like a worn, tired old tale that he himself could not take seriously any more. ". . . . Now all we have to do is spread the word as quickly as possible over all Jerusalem that the chief priests have thrown Jesus into prison. Then the crowds will tear him out of their grasp and proclaim him king."

He could see that his words had made no impression on Thomas. Just the opposite; he eyed him more suspiciously now. Finally Thomas spoke: "Why are you telling me this? You know it's all a lie."

"What do you mean, a lie?" Judas exclaimed angrily. "You don't believe me? Who do you take me for?"

Thomas was silent for a moment. Still eyeing him distrustfully, he began to speak: "You knew what the chief priests were circulating round the city yesterday. Telling everyone that Jesus wants to seize command, and that Herod would then march in with his divisions and a fratricidal war would break out. And that the Romans are just waiting for an opportunity like that so they can force the entire nation into slavery. Didn't you see them? On every corner, priests, Pharisees, scribes, gathering people around and explaining all this to them. Didn't you see them?"

It was true, he had in fact heard about them. His fears began to grow. "I heard. But no one will believe them." He started to repeat his arguments again: "The whole city is full of our people. As soon as they hear about the arrest—"

"You talk as if you didn't know our people," Thomas interrupted curtly. "No one will budge."

Thomas's voice seemed to have returned to normal, as if the coldness in him had thawed. Judas answered impulsively, "You were always so timid. You'll see, everything will work out—just so long as we make sure that everyone is informed about it first thing in the morning."

He wanted to believe it, he wanted Thomas to believe him, he wanted his other companions to believe him. "Where are Peter and the others?" he asked.

Thomas shrank at the question. He would not answer. Judas was piqued. "Why don't you answer me?" he shouted. "Don't you believe me?"

"No," the other said very simply.

Judas's strength suddenly flagged, he crumbled. The last thread on which he had been depending was cut.

Thomas suddenly broke free of his grasp and ran out. The rapid clapping sound of his sandals echoed in the empty street, then faded into the distance. Judas shivered—what now? Something had to be done. Not all was lost. Even if the others refused to help him, there were still some who would understand. Jesus had to be saved. That fact, put in those words, terrified him. He suddenly thought of Mary Magdalene and Lazarus. He would go to them. At least he could talk to them; they would finally understand him and help him once he explained what he had in mind.

He dashed into the street—if only he could find the fastest route out of this accursed city. Again he blundered hopelessly through the maze of lanes and alleys, falling over stones and over sprawled and sleeping pilgrims. At last, a gate—not the right one. To find the Bethany road, he would have to circle nearly half the city. He half ran, took shortcuts that led nowhere, tumbled into holes, caught and ripped his clothing on thorns and bushes. His frantic rushing brought him to the edge of collapse. By the time he found the Bethany road, dawn had broken and the sunrise was just over the horizon. The road ahead of him was easy, but even so, it seemed to lengthen interminably. Alternately, he ran till his lungs burned, slowed to a fast march to catch his breath, then ran again. Thomas's words still hammered in his ears—but Thomas was a born pessimist. All those times the others had laughed and teased him because he would not believe anything he was unable to touch with his own two hands. . . . "Well," he muttered to himself, "people like that never get far in the world. He'll come around when he finds I am right."

The entrance to Lazarus' enclosure was locked. Judas feared he would lose precious time rattling and pounding on the gate, trying to rouse someone, but he was pleasantly surprised to see the gate swing open at the first knock. A pair of servants stood in the entrance. Judas did not recognize either of them.

"I want to speak to Lazarus," he said.

"I'll summon the steward at once," one of the two replied and ran off.

All round the courtyard, in front of the house, large numbers of servants were milling about. He was puzzled—up so early? Were they celebrating the holiday already? He did not know what to make of it. He noticed that they hurriedly bolted the door behind him. Since when did they have such strange customs here? he wondered. He saw the steward approach, he greeted him. For a moment, the steward failed to recognize him, then he recoiled with a startled look on his face.

"What's the matter? Don't you recognize me?" Judas asked.

"I recognize you. You're Judas, the traitor."

They already know, Judas thought to himself.

"Are you alone?" The steward shot the question at him like an interrogator.

"And who am I supposed to be with? I'm alone."

"What do you want here?"

"I want to speak to Lazarus."

The servants began to crowd around them. Another instant and they had closed around them in a tight ring. Judas noticed then that each man was armed. The steward threw them a quick look, then demanded, "Why? Do you want to hand him over to the chief priests, as well?"

Judas had had just about enough. "I'm not interested in talking to you," he said coldly.

"If I were in Lazarus' place," the steward growled, "I would have you killed right here as you stand. But I haven't the right, and I know that he wouldn't do that either. So I'm letting you go free, but get out now, and never show your face here again, because you will be sorry if you do."

"I won't leave until I talk to Lazarus," Judas insisted. "It's not just concerning him or me, it's a question of Jesus' life."

"I don't believe anything you say. And don't you dare even speak his name. For the last time, I'm warning you: get out. Lazarus isn't here."

"What about Mary?"

"She isn't here either."

"Where did they go?"

"That is not your concern."

The men began to press forward threateningly. Judas asked no more questions. Badly shaken, he backed out of their circle and out through the gate. He could feel their eyes burning into him full of hatred. There was nothing to do but return to Jerusalem. They stood a long time in the gate watching him. Someone yelled something to him; he ignored it. Then someone else. Then they all broke into long harsh laughter. The sound carried over the field, followed him at his back, jeering laughter—would they never stop? He quickened his steps, and then ran, trying to outdistance the sound. He could not listen to that laughter. Beyond a hill, out of sight, he finally managed to compse himself. The blood pulsed like drum beats in his temples. Rest, he had to rest, at least for a moment, then he would continue on his way. He stretched out on the ground; the sky shimmered brilliantly overhead— it augured a beautiful day.

He collected his thoughts. In the end, everything had turned out well after all: if Lazarus and Mary Magdalene had already gone to look into the affair, then his mission was accomplished; his role in the matter was ended. The ferment that he had planned and predicted around the arrest of Jesus was beginning to stir. But he could not just lie there, he had to get back to the city. Although he felt as though he could not take another step without collapsing, although he hurt in every muscle of his body, he struggled to his feet and forced himself to walk in the direction of Jerusalem.

By now it was fully daylight. The closer he got to the city, the more pilgrims he met trudging along the way. The city gate was jammed with them, the crush thickening by the minute. The clamor of human voices merged with the lowing of cows and the bleating of sheep into an ear-splitting uproar. He could discern no signs of unrest; the life of the city seemed to be trundling on as usual toward another loud, busy day.

He elbowed his way through the crowds in the direction of the temple. First he had to find out what was happening with Jesus, what kind of arrest they were holding him in. As he squeezed along the wall, he noticed a group of women huddled in a recess, weeping. Could they have heard the news already? he wondered. Then he recognized one of the women among them—she had helped them somewhere along the road during their travels with Jesus.

"Why are you weeping?" he asked her.

The woman lifted a frightened face to him, recognized him, stopped her crying. "You are Judas, one of the Twelve, aren't you?"

"Yes."

"And you don't know?"

"I know.The chief priests have arrested Jesus."

"Is that all?"

"Yes. He's under arrest now somewhere. I'm looking for him."

The woman stared at him, a look of astonishment on her face. Slowly her face crumpled in a spasm of weeping. "Then you don't know?" she sobbed. "They have condemned him to death. He passed this way with a cross just a short time ago."

He felt the hair in his scalp stand on end. An icy chill washed over him. "Woman, you must be mistaken. They were leading someone else out to die." He could barely choke out the words.

"No, I'm not mistaken." She broke into another surge of sobs.

"When was this?" His voice was barely audible.

"Around eight. We were walking along this street quite by chance—I'm not from this city, I'm from Galilee. Suddenly I looked—I saw them leading criminals to their execution. The soldiers pushed us out of the way up against the wall here, and then one of the condemned men stopped here in front of us because he didn't have the strength to go on. It was Jesus."

"You must be mistaken," he repeated in a daze.

"It was him,," she insisted. "He started to speak to us—it was only then that I recognized him, because his face was so covered with blood."

Judas fell back heavily against the wall. "Where were they going?" he asked.

"To Golgotha."

Groping and pushing against the wall with his hands, he tore frantically up the hill, thrusting people roughly out of his way to get to the gate. From there, a wide unobstructed expanse opened out before him, terminating in the hill of Golgotha, where the scene at the top chilled his blood: three crosses, three men suspended from them; in the middle Jesus, coated with blood. He felt himself reeling and sinking in blackness to the ground; he tried to cry out: "People, people . . .!" but no one could hear; his throat had tightened and choked off the sound.

When he recovered his senses, he found that he was clawing the ground with his hands and heaping dust over his head. Something familiar, something Jesus had once said echoed in the back of his mind . . . what was it he had said? He tried to recall his exact words: ". . . . And when you do penance, wash your faces and brush your hair, so you won't be like the Pharisees, who want to be seen by all the people."

He picked himself up, stiff-legged, brushed himself off, straightened up and smiled in his characteristic fashion very faintly, just lightly under the mustache, with a slight squint of his eyes. He turned and started back toward the city. As he threw his coat over his arm, his hand brushed against the little purse of money bulging at his waist. "In matters of business, all things should be settled to the last detail"—he was quoting himself. "The matter of this money, then, ought to be put in order as quickly as possible," he muttered to himself. What was it Jesus once said? "You cannot serve God and Mammon." A fresh wave of memories blew over him.

He directed his steps toward the temple grounds. He plunged through the snarl of alleys where the everyday throb of city life and business was already in full swing: pedlars shouting, inviting, exhorting, pressing to examine their merchandise; buyers trying, testing, bargaining, quarrelling with them; the pungent odors of hot olive oil, garlic, and meats roasting and smoking on spits, saturating the air. Judas saw it all now with cold, brutal clarity. He thought to himself ironically: and these were the people who were going to fight for a new kingdom.

The temple grounds were teeming with pilgrims. Faces and attire from every part of the world swirled before his eyes. Singing, shouting, talking, bleating, lowing—every sound imaginable assaulted his ears. He thrust his way through the sea of humanity, so busily absorbed in its own affairs. He found the hall where he had last spoken with the chief priests. Pushing aside the heavy curtain, he stepped inside. It was dark within. He could not distinguish anything in the gloom, yet he was certain that, as he entered, he had distinctly heard voices. They ceased with his appearance. Flattened against a wall, he waited for his eyes to adjust to the dusk. Now he could make out two figures in the room. They did not notice him; they did not want to notice him. The conversation was resumed. He stood motionless, with his head and back pressed against the wall, afraid that in another instant he would simply topple over. Who of them would understand? Or even want to understand? He heard his own voice in the room: "I have sinned. I have betrayed innocent blood." He said it to no one in particular, really to himself. His whisper carried widely around the hall. The murmuring stopped abruptly. Through half-closed lids, he saw one of the two men detach himself from where he was standing up against the wall, and come toward him. He recognized one of the priests who had been with him yesterday.

"Caiaphas and the other chief priests are all at Golgotha," he said. "Annas is the only one here. Shall I call him for you? Do you want to speak with him?"

He had hardly thought about that, all he wanted to do was leave the money and go. Speak with Annas? All right. And maybe tell him everything. He nodded his head, too weak to answer. The priest disappeared. Judas watched the other one bustling about the room. He seemed to see him in another dimension. . . . After all that had happened, that someone could still occupy himself with these kinds of things. . . . Did anything make sense any more?

Annas entered in the company of a servant. He paused, peered around. At least he appeared not to recognize Judas.

Finally he stumped over to him and stopped, as he had done the last time, very close, so close that Judas could feel his breath on his face.

"What do you want?"

Judas sensed uncertainty in his voice. He thinks I want something else from him, he thought to himself. All his tenseness suddenly fell away. It was no use, what could Annas possibly understand? Why bother to explain? So that he could have one more satisfaction?

"What do you want?" he asked again.

Judas was about to turn and walk out without a word, when he felt the purse of money in his hand. "I have betrayed innocent blood," he said mechanically.

He saw the tightened muscles in the other's face suddenly relax. The two men stared at each other a long moment. Then Annas hissed, "What has that to do with me? That's your affair." He spun around and started from the room.

Judas watched him go. What had he expected from him? That Annas would cheer him? Explain it all away? Take the blame upon himself? As it was, Annas was gracious enough not to burst out laughing. No, he would never have been able to stand it if Annas had laughed.

He wanted to escape that place as quickly as possible. But . . . there was still the money. He wanted to throw it after Annas, but he had not the strength and, anyway, it would have been a melodramatic gesture. He placed the money purse on the tiling—or rather, he let it fall out of his hands. Then practically feeling his way along the wall, he left and went out into the gallery.

Outside he was struck by the brilliant sunlight and the commotion. He made his way rapidly through the crowds, anxious to get away from the temple. Over the din, he thought he heard his name. Someone was calling him. No, he must have imagined it, who would still want him? Or maybe . . .? Maybe something had changed? Maybe there was someone waiting with good news for him? He looked around hopefully. Through the milling crowd he saw the priest he had led to Gethsemane, now sitting and collecting the temple tax from the swarming pilgrims. He came up alongside him and stood a few minutes watching his hands: the speed with which they collected the money, counted it, tossed it into the coffer, jotted notes and figures in the scrolls. Finally the priest looked up. Without interrupting the rhythm of collecting, tossing, counting, jotting, he said, "Well, with your help we finally got rid of that teacher from Nazareth. We had to work fast, otherwise we would have had a disaster on our hands. Don't be surprised—we couldn't keep him in prison and wait around for the rabble to demolish the temple—so his prophecy would come to pass. You don't even know how meticulously every last detail was thought out and arranged beforehand. We had to sentence him before the people could get wind of it. The trial with Annas and Caiaphas was very quick—at night, right after bringing him from Gethsemane. I was there."

"Did he defend himself?"

"Not in the least. To the High Priest's questions, he admitted that he was the Son of God."

Judas thought he could hear the words ringing in his ears: ". . . And when they will lead you into the synagogues and question you, do not be anxious about how or what you will answer. The Spirit will help you."

"Did you beat him?" Judas asked quietly.

"I didn't, but there were some who did. They even spat at him."

Judas half closed his eyes. Again, like a far off echo he heard: ". . . And if they strike you on the left cheek, turn then the right. And if they take away your coat, give them also your cloak."

The priest's words buzzed, superimposed themselves over those other memories; he felt as if he were existing in two worlds, the priest's narrative, and that other world, the world of Jesus.

". . . . Then the chief priests took him to Pilate. Very early in the morning—he did not even want to see them. But they warned him that he'd better see them or rioting could break out. Just as we expected, Pilate wanted to save him. He sent them packing to Herod. That was something none of us had anticipated—it was an extremely dangerous delay. When they got there, Herod was just finishing off a feast. He was drunk, but still sober enough not to do anything foolish. He amused himself a bit with Jesus and then sent him back to Pilate. Our chief priests are always very farsighted. All our people were ordered to assemble in the square and clamor for the death of Jesus. As many Pharisees as were available came, as well— I never thought there were so many of them in Jerusalem. We screamed and shouted so hard that I'm hoarse. I can hardly talk now."

"What did you shout?"

"What they told us to shout, mostly 'Crucify him!' Pilate shouted at us so many times, now we shouted back at him. We wouldn't stop until Pilate agreed. He agreed finally, though he did his best to save him. He even ordered him to be scourged."

"He was scourged?"

Like a ghostly voice out of the past came the words: ". . . And the Son of Man will be taken, and scourged, and then they will crucify him." Why, he already knew everything ahead of time!

The priest went on, pausing every few minutes to make an inscription in the scrolls: "The chief priests had an idea. They told the soldiers to go ahead and amuse themselves with the 'King of the Jews' if they wanted to. The soldiers crammed a crown made out of thorns on his head. It didn't spill a lot of blood, but enough to change his appearance. Just in case— it made it more difficult to recognize him with that thing on his head."

A fresh wave of despair swept over Judas. Had not Jesus always talked about his kingdom? About how a new kingdom was at hand, about how he was a king?

"But he didn't inspire any pity," the priest drawled on. "Pilate didn't realize exactly who had come before his palace. Finally the chief priests threatened to denounce him to Caesar, and then he consented to Jesus' death. The chief priests wanted to have Jesus hanged by eight, before the city was up. He was crucified at nine, finally."

"What happened after that?"

"After that, I don't really know myself, because I came back here. I have to hurry, see how many people? I only know this: to the very end every possible precaution was taken. He was led along with two criminals. They were surrounded by a very tight cordon. In fact, the people still don't know what has happened, and they won't find out very quickly either, because he won't be hanging there very much longer. A delegation has already gone to Pilate for permission to break the bones of all three and take them down from the crosses." He stopped. After a moment he said, "You know everything now."

"Yes, everything," he murmured.

"What are you going to do now?" the priest asked.

But Judas had already turned away and was pushing his way off the temple grounds.

He knew everything, he had settled everything. What next? He had just noticed that a black cover of storm clouds had spread across the sky, darkening the air like dusk. Heavy drops of rain began to pummel the ground. Where should he go? Home? He smiled bitterly to himself. There was only one person to whom he would want to go now, with whom he would want to speak. For whom he lived. What was it he had said? "Woe to that man by whom the Son of Man will be betrayed. It were better for him if he had not been born."

Suddenly, urgently, Judas had to know—had Jesus been thinking of him when he said that? Yet, if he knew so much, then surely he must have known his intentions as well. Then why had he used the word "traitor"? The plan simply had not worked, all they had needed was a bit more luck. It was not a bad plan, there was a chance he might have become king. Except the others were faster and shrewder. So why had he cursed him?. . . Perhaps Jesus never really wanted to be king? Perhaps he had said all those other things as a warning to stop him? Maybe he had never understood Jesus at all? But now he was hanging on a cross. Judas quickened his steps, he had to get to him, maybe he would speak, say something to him. Maybe he would give him a sign of forgiveness.

The storm broke with an insane fury. Fingers of white lightning stabbed across the opaque sky. Heavy peals of thunder shook the air, rolled across the rooftops. Streams of water bathed the streets, over his feet and sandals. The streets were completely deserted. He pressed forward against the rain, slipping on the wet stones. He passed the city gate, climbed the rising plateau. Through the spatter of rain and incessant claps of thunder, he thought he heard the sound of voices. Figures moving up ahead--definitely returning from Golgotha. His heart leaped to his throat—could Jesus already be dead? In a blaze of lightning, he saw priests and Pharisees among the descending group. He hastened off the road, pulled his hood over his eyes; he was afraid of being recognized. He huddled off to one side, straining to hear what they were saying. Words, scraps of conversation reached him . . . no, it couldn't be . . . yes, it was true, Jesus was already dead. It was not possible. He still had to see him, he still had to hear him. He broke into a mad run up the slope, stumbling, sliding on the mud to his knees, clawing over rocks, stones. His hood flew back from his head; rain water, dripping from his hair, seeped into his eyes. He could hardly breathe; his heart pounded so hard, he thought it would shatter his rib cage. At last, the top of the hill. He looked up. Through the gray streaming rain he could see three shadowy crosses. Which one? He shaded his eyes with his hand to keep out the driving rain. The sky erupted with a blinding bolt of lightning. He saw . . . two definitely alive, neither of them Jesus. Then the one in the middle—could it be? He did not recognize him, how was that possible. Maybe it wasn't true after all. Maybe they did not really crucify him, maybe that was not him up there at all. Maybe the priest had lied, maybe they had simply nailed up another criminal instead. Maybe they had secreted him away, hidden him, were holding him somewhere. Maybe he was still alive. A wave of hope swept over him. It had to be true, otherwise he would have recognized him. How could he not recognize him? A shaft of light tore across the sky just over the top of the hill. For an instant it was bright as a sunny day. In the moment of brilliance, he saw: it *was* his body. Bluish, lacerated, streaked with thick crimson tracks, wet and shiny and slippery from rain and blood, frozen, hardened in agony; his torso twisted with a grotesque posture, his head hanging, staring with vacant, unseeing eyes, his beard terminating in a red congealed clot from the blood trickling down his face from under the crown of thorns. Judas stared, transfixed in horror by that alien, remote body. As suddenly as it had appeared, the scene vanished. He turned his head away quickly, afraid that at any moment another flash of lightning might bring it back. And he could not look at it again, not a second time. He felt as if his lungs had collapsed, as if he were suffocating. An inhuman cry suddenly issued from his mouth. He plunged down the hill, sliding, falling, springing back up again, faster, farther, screaming like a man possessed—like the possessed man near the cemetery in Galilee, he thought. But no, he was not mad, he knew what he was doing. But he could not hold back the screams, he had to keep on running. As far as possible from that cross on the hill. He ran till he fell, spent, numb. He lay against some rocks, hugging them, panting for air, then he sprang to his feet again—he had to keep on going. He was quiet now. He walked. He knew he would never rid himself of that image. That body—contorted, pinned to the wood—it had no relation to Jesus. It was a stranger's body, ghostly, horrible. Jesus had never been there.

Suddenly he realized how completely alone he was. In an instant his life had suddenly become devoid of meaning. The ground seemed to be shifting beneath his feet. His world, in which he had moved, in which he had lived, was gone. And he wanted no other. He had no desire to seek or build a new world. He had never realized before how Jesus had become the point of reference for everything that occurred in his life. Everything he was, everything he lived for, was bound up with Jesus. All things gained confirmation or condemnation accordingly: Jesus was his rule, his standard for thought and action. And now he was gone.

The rain whipped him mercilessly. "Where am I anyway?" he wondered aloud. The city sounds and voices had stayed far behind. He peered around through the rain—he was on the road to Bethany. The road he had tramped so many times with Jesus. He felt cold. His wet clothing clung to him like so many clammy hands. Unexpectedly, with brutal impact, the realization hit him: he, Judas, was to blame for Jesus' death.

Stubbornly he kept up a wall of defense against the thought, telling himself that he never intended to hurt Jesus, that he only wanted to save him. Now the truth began to surge in through a widening chink in the wall—he was a partner to the crime. Maybe they would not have found Jesus were it not for him. Maybe the chief priests were only bluffing about how omnipotent they were. Maybe Jesus would have managed to escape. Maybe he would still be alive. The thought utterly crushed him. He wanted to lie down, but there was nowhere to lie, only mud and puddles and the indifferent rain. So he walked, just to walk, weaving across and across the road like a drunkard.

He searched his mind for arguments in his own defense. Then he remembered a text from the Law: ". . . . Because cursed by God is he who hangs from a tree". He spoke to himself out loud on the deserted road: "If Jesus was hanged on a cross, then it was because he was cursed by God. After all, it is written in the Scriptures. In that case, I am a decent man and he is the criminal." He laughed lightly to himself. "But if he is cursed, then so am I. My place is near him; we are bound together. His fate is my fate. I am nothing without him. If he is hanging from a cross, then I should be hanged alongside him. The only trouble is, there were plenty of them happy to crucify him; there are no volunteers to crucify me." He laughed again to himself: no volunteers to crucify him. So many of them ready and eager to hang Jesus, but no one available to hang him. They had no reason to do so. It was too bad that Jesus had a different opinion on that matter. Again the words stood before him in sharp focus: "Woe to that man by whom the Son of Man will be betrayed. It were better for him if he had never been born".

He stopped short in the middle of the road and said aloud, "With my own ears I heard what he was saying to me, and I didn't understand. How could I not have understood? He must have known everything about me and my agreement with the chief priests. He was warning me. He could not have said it more clearly. And I thought that I knew better than he what was going on. I wanted to save him and I turned him over to the chief priests." He smiled. "Now if it wasn't

for that money, the whole episode would be a lot cleaner.''
Automatically he reached for the rope around his waist where
the pouch of silver had been tied. He tightened it around
him. "How did Jesus put it? Woe to that man? So that means
it is woe to me. I am that man who should never have been
born.''

But there was someone, something else he had once cursed.
What was it? Then he remembered: the barren fig tree.

They had been on their way from Bethany then, they were
hungry, they stopped under the tree and searched it for fruit.
Later, when they were returning that way again, they saw
that the tree had withered.

Suddenly a spark of hope ignited in him: maybe the tree
had revived? Jesus himself once said that a barren tree should
be left alone for a time, then dug around with a trench and
watered, and maybe then it would bear fruit. Maybe that fig
tree had revived? He felt an irresistible urge to see it, check
it; he had to know. He looked through the heavy rain, surely
it could not be too far away from here? A form up ahead, that
was it, about a stone's throw from where he was. He ran
toward it, trying to see through the blur of water in his eyes.
He cupped his hand over his forehead and stared: the tree
was bare. Thin branches like wires bristled stiffly in the air.
Drops of rain were beating down on the scant dried leaves.

ANNAS

"That is none of my concern," Annas grumbled, shuffling in circles around the room. "You have your own High Priest, let him manage your affairs. I want some peace and quiet. I'm entitled to it by now, don't you think?"

He said it mechanically, like a formula, he had used it so often. Suddenly he stopped short, as if the gist of the message had only now hit him. "What did you say? What has Caiaphas decided to do?"

"To kill Lazarus," came the reply a second time.

Imbecile, he thought to himself. Why was he always so stupid? "Bring him here at once," he snapped to the priest.

He was rankled; he resented being called away from his place in front of the Holy of Holies, where he sat whole days before the veil separating the Sanctuary from the rest of the temple. It was how he spent his days ever since Caiaphas was made High Priest. He was content in his declining years to give himself over wholly to prayer. The atmosphere of silence broken only by liturgy suited him. He liked the singing, the smoking incense, the processions. It was his world. "This is my role," he would say. "For this I am responsible, that the chosen nation renders God his due tribute." Called away to his home now, he paced the room impatiently with small mincing steps.

How did Caiaphas even dream up a scheme like that? He must have completely lost his head. But Annas had to admit, he too had begun to lose his head. Nothing like this had ever happened in his entire life. Instinctively, he moved towards the window to listen to the hum of the city. He had learned this habit of listening to the city a long time ago. The noise

97

was bad again today. Hostile, menacing. Hostile toward the priests, menacing to the temple.

But he had only himself to blame. He had ignored that carpenter. He and the whole temple with him. He had ignored him, or rather had tried to ignore him. Even in his mind, he had dismissed any idea of danger on his part. He had simply refused to be defiled by contact with that Galilean even by thinking about him. He was not a worthy enough opponent. He had never even wanted to discuss him, nor—following his examples—had the other temple servants. Now he was forced to admit that he had only been deceiving himself, just as they had been deceiving themselves. Though it was true that their discussions had, at times, touched upon the topic of the Galilean, but in a different way: they had enjoyed themselves immensely at the expense of the Pharisees, watching them suffer defeat after defeat in their encounters with Jesus.

At that stage, he had not considered Jesus an antagonist; quite the opposite, he was almost an ally. Personally, he was delighted to see someone finally telling those mules to their faces about how ridiculous they were. How satisfying to see those swell-headed Pharisees getting their eyes blackened. Privately, he even sympathized with Jesus, wished him well. He considered him an accomplished tactician. Until the moment he heard about that speech of his in which he summed up his point with that last statement: "God wants compassion, and not sacrifices". Then he had felt personally attacked; that was direct provocation. He had better not dare start on us, he had threatened him in his mind, because he won't win against us.

That was all the more reason why Caiaphas's decision infuriated him now. Where was he anyway? When he needed him he was never around, but when he wanted a moment of peace, there was no getting rid of him. The fool did not even ask if it was the right thing to do. Just like the time he had sent some priests to conduct discussions with Jesus. Of course, it was something that should have been done, but it should have been prepared in advance. How could they have tried the tired old riddle about the woman with seven brother-husbands on such an opponent to demonstrate the absurdity of the resurrection? He could just see them, with that crafty gleam in their eyes, asking him, ".... And in the resurrection, whose wife of them will she be? The first, the second ... or the seventh?" They might try to dupe some dimwitted fisherman from the Lake of Tiberias with a question like that, but not him, not the master of dispute, who could not only maneuver himself out of the trickiest, most cunning questions put to him by the scribes and Pharisees, but could destroy his opponents with their own weapons as well.

Caiaphas came in. As usual—first the timorous face in the door, then the rapidly shifting eyes squinting carefully around the room, then the rest of him sliding in like a cat.

All that shilly-shallying irked Annas—would he never learn to behave as befitted the High Priest? And this was supposed to be his son-in-law to boot.

"Is there something new? Why did you call me?" he asked in a loud raspy whisper.

Instantly Annas felt his temper flare. He would not answer, he forced himself to say nothing. He paced the floor trying to compose himself. Finally he halted in front of Caiaphas, very close, eye to eye. "Have you gone mad?" he hissed.

Caiaphas fell back. He spread his palms out in front of him "What do you mean? I beg your pardon, but I don't understand that. What do you want from me?"

"And what do you think?" Annas moved away from him to continue his circling around the room.

"You mean about Lazarus?" His voice was shrill. "Well then, I very politely ask you, what alternative do you see? Do you not see what's happening? All of Jerusalem is flocking to see him. He's not just anybody. He's no cured street beggar. Hundreds of people were at his funeral. All Jerusalem knew him. And now that dead man is walking about the earth and telling everyone that Jesus raised him from the dead."

"And you believe that he raised him from the dead?"

Confusion flickered across his face. He fluttered his eyelids, tried to say something; he mumbled out an incoherent word and shifted his eyes around.

Annas did not miss his reaction. He resumed his pacing. So, even that fool Caiaphas believed. . . . What would happen, he wondered, when it got to the point where he, too, would begin to vacillate. He felt completely isolated.

"And may I ask your opinion about what happened?" Caiaphas tried to answer the attack with a clumsy counterattack.

"I think that it isn't Lazarus who should be killed, but someone else," he snapped.

"Who? Jesus? For what?" Caiaphas blurted out, then instantly regretted it.

Annas held him captive in a long cold gaze. How radically he has changed in relation to Jesus, he thought to himself. And in such a short time. Aloud he said, "You'll see that I was right. And probably very soon, too. But now go and recall your orders. Then come right back. We have to talk."

Caiaphas edged red-faced out the door.

So . . . that's how it is. Even that idiot Caiaphas. . . . Yet, there had been warning signals all along . . . that time Jesus healed that beggar who begged outside the temple—the one who was born blind.

. . . . Yes, it was Caiaphas—always Caiaphas—who came running with the news of the rumour running through Jerusalem—and more significantly among the people of the temple—that Jesus had performed a new "miracle". And not somewhere remote, on the banks of the Lake of Gennesaret, or on the outskirts of the city, but right inside the very temple itself. Like a challenge tossed into all their faces. And that naive Caiaphas claimed he was finally going to put a stop to all that quackery and prove to the world that the Galilean was nothing but a cheat. "Leave it," he told him then. "No," Caiaphas retorted, "let the truth finally come out into the open." "Leave it," he said again. "Why? Anyway, I have already suggested to the Pharisees that they should handle the matter. They took to the idea with gusto." "Imbecile," he called him then. He was insulted. "Imbecile," he repeated a second time. Then he strode up to him, very close the way he always did, within inches of his face, and stared him straight in the eyes. But Caiaphas averted his head, stared demonstratively out the window to show that he did not care, he was not going to accept it. "Don't you understand that

it's not important whether it happened like that or not?"
Caiaphas bristled. "No, I don't understand. Then what, what
is important?" "If you don't understand that, then I'm not
going to explain it to you. You're the High Priest, it's your
affair." Unexpectedly Caiaphas burst out with, "Yes, that's
right, I know you're jealous of me." He felt the blood rush to
his head, he saw red. He never expected Caiaphas to be so
insolent. He pointed with his arm to the door. "Get out. Get
out this instant." Sure enough, Caiaphas came back later to
apologize, but he really came to boast about all the detailed
reports he had collected involving the temple healing.

". . . . Can you imagine, they say Jesus spat on the ground
and made mud of the spittle and smeared the man's eyes
with it, and then told him to go and wash in the pool of Siloe.
A few people led him away to wash, and he began to see.
They say he went back to Jesus crying for joy like a baby.
Then he came to us. In fact, that was when I suggested to
the Pharisees that they ought to look into the matter. As I
was later informed, the Pharisees questioned him very
thoroughly. The beggar told them: 'He put mud on my eyes,
I washed, and I see.' But as you recall, it was Saturday. A
few of the Pharisees fell on him, saying, 'This man is not of
God who doesn't keep the Sabbath.' But there were others
who disagreed, who defended Jesus. They said, 'How can a
man who is a sinner perform such miracles?' And can you
imagine, they started quarelling fiercely among
themselves. . . ."

He seethed as Caiaphas prattled on, he could barely hold
back his fury. And the High Priest, completely oblivious,
continued to talk.

". . . . Imagine, right there in front of that man they started
quarrelling among themselves like thieves. I thought they
would never stop. Finally they all decided that this was not
the same man but someone else altogether, an imposter
planted by Jesus. Just one big masquerade. Nothing could be
simpler than to contact the beggar's family. They summoned
his parents—as it happens, they live in Jerusalem. I was there
when they questioned them. They arranged a type of official
hearing. When asked, Is this your son whom you say was

blind at birth? they replied in the affirmative. Then they were
asked, How is it that he now sees? It was a sly, deliberate
question, meant to trip them up, find out if they were in
collusion with Jesus or his disciples. But these were Jerusalem
people; they could smell a rat, they knew better than to play
with fire. They were very cautious. They said, 'We know that
he is our son, and we know that he was born blind, but in
what way he now sees, this we don't know'. They didn't want
to say any more. Though we pressed them, they denied knowing anything else, as if they knew something else. All they
repeated was, 'We know nothing'. Until one of our own people
blurted out to them that their son was now able to see because
someone had given him sight. They did not look at all surprised by that bit of information, and all they said was, 'We
don't know who opened his eyes'. Finally they became downright rude and left, saying, 'Why don't you ask him? He is of
age, he'll know how to speak for himself'."

By now Annas was staring at Caiaphas in wide-eyed disbelief. Caiaphas talked and acted like a small boy bent on
finding out what was inside his toy, only to be disappointed
when he found sawdust.

". . . . So we all finally agreed that he really was their son
after all."

He stared at him flabbergasted. Why, the man understood
absolutely nothing about what was happening. It must have
been for that very reason that he let Caiaphas talk him into
attending a repeat hearing of the beggar. What he saw and
heard only bore out his suspicions.

He had felt intensely embarrassed in the presence of that
man. He had known him for so many years, but now he was
a different man altogether. He never thought anyone could
change that much, and so suddenly. Now he could understand
why the others had mistaken him for someone else, insisting
that he was not the same beggar. He was somehow free,
liberated, at his ease. And the way he talked: "I don't know
if he who opened my eyes is a sinner. One thing I do know,
whereas I was blind, now I can see." Yes, he was a changed
man. They flooded him with questions: What did he do to
you? How did he open your eyes? How's that?—clay made of

spittle? Mud from the pool of Siloe? Who were the people
with you? The beggar looked around at them, smiling, con-
versing at his ease like a man among equals. No, more like
a man who knows, among men who are lying to themselves.
"I have already told you once, and you did not listen to me.
Why do you want to hear it again? Do you also want to
become his disciples?" He mocked them to their faces. He
drove them to such a passion that some lost control and
behaved like immature schoolboys with no regard for their
dignity: "You're the one who is his disciple, we are the disciples of Moses. We know that God spoke to Moses, but as
to this man, we don't know where he is from.' They were
spluttering fatuities now, and Annas felt all the more embarrassed for them when he saw the beggar amusedly wait out
the flurry of retorts and then say to them, "Now isn't it very
strange that you don't know where he is from, and he has
opened my eyes. Especially when you teach that God does
not hear sinners, but hears him who is a server of God and
does his will." He was mocking them mightily. and then, very
calmly, very confidently, he addressed them as if they were
an assembly of little children: "From the beginning of the
world, it has never been heard that any man has opened the
eyes of one born blind. If this man were not of God, he could
not do anything." The Pharisees flew into a blind range,
screamed at him like men possessed: "Get out! Who do you
think you are preaching to?" Caiaphas was delighted to see
them humiliated and behaving so immaturely.

And that was what terrified Annas most: Caiaphas did not
see the problem. Nor did he see the danger.

That was the first warning signal, and that was when he
should have come to a decision. But he did not take up the
challenge. He must have been afraid. Maybe he wanted to
spare himself. Maybe he thought someone else would take up
the matter. . . . Or maybe it was that he himself was influ-
enced by what had happened. . .? Why had he not reacted?
He could not really answer that question. And since then,
how much had changed! How Caiaphas himself had changed!
Then he had talked about Jesus as if he were a charlatan.
But now. . . .

The second signal came a little later and was related in a way to the first. It was at the time of the last Feast of Tabernacles. The temple guards had received orders to arrest Jesus—another of Caiaphas's brilliant ideas. Of course, the idea was absolute foolishness, but that was not the point. The point was that the guards returned empty-handed. They had simply refused to carry out their orders. An unprecedented act of insubordination! They should have been severely punished, but they were not, out of fear that it might incite greater defiance from them, or even outright revolt. But the most characteristic aspect of the whole episode was their explanation: "No man has ever spoken like that, the way he does". And when the Pharisees and priests lost their tempers and started to berate them—Have you, too, let yourselves be deceived? Have any of the priests or Pharisees believed in him? The rabble that follows around after him doesn't know the Law and the Prophets and is cursed—that was when Nicodemus came to their defense, humiliating the priests right in front of the guards. He said, "Does our Law condemn a man before it hears him and examines his deeds?" So it was not enough that the guards were for him, now it turned out that Nicodemus—whom he considered one of the finest minds in the Sanhedrin—supported him as well.

He turned abruptly and saw Caiaphas standing in the room. As usual, he had slid in undetected.

Without breaking the rhythm of his pacing, he said, "Let's begin with the healings. Do you remember? You once took an interest in the case of that blind beggar outside the temple."

"I beg your pardon," Caiaphas began in that oily tone of voice Annas could not stand, "but why do you keep returning to the subject of healing? He isn't the first prophet to heal. And there were non-prophets who healed as well."

He was clearly in no mood for a serious discussion.

"Did I say there weren't any?" He pretended not to notice his reluctance. "Certainly there were prophets and there were non-prophets, but when they performed miracles, they always intended them as praise to God, to prove that Adonai was more powerful than the pagan gods. You have, for example,

Elisha, who healed Naaman the Syrian. But it's entirely different with this, this . . . trickster. He acts as if healing were his primary function. Do you remember what he said to the disciples of John when they came to ask him, 'Are you the One for whom we are waiting?' "

"If I'm not mistaken, he answered, 'The deaf hear, the blind see, lepers become clean'. But please be so kind as to remember that it was a quotation from Isaiah."

"Yes, and don't you forget that he also added, 'Blessed is he who is not scandalized by me.' Which means he knew something was wrong, that he was overturning God's order."

Caiaphas looked patently unimpressed.

"Does God govern all things, or doesn't he?" Annas went on emphatically. "If yes, then it's up to him if someone is ill or healthy. And we know that God only rewards good. And he punishes evil. By what right does Jesus remove God's punishment? By what right does he heal? With whose power does he oppose God's will? With God's power? Can God act against himself?" Annas could hear his voice rising in impassioned pitch.

"Of course he can't. But if that is the case, then permit me to ask, then with whose power?"

"With Satan's power! And not just Satan's, but with the power of Beelzebub himself, prince of darkness."

"Am I to understand, then, that Satan is more powerful than God?" It had the coy ring of a question put to a child in the heder.

Annas' temper flared. "Don't talk stupid to me, I'm not an infant. If God allows something like this, then it's only to warn us, to point out to us those who are in league with Satan."

"Maybe yes, maybe no. Maybe it's something else altogether."

This wordplay on the part of Caiaphas irked him. He hardly recognized him. Always so submissive and frightened. Now he was suddenly almost defiant. "Explain," he said.

"I don't wish to offend you, but in your opinion the teacher from Nazareth acts to spite the Lord God. Or at least to spite the temple. And with the help of Satan."

"And is it otherwise?"

"I'm truly sorry, but it really seems to me that it's not like that at all. He talks about God altogether differently than we do."

Annas stared incredulously at him, scarcely believing his own ears. As if he were seeing Caiaphas for the first time in his life. So, something had lit up in that empty head of his after all. "Go on," he said quietly. "Unfortunately it seems that way to me too."

A look of confusion crossed Caiaphas's face but he went on resolutely: "Jesus says, 'Blessed are those who weep, those who hunger; blessed are the meek'. In my opinion, his most significant parable is the one about Lazarus and the rich man. In it it's the suffering Lazarus who goes to the bosom of Abraham after death, and not the rich man. Of course, that doesn't particularly appeal to you. Forgive me, according to you the rich man ought to enter into heaven—he was ill because he was a sinner. That's all I have to say. But if you'll permit me, I do want to add this: Jesus didn't think all that up by himself. He refers back to the Prophets, except that he is more radical than they."

Annas bristled; he did not like the Prophets, and he especially did not like it when somebody cited them. "Please, don't start with the Prophets. Stick to the Law. You can go too far with the Prophets."

"Forgive me, but are we permitted to ignore them?"

Annas strutted and fumed across the room. "Who governs the world?" he snapped.

Caiaphas was silent.

"If it's God, then he decides who is rich or poor. And if God is just, then he is rich who deserves to be by an honest and decent life. Isn't that right?"

Caiaphas was uncompromising in his silence.

"Now think, can God contradict himself?"

"As far as I was able to understand Jesus," Caiaphas began slowly, "then according to him, God has mercy on the sick, the suffering—"

"That's not God," Annas broke in. "At best, that's some pagan divinity or a good spirit, but not Almighty God. The things that carpenter teaches are not only blasphemy, but pure and utter drivel."

Again Caiaphas did not answer.

Annas thought to himself, I must have shouted too loud and scared him. "Well, am I right or not?" he asked quietly.

"Well . . . I wouldn't say that. One thing he's not is illogical." His voice drifted; he had no inclination to pursue the conversation.

"Then tell me how you see it. After all, we have to consider these things jointly." Annas spoke gently, as if to a child.

"I think he is very consistent. Who does he surround himself with? Whom does he associate with? Sinners, publicans, prostitutes. Is it because he especially likes them? Maybe he does like them, maybe he doesn't. But there's more to it than that."

Annas thought it must be the first time he had heard Caiaphas talk seriously.

Caiaphas went on shrilly, "I'm not sure, but I think he once said, 'It is not the healthy who need a physician, but they who are ill'. I think he expressed all that in the parable of the prodigal son. You no doubt remember it better than I do."

"Do you mean the parable about the father patiently waiting around for the return of his wastrel son? Who when he caught sight of him from a distance ran out to meet him and covered him with his own coat, and put his own ring on his finger, and made him a great feast? Why, that's so much absolute nonsense. All for a profligate son who couldn't even bring himself to feel truly sorry, but who was returning home because, as he himself said, the hired servants in his father's house were better off than he was? Show me a father anywhere in the world who would treat such a degenerate son that way. Is it proper conduct? Can it be taken as a model? Recommended? And he, the master of Nazareth, is trying to tell us that God is exactly like that."

Indignation swelled like a wave in Annas' chest, rose to his throat and made him gasp and swallow his words and air together. "Is that the way to treat God?! Is that the way to treat sinners?! Who ever heard of such a thing? He makes it

sound as if sinners are doing God a favor when they return
to him. How does he treat God? Not like the Lord, the creator
of heaven and earth, but like a servant who washes men's
feet. How does he dare talk that way about God? How can
God allow it? He ought to punish him with lightning!"

He pulled himself together. Caiaphas was staring at him
hunched up. "Forgive me for flying off the handle like this,"
he said hastily, "but all this worries me dreadfully, and I
have no one to discuss it with. Those priests of yours fear me
like fire—though I can't imagine why—and before I even
begin to speak they start agreeing with me. You are the only
one with whom I can converse honestly, openly. Did you ever
stop to think that the world that Nazarene proposes to his
followers is a world totally different from what they imagine
to themselves? The fact is, they understand little or nothing
of what he preaches. Maybe that's not important to them.
The miracles are what count. And that is why, in my opinion,
this is the biggest misunderstanding in the history of our
nation. They call him the Messiah. In other words, they
consider him the one whom God has chosen to lead the Jewish
nation. But the simple fact is that he is an enemy of this
nation." He paused to give Caiaphas a chance to speak.

Finally Caiaphas did speak. "I don't know . . . I'm not that
knowledgeable in these things, as you yourself keep reminding
me, but be so kind as to be specific—what fault do you find
in him?"

"What fault do I find in him? He calls himself the Messiah!
And I tell you again, that is a pure and shameless lie. He
misleads everyone who listens to him. He's no Messiah. He's
not even a Jew. Worse yet, he covers himself with the patri-
archs and prophets. He calls himself a teacher, but he really
doesn't understand either the Law or the Prophets—or rather,
he doesn't 'not understand'. If he didn't understand, he would
have some justification, but he deliberately and perfidiously
bends the sacred writings to suit his subversive ideas. He
interprets them to suit his own purposes—"

"Yes, thank you," Caiaphas interrupted. You were kind
enough to tell me all this many times in the past. Would you
be so gracious as to tell me something new."

"You want something new? Did you hear what he said in Nazareth? 'Though there were many widows in Israel in the days of Elijah, when heaven was shut up three years and six months, when there was a great famine throughout all the earth, Elijah was not sent to any of them, except to the widowed woman, Sarepta of Sidon. And there were many lepers in Israel in the time of the prophet Elisha, but none of them were cleansed but Naaman the Syrian.' Do you know what that means? Have you ever stopped to think about it? But luckily he missed his mark, because his compatriots figured him out, someone finally grasped his meaning. Remember? They cast their compatriot out of the city and tried to throw him off a cliff. Unfortunately he managed to free himself and get away. Too bad," he sighed. "We wouldn't have all this trouble now with him and his deceit. You want me to be specific about how he is not a Jew? Well, do you remember what he said at the time he spoke to the centurion whose servant he supposedly cured? 'And I say to you, that many shall come from the east and the west, and shall sit down with Abraham and Isaac and Jacob in the kingdom of heaven, but the children of the kingdom shall be cast out into the exterior darkness. There shall be weeping and gnashing of teeth.' Did you understand that?"

He suddenly realized he was shouting again. He felt his face hot and swollen with anger, but he could not control himself: "Here he's no longer Greek or Jew—a pagan or a member of the chosen nation. Now it's no longer important, circumcision or no circumcision. Now it's even the opposite! People call him the Christ, the Messiah. And he concedes it, admits that he is. There's just one small difference: the people understand one thing by the word, he understands quite another."

He stopped. He saw that his words had not made the slightest impact on Caiaphas. This was not the same Caiaphas. These were not the old days anymore. Caiaphas had his own opinions about Jesus and wouldn't give in easily. "What's your opinion about all this?" he asked abruptly.

Caiaphas evaded his gaze and his question. His eyes slipped

around the room. "Me? Nothing. I'm just listening. I'm listening to what you have to say."

Annas saw he would not be able to get any more out of him. He paused to calm himself and, recovering his normal pitch of voice, he went on, "What he proposes is not a Jewish nation, but some kind of supernatural kingdom, to which every individual belongs if he is so-called honest. Anyone who listens carefully to the teachings of this godless man can see that he aims at the destruction of the chosen nation. With him it's no longer important if one derives from the Jewish tribes or if one belongs to the Jewish nation or not. And He still has the nerve to consider himself one of us and the audacity to call himself the Messiah." He was getting excited again. "Do you know what he said? That a Samaritan can be better than a Jew. That harlots and publicans will come before the sons of the chosen nation. That's right. I wonder if you really understand all this."

He glared at Caiaphas, he wanted to make sure it was all sinking in. Now came his most incisive argument: "Did you hear what, in his opinion, God will ask men at the end of the world? Not whether or not they were Jews, or if they went to the temple, or if they offered him sacrifices—when and how many lambs and doves, and if they paid their taxes of caraway and anise on time, as he scoffed. No, no, and once again no. He claims that God will say to them: I was hungry and you gave me to eat; I was thirsty and you gave me to drink; I was in prison and you visited me. And so on, without end. It's that commandment of love of God and neighbor that he always thrusts down our throats. Do you understand that? Only service to men—that's what, in his opinion, we will be judged for. Not a word about being an Israelite, not a word about sacrifices, not a word about prayers."

Caiaphas blinked his eyes and smiled ironically. "I beg your pardon, but I marvel at the trouble you have taken to collect so much information about what he teaches."

"Don't interrupt, this is important. He is wrong. First comes concern about the nation, about those whom God chose to give him glory. First comes concern about the descendants of Abraham—and all their enemies be damned!"

He felt the blood rush to his face. "And what does he teach? The exact opposite. Love your enemies. Do good to those who persecute you. That's the first thing. Secondly, how can you compare visiting a thief in prison—or even feeding a hungry man—to prayer, or to making sacrifices? The temple is paramount! The temple!" He stood over Caiaphas, shouting. "The Tabernacle! The Holy of Holies!"

The same slight foxy smile curled Caiaphas's lips. In the same politely ironic tone of voice, he said, "Perhaps I'm mistaken, but I thought I actually saw that unbeliever in the temple, and it looked to me as if he not only conducted himself reverently, but that he was even praying."

"I heard about that," Annas said in a conciliatory tone.

Caiaphas is certainly defending him, he thought to himself. He went on, "But he only treats all those things as an aid to a good and honest life. But it should be just the opposite. All things must serve God. His glory, his honor. A whole secular life isn't worth one prayer, one sacrifice. Temporal work, toil, is only a necessary evil. The individual's essential function— his most sacred act—is prayer and sacrifice, and men must give themselves up to that. Nothing is sacred to Jesus. Did you hear what he said to the Pharisees when they reproached his disciples for plucking ears of corn on the Sabbath and shelling and eating them? Naturally he quoted the Scriptures. He said, 'Have you never read what David did when he was hungry and those who were with him? How he went into the house of God and taking the loaves of proposition, which were not lawful to eat but for the priests, gave them to those who were with him?' The Sabbath is unimportant to him—the holy day, which God commanded us to honor. Did you hear what he said? 'The Sabbath was made for man and not man for the Sabbath.' Do you know what that means? That's blasphemy. That's sacrilege. Do you understand what kind of danger that epigram conceals? With it he overturns everything. In spite of everything he says, I maintain—to use his wording—that man is made for the Sabbath and must blindly keep it holy. Yes, I repeat, blindly keep it holy. The world he proposes is one in which the temple is dispensable. And even if it were needed, its significance would be reduced to barely nothing. To him sacrifices are unimportant; worldly life is all that matters. What does he always call it—love. He talks about it constantly, everywhere, every chance he gets."

Annas realized he was repeating himself. He stopped, took a deep breath. "You ask me what I mean? This is exactly what I mean, I told you so many times, but nothing seems to sink into that head of yours." His temper flared again. "Did you hear his warning? 'Not all who cry Lord, Lord, will enter into the Kingdom of Heaven, but everyone who does the will of my Father.' There's that 'my Father' again, but that's not what interests me this minute. His is a wholly new concept of life: the relationship between religion and temporal life. That motley lot that straggle along behind him, always on the lookout for new miracles, understands nothing of all this. How many of those half-wits really understand that everything in his world is different? And just to make things a little more amusing, he quotes the Law and the Prophets— in large measure spaciously. How many of those simpletons are capable of understanding? Let's take as an example—did you understand what Jesus meant by his parable about the Samaritan?"

"Why should I have understood it? For what purpose? He wasn't talking to me. I am not his disciple. He's not my teacher. I have the Law. I have you. You are the greatest teacher of the Law. Do I need anything else?"

Annas eyed him coldly. It was difficult for him to show open offense at the sarcasm in Caiaphas's words, spoken as they were in an innocuous tone of voice.

"You are ignorant," he answered. "You have to know your enemy, know who you're up against. That's right, I heard how your friends spat left and right when Jesus dared to say that it was the Samaritan who was good and that he saved the Jew, while the priests and Levites did not help him. Agreed. But did you ever ask yourself the question why didn't Jesus point his finger at some ordinary Jew, but only at the priest and Levite? Why didn't the priest or the Levite stop to save the wounded man? Well, tell me! Because they were hurrying to the temple for services! Do you understand? He rebuked them because their devotions were more important to them than stopping to help the distressed man. Only when you look at that parable from this angle can you grasp its real meaning And I say no! Sacrifices are absolutely more important. That is why he has to die."

But he could see by the doubtful look on Caiaphas's face that he did not agree with him.

Though nothing was actually happening in the city for the next several days, Annas could feel the tension mounting. He had to admit, bitterly, that the initiative belonged wholly to Jesus. We can only defend ourselves, he repeated grimly to himself. Every day seemed like a repetition of the one before it: nothing new, yet an atmosphere of some kind of expectation gathering strength in the air. Though no one talked about it, everyone knew it: something had to happen. And happen it did.

He had just come back from the temple—earlier than usual, because he was disturbed by the little groups of men murmuring in low confidential tones who suddenly broke off every time he approached, and by his friends now edging away from him furtively. A priest hurried into his room. "Jesus is entering the city!" he cried out, then disappeared.

Somehow the words did not affect him. Maybe because he was ready for anything. "Now at least I know," he muttered under his breath. "Better this than that hopeless waiting." He expected that at any moment Caiaphas would slide in and start raving hysterically, but somehow he failed to appear. Maybe he has run away, he thought. Maybe some of the others have fled too. He went over to the other side of the palace. He searched the courtyard. It was ominously quiet and empty. Like a deserted house, he sighed. Well, that means the mob will be here any minute to take care of us. I ought to take something from my rooms with me, in case I have to abandon them, he thought. That is, if they let me take something. I just hope they don't burn anything. And if it is prison for me? No, I wouldn't want that. Perhaps I should leave now, before the fighting erupts? He was dreadfully afraid of getting pushed around by the street rabble. But it was probably too late to escape now anyway.

He returned to his chamber. As he entered, he heard sing-ing. He went to the window and looked down at the advancing throngs. They poured through the streets like a wide splashing river. Exuberant cheering, chanting, and singing filled the air. They sang triumphantly, exultantly. They came closer. More shouting, more singing, the two sounds fused. Annas watched them spellbound. Vaguely he was reminded of a great liturgical procession. He leaned out farther. The thun-derous din from the street struck him full force. And the color green. A forest of branches—where did they get that idea from? he wondered. A sea of bobbing heads, palm branches swung aloft like torches. Finally he saw Jesus. He was riding on the back of a donkey. His head was bent slightly forward, as if he were listening carefully to the singing.

"Ho-san-na, Ho-san-na, Ho-san-na to the Son of David!"

They chanted in ebullient rhythm: "Bles-sed is he, who comes in the name of the Lord!"

Annas scanned the crowd for signs of fighting, beating, pillaging. There were none. Just like a procession, he mused. The scene calmed his serves—this was not the way men proceeded who were bent on seizing power.

For a long time they came on, streaming endlessly past his window. He felt bitterness. And envy. I have lost, anyway, he said to himself in his mind, as he watched the streets slowly empty. No matter what happens next, I have already lost. In my old age, to see the nation choose itself another leader. I am alone. He felt suddenly old, tired.

Caiaphas flew through the door, disheveled, trembling, ranting distractedly. Annas watched him in contemptuous silence: the High Priest was a pitiful sight. He had completely fallen to pieces. What would he look like, Annas wondered scornfully, if something worse ever happened?

He began his rambling around the room to listen to Caia-phas's account of Jesus' entry into Jerusalem. As he listened, he thought smugly to himself: his eyes have finally been opened; he did not want to believe me, or accept what I told him, now look at him. He was under the delusion that the Nazarene would content himself with simply philosophizing.

No, none of that; philosophy always ends in practical consequences—usually with social upheavals.

Caiaphas had managed to calm himself somewhat and now was indignantly repeating how Jesus had censured the Pharisees who were trying to silence the enthusiastic crowds.

". . . . Do you know what he said to them? He said, 'If they would be silent, then the stones would cry out'. How arrogant!"

Annas cut him short impatiently. "Where did he go with that mob?"

"To the temple."

"And what is he doing there?"

"Probably what he always does—teaching."

"I would prefer it if you were there minding the temple. I don't like surprises, and I don't want to go through the same thing as the last time. Only, I don't understand why he didn't do it. . . ."

"Do what?"

"Why he didn't simply come and do away with us," he snapped impatiently.

"Do away with us? Him?"

It came home to him once more how little Caiaphas still understood. His next statement bore it out.

"But we can arrest him."

Annas looked at him as if he were a lunatic. "Maybe you can, because I certainly can't, and neither can anyone else from the temple, that's for sure."

A flurry of footsteps sounded outside the room. A priest hurried in. "I was looking for you." He addressed Caiaphas.

"What has happened?"

"Jesus of Nazareth is throwing the merchants out of the temple."

Caiaphas sprang up without a word and ran from the room.

Annas ran after him. "I told you, I told you," he screeched at their backs. "Mind the temple."

Well, well, he shook his head. Who would have expected it? Throwing the merchants out of the temple! So he has already started to rule the roost, making himself at home like the master of the house. The thought cut him to the quick;

it was as if someone had robbed him of his dearest possession. "No, I won't allow it!" he muttered, and pounded the floor angrily with his staff.

So absorbed was he in his thoughts that he had not noticed the droves of people running from every direction toward the temple. He saw them now, anxiously. Already an immense number were gathered there. With much pushing and shoving, the temple servants cleared a path for him to the interior. What he saw set his hair on end: his temple was his temple no longer. Jesus of Nazareth, grasping a tangle of ropes in his hand, was striding down the aisles, overturning the tables of the merchants and moneychangers. The temple rang with the crack of splintering wood, the metallic clang of scattering, rolling coins, and the curses of the scurrying merchants. That's right, Annas chafed, the merchants were swearing, but no one tried to stop him. Behind him, his people surged—the throng, with its eyes fixed raptly on him; the throng that would not let a finger be raised against its leader. They trod delightedly on the heels of the dealers.

Suddenly Jesus halted, threw his hand with the ropes severely into the air—he wanted to speak. An instant hush fell over the temple, and in the disquieting stillness, Annas heard him thrust words of condemnation into the face of every priest, but especially into his, because he considered himself the master of this house: "My house is a house of prayer, and you have made it a den of thieves."

Every word that followed was one big blasphemy. Annas, leaning heavily against the wall, wanted to get away—just listening was sin enough—but his legs refused to respond.

". . . . God does not need sacrifices of bulls or lambs. . . . God does not need spilled blood or the burning of animal fats."

That son of a carpenter had dared to challenge the whole temple! So, Annas fumed to himself, he has finally told us unequivocally that in his world, there is no room for the temple, nor for us. In that case, we have to explain to him that in our world there is no room for him. He has opposed the teachings of Moses, those things that Moses promised God when he entered into the Covenant. He denies everything that the nation of Israel represents. He has raised his hand against the temple, against the Sanctuary of God, and so now the temple must raise its hand against him.

He pushed his way out to the gallery and stopped a moment to quiet his pounding heart. He began slowly to walk the length of the colonnade. Caiaphas suddenly darted out at him from somewhere.

"Were you there? Did you see it all?" he panted.

"Yes."

Annas walked along in silence. He wanted to be alone. He wished Caiaphas would go away. but he could not think of an excuse for getting rid of him. After a moment he asked, "So, what do you think?"

Caiaphas stared at him with a bewildered look on his face.

Without waiting for a reply, Annas said, "What right does he have to lord it over our temple? That's right, go to him and ask him. And if you don't want to go—and that might be better—then send one of your priests."

Caiaphas left reluctantly.

Annas followed him with his eyes, afraid that he might come back. Then he limped over and sat down in his place in front of the Holy of Holies.

Now he felt calm, he was in his favourite of all places. He hardly noticed that he had begun to carry on a dialogue in his mind with Jesus. . . . What is it you said? God wants man himself, his goodwill? The only sacrifice for which he waits is a good and honest life? The greatest gift is service to one's neighbor? The happiness a man can give God is in forgiving his enemies? One thing is certain in all this: you are too difficult. Who can possibly understand you? Those admirers who constantly follow you around? That is why you will lose. People need to give sacrifices. They need to bring God a sack of wheat or the most flawless lamb when they petition him for favors, or when they want to thank him for favors received, or when they beg pardon for wrongs committed. That is when they know that God is, when it costs them materially. If you eliminate the sacrifices, then you eliminate the religion as well, and maybe even faith in God. God is love? Maybe that might even be true, but spiritual sacrifices? He smiled a tolerant, wordly-wise smile to himself. You say that because you do not understand men. Maybe someday men will measure up to it, though I doubt it. At any rate, a lot more water will flow down the Jordan before that happens. You're young, a fantasist, a dreamer. You want too much all at once, in one fell swoop. . . .

One thing puzzled him. Why had he done it? Why had he gone to extremes like that? Did he want to have the Essenes behind him? But he had them behind him long ago. But who takes them seriously? Did he want to win over the Pharisees? Oh no it was too late for that now. First of all, he had antagonized them enough times already, and secondly, though they might even think along his lines, they certainly were not going to risk following him on the dangerous road he was taking now. So why then?

He started talking to Jesus again in his mind, questioning him. . . . Did you need to create some kind of sensation for the hordes of pilgrims here for the festival days? You can't depend on the mob, because it's a herd—here today, there tomorrow. First they're behind you, then the next thing they trample you in a panic. If you don't know that, then you don't know anything. You can only operate with a basis in an institution, and you have made the fundamental mistake of neither creating a new institution, nor joining an existing one. You are alone. And that is why you have to die.

Caiaphas appeared. For a moment Annas could not remember why he was back. Then he remembered. He took him by the arm. "Let's go home," he said.

He waited impatiently for Caiaphas report.

"I sent a few of our people," Caiaphas began, "just as you, Annas, suggested to ask Jesus by what authority he threw out the merchants."

"What did he say to that?"

"He evaded the question with another question. He said, 'You tell me first, was the baptism of John from heaven or from men? Then I will tell you by what authority I do these things.' Our people conferred a moment about what to do. If they admitted that it was from heaven, he would reproach them saying, then why did you not believe John when he pointed to me? And if they claimed that it was a purely human institution, then all the people who consider John a prophet would turn against them."

"So what happened?"

"They couldn't think what to say. Very cautiously they answered, 'We don't know'. So then he said, 'Well, then, neither will I tell you by what authority I do these things'."

"There, you see! That's him all right. And naturally, all of you lost your heads."

"I beg your pardon, but what would you have done?"

"I'm not the High Priest. You're in charge. I'm entitled to a little rest and relaxation finally."

Annas never thought the incidents involving Jesus would so completely crush him: he took to isolating himself in his rooms, even absenting himself from the temple; he refused to see anyone, talk to anyone; he did not dare look people in the eye. He suffered. Officially, the word went around that Annas was doing penance. But the truth was, he simply did not know what to do next, and that drove him to distraction and helpless rage. He could not see a single solution. Every move that came to his mind could only worsen the situation or lead to total disaster. And that he could not afford now, not any more. Experimentation was done with, once and for all. It was a type of situation he had never been in before. He, the old fox who had competed against Romans and Pharisees alike; he, who could lead masters of the political game by the nose, and just when they were confident of victory, destroy them with a sudden move—now he felt like a helpless child. He had no idea what to do next. Go to the Romans for help? No, he would never condescend to appeal to them. He could not afford the disgrace. He had lived too long not to know that there were no secrets that sooner or later would not leak out.

Kill him secretly? First, it was not technically feasible. Jesus had very obviously reckoned with that eventuality, surrounding himself day and night with his men, constantly changing lodgings and sleeping quarters; and that could carry incalculable consequences.

An official trial? That blasphemer had to be caught first.

In the daytime the crowds made that impossible. And even if he were captured at night, what would they do with him during the day? As soon as his followers got wind of it, they would storm the prison with a vengeance. Was there no way out? Worse yet, time was on his side: the closer the festival days came, more and more people crammed into Jerusalem. People from the provinces—his people. Even at that very moment it would be child's play for him to seize power if he wanted to. There was just one comforting, consoling thought, like a salve on his abrasions, which Annas had not disclosed in his conversations with Caiaphas, yet had always kept in the front of his mind: the carpenter's son had committed blasphemy, not just blasphemy, but the worst blasphemy any man on earth could possibly utter. And it was not speculation or conjecture any more; it was not the indignant gossip of the priests and Pharisees any more. He, Annas himself, had heard it with his own ears, and he had witnesses who would swear to it. "He is a blasphemer." He caressed the indictment in his mind like a favorite child, savored it, saved it like a choice arrow in his quiver, like an unfailing dagger concealed against his breast, ready for the opportune moment, for the decisive battle. Yet why had the Nazarene handed the weapon to the priests, and especially himself, right into their hands? A moment of weakness or impetuousness? But surely he would have realized the danger he could expect from the priests, and particularly from him. And how exquisitely satisfying it was to think that it was his handiwork, his plan that had forced that juggler of words to unmask himself. He loved to return to the scene in his mind, not just to bask in those glorious days, but to keep the weapon always fresh and handy in his mind, instantly ready for battle, like a sword that slides smoothly and swiftly out of its scabbard.

Much, much earlier he had been perturbed by certain signals coming from the countryside. It was not so much the polemics or the disputes or debates—in which, for that matter, Jesus emerged, then as now, triumphant. It was not even the miracles he performed. It was the titles he used to describe himself, and which his followers eagerly seized upon: Son of Man, Messiah, Son of David.

Caiaphas had come to him with a list of his titles. Annas could still remember the way he interrupted him every few minutes with derisive commentary:

". . . . That teacher from Nazareth calls himself a shepherd. He says, 'I am the Good Shepherd'."

"So let him go ahead and be a shepherd," he had thrown in sarcastically.

"He teaches, 'Without me you can do nothing'."

"What does that mean, 'without me'? What does 'you can do nothing' mean?"

Caiaphas had not answered, only glued his eyes to the scroll and muttered: " 'Behold one who is greater than Jonah, greater even than Solomon'."

"Well, Jonah was only Jonah, but Solomon? Only a fool or a madman would compare himself to him. I knew he was pompous and swell-headed, but not to that extent."

" 'The Son of Man has not come to lose souls, but to redeem them'."

"Fine, fine, let him go ahead and redeem those souls, but just what does 'Son of Man' mean? What does he understand by 'Son of Man'? Why, that's what the Scriptures call the Messiah!"

" 'Everything was given to me by my Father'."

"It doesn't matter what 'everything' means, but who is his 'Father' to him? Does that mean God? That he is his son? Different from all other men?"

But the next pronouncement was clearer still: " 'No one knows who the Father is but the Son'."

"Well, that's clear enough. He is speaking very plainly."

"He says, 'I am the Resurrection and the Life'. And, 'I am the Way, the Truth, and the Life'."

"No, no, no," he had bellowed. "He's a fanatic, a madman, possessed not by one devil, not by seven devils, but by Beelzebub himself. How can they listen patiently to all that? Why is he still alive? Isn't there a true Israelite left in this nation? Isn't there one man left who will take up a stone and put an end to this outrage? Why didn't you stone him?" he had screamed at Caiaphas. "Stone him! That's what the Law and the Prophets command us to do! Why does the holy earth

still carry him? Why doesn't hell suck him down. Damn him!"
Then he spit to the left and right to rid himself of Jesus'
presence and the presence of every evil spirit.

He remembered how his heart had leaped the first time he
received word that there had been an attempt to throw Jesus
off a cliff in his own city. The fact that the attempt failed had
not been that important to him—they might fail once, they
could fail ten more times, but they would succeed on the
eleventh try. The important thing was that the nation's spirit
had not died, that the people still understood the difference
between truth and fallacy. Though in his heart he often sighed
in regret that they had not managed to push him off after all.
The situation was almost ideal, at least according to the
eyewitness reports: Jesus had arrived in Nazareth on the
Sabbath and, as he usually did, he went into the synagogue.
During prayer service, he presented himself for the reading.
What happened next was fully written up in the report sent
to the temple by the elder of the Nazareth synagogue: "He
was handed the book of the Prophet Isaiah. Unrolling it, he
came upon the place where it is written:

The Spirit of the Lord is upon me.
Wherefore He has anointed me
to preach the gospel to the poor,
He has sent me to heal the contrite of heart,
to preach deliverance to the captives,
and sight to the blind,
to set at liberty them that are bruised,
to preach the acceptable year of the Lord and the day of
reward.

Rolling up the book, he returned it to the minister and sat
down. The eyes of everyone in the synagogue were fixed on
him. Then he said to them, 'This day are fulfilled the words
of this Scripture which you have heard.'

"They began to ask among themselves, 'Is this not the son
of Joseph, the carpenter?' And, 'Do his brethren not live
among us?' Then he said to them, 'Doubtless you will say to
me this similitude: Physician, heal thyself. Do here in your
own country such great things as we have heard done in

Capernaum. I say to you that no prophet is accepted in his own country. In truth I say to you, there were many widows in Israel in the days of Elijah, when heaven was closed three years and six months, when there was a great famine throughout all the earth. And Elijah was sent to none of them, but to the widow woman, Sarepta of Sidon. And there were many lepers in Israel in the time of Elisha the prophet, and none of them were cleansed but Naaman the Syrian.'

"Hearing these words, everyone in the synagogue rose up in anger. They seized him at once, and turned him out of the city, and brought him to the brow of the hill on which the city is built to cast him down. But passing through the midst of them, he went his way."

So ended the report from Nazareth.

That last sentence was something Annas could never quite figure out. How was it that he passed through their midst? What was that supposed to mean, "passed through"? How could they not have thrown him off the cliff?! Did they panic and turn tail and let him go? What were they afraid of that they let him go? They should not have let him go, they should have pushed him! He would never forgive them.

But Annas had one quality that, even his worst predicaments, had saved him from blundering: he knew how to wait. He never hurried. He knew that sooner or later Jesus would come to Jerusalem, that someday they would meet, and he was confident that he could play the winning hand against him in the way he had so many times in the past with a variety of more dangerous opponents. He waited. Once, he had managed to corner Caiaphas and his priests from spoiling all his plans when Jesus finally did appear in Jerusalem. Even then Caiaphas was reluctant to discuss Jesus, even then he resisted. He could still see those rapidly flitting rat's eyes of his as he cornered the High Priest. . . .

". . . . I can promise you, he will definitely come here. How can he not show up after everything he's said. He'll be back, just wait and see. Because Jerusalem is the city of the Messiah, and that's what he thinks he is. So when he comes, listen carefully." He stood insinuatingly close to him, eye to eye. "And when he comes, there'll be no silly talk. No jokes. Save your jokes for your advisers," he rasped. Caiaphas was silenced by the contempt in his voice. "No jokes. You only need to find out from him who he is. Is that understood?" He started to hobble in circles around the room. Only when his back was turned did Caiaphas venture to speak.

"Is it so important that he tells us who he is? Isn't all you know already about him enough? Isn't everything he has done and said about himself sufficient? Is anything else needed."

He limped over to him instantly. "You are feeble-minded. I want him, in front of all the priests who will be listening, in front of all the people who will be listening, to state exactly who he is, and that is what you have to ask him. I want him finally to state his name. Do you understand?"

He stopped, walked over to the window to give Caiaphas another chance to say something—he did not want the High Priest catching him off guard in future with another of his half-baked ideas. Sure enough, as soon as his back was turned, Caiaphas squeaked, "Why do you need to find out his name? Why are you so obsessed with it?"

He was just waiting for those words. He fairly flew over to Caiaphas and, between clenched teeth, hissed, "Because I want you finally to stone him!"

Caiaphas's face froze. It was too much. "Me . . .? Me . . .?" he stuttered.

"Yes, you." Then after a moment, to ease him out of his panic, he said to him. "You and everyone who hears it. Surely there must still be true, God-fearing Israelites among us. At least I believe so. I believe that if a true Israelite hears such blasphemy, he will reach for a stone in order to keep the Law and destroy the criminal. I believe there still are such Israelites left. . . ."

And so he had waited. Until his waiting was finally rewarded. He remembered the occasion well. It was the Feast of Tabernacles.

. . . . It was unusually cold for autumn. The chill had crept into his bones; he felt out of sorts. Around noon, Caiaphas hurried in breathlessly with the news: "He's here!"

"Where is he?" He didn't have to ask whom Caiaphas meant.

"He's preaching in the temple."

"What are you so afraid of . . .? Wait a minute, where are you running off to?" He dragged himself painfully out of his bed. All his bones ached. "I'm coming, just let me get myself dressed. Bring me my staff . . . well, move already. Give me your hand . . . slowly. Don't be in such a hurry, we'll get there in time. Tell me everything that has happened so far."

"I wasn't there from the beginning. He got there first–"

"I know, I know, you're always late, especially when I need you most. Well, then what? Go on, go on, I won't interrupt again."

He had already started to speak with our people."

"About what?"

"What you instructed us to say. I told them so many times, I told them exactly what it was you wanted us to say."

"Yes, but that was a long time ago. They could have forgotten by now, couldn't they?"

He was hotly stimulated by the news. Once again, things were happening around the temple—and in his empty life as well. He could feel the energy surge inside him; he could feel the sudden sharpness of thought, just like in the old, glorious days when he was High Priest, when he held the whole power of the temple in his hand—the power this imbecile here now wielded. He glanced disdainfully at Caiaphas. He had not stopped talking, but as usual it was disjointed, chaotic prating. He could not stand that stammering of his—where was he when everyone else was in school? How could they have ever let him fill such an important post? The Romans certainly knew whom to pick for High Priest.

They entered the temple and immediately saw a tightly-packed crowd in Solomon's portico. Yes, he must be over there. Annas took in the whole situation instantly. "Let's circle around from the rear. This way, this way," he rushed Caiaphas along impatiently, pushing and puffing his way through a network of stairwells, vestibules, halls. Finally they emerged again in the gallery, only a few steps from where Jesus was standing in the midst of a crowd of priests, Levites, Pharisees, and pilgrims. But the pilgrims were only silent

observers of the exchanges between Jesus, the priests, and the
Pharisees.

Every sentence, every word uttered at that meeting etched
itself indelibly on Annas' mind. He was seeing Jesus for the
first time at close range, his every gesture, every twitch of
every muscle in his face. And he was listening to him for the
first time in such a dialogue with the priests.

". . . . You are from below, I am from above. You are of
this world, I am not of this world. That is why I have said
to you that you will die in your sins. Yes, if you do not believe
that I am he, you shall die in your sins."

How insolent! How insolent he is! he fumed. Insulting us
to our faces! But one phrase in particular stuck in his mind—
what was it? That "I am he". Why did he say that? Those
were the very same words that Adonai had spoken to Moses
when he appeared to him in the burning bush! What did this
Nazarene mean by using them? Did he use them accidentally
or intentionally? One thing was sure—he certainly knew how
to speak! Too bad Caiaphas could not talk like that. If only
one of our priests knew how to talk like that.

He turned his attention back again. His heart beat excitedly, his mouth was dry as linen, his muscles sorely tensed.
He didn't want to miss a word of what Jesus said.

". . . I am the bread of life. Your fathers ate manna in the
desert and are dead. This is the bread which comes down
from heaven, that if any man eat of it, he may not die."

He could not quite follow his meaning, he must have fo-
cussed on the words too late, missed something in the beginning. Suddenly he heard Jesus' voice: "Amen, Amen, if any
man keeps my word, he will not see death forever."

Over the buzz of the crowd, he heard individual voices
raised in protest: ". . . . Now we know that you are possessed
by the devil. Abraham is dead, and so are the prophets. And
you say, if anyone keeps my word, he shall never taste death.
Are you greater than our father Abraham, who is dead, as
the prophets are also dead? Whom do you claim yourself to
be?"

Yes, yes, that was good! The question he had been waiting
for. Oh, if only he would stick to the question, just answer

the question, just answer who he is! He would have to give himself away, compromise himself. He clenched his fists tight. His heart was thumping up in his throat. He tightened his jaw, hoping they would not stop baiting him.

"Abraham, your father, rejoiced that he might see my day: he saw it and was glad."

What was he mouthing now? What kind of nonsense was this? He was going mad. Suddenly a voice from the crowd— he could not see whose—jeered, "What! You're not yet fifty years old, and you have seen Abraham?" Derisive laughter rippled through the onlookers. Annas was jubilant. Yes, yes, Jesus was losing. They were pointing their fingers at him and laughing. The master of debate was being defeated, ensnared in his own trap.

He watched Jesus anxiously, saw him wait for the noise to subside, saw the anger rise in his face. The crowd quieted down more quickly than he had expected, somehow suddenly subdued by his countenance. Then he heard the words, spoken with his own lips, the awful staggering words: "Amen, Amen, I say to you, before Abraham was, I exist."

A stunned hush fell over the assembly: a collective gasp sucked through the air—no one had expected anything like it. For as long as the temple was the temple, for as long as the world was the world, no one had ever dared to utter words of such shocking blasphemy.

He felt as if he had been struck a hammer blow; he could scarcely catch a breath. He had been waiting for some kind of blasphemous pronouncement, but he had never dreamed it would be so outrageous. He threw his arms into the air. "Stone him!" he choked out to the mute onlookers. He thought he was going to fall over with a heart seizure.

. . . . And although so much time had elapsed since that day, every time he thought about it, his heart started thumping painfully in his chest again, and his arms shot up into the air again by themselves.

His cry had been instantly picked up and repeated; the whole crowd began to shriek like men possessed. Some of them threw themselves at Jesus to drag him out of the temple to stone him outside its grounds, while others cast around for rocks and stones . . .and he got away, he simply slipped away.

Even now, when he thought about it, he just could not understand it. By what manner had that blasphemer managed to pull free of so many hands reaching for him, so much hatred demanding his instant death?

But it did not matter. His words were left. For all time. To be returned to, cited, pointed at. To accuse with. To sentence with. To comdemn with. To kill with.

Annas was roughly jarred out of his reverie by Caiaphas bursting into his room.

"One of the Twelve is here with a proposition to turn Jesus over to us."

He did not understand. "What is he here for?"

"For money. He wants to reveal where Jesus spends the night."

He stared fearfully at Caiaphas. Either the High Priest had gone mad or he had. He stumped over to him, scrutinized his face. Caiaphas was elated, grinning delightedly. Annas thought he had never seen Caiaphas in quite such spirits. "Which one of them?" he demanded.

"Judas."

Judas. That did not tell him very much. He could not recall anything about him. "Let's go," he said tersely, not wholly convinced.

He went along behind Caiaphas to the conference hall, which was swarming with priests and Levites. They were euphoric. A buzzing, droning hive of excitement, flapping hands, laughter—they did not even notice the two of them enter. "They're either drunk or mad," he muttered to himself.

Only after Caiaphas began to bring them to order did they notice Annas and rush up to him from every direction, shouting and wildly gesticulating. He swung his arms in front of him to ward them off and started backing up against the wall, afraid they might trample him, shout him down. Another instant and his temper ignited. He rapped his staff ill-temperedly against the floor. "Silence!" he screamed. "Calm yourselves! Where is he?"

"He's waiting in the next room."

"I want to see him."

The chatter erupted again:

"Do you want to find out how much he wants . . .?"

". . . We'll give him as much as he wants. . . ."

"Even twice as much, ten times as much. . . ."

He looked at them with unseeing eyes. He would not even bother to tell them what he thought of them: cretins. He passed through them; they moved aside respectfully. He went into the next room. It was nearly empty. A scribe sat in one corner with another figure. No, that was not him. He glanced around. There he was, up against the wall. Yes, that was definitely Judas, though he did not know him and had never seen him. But that was somehow the way he had pictured him—though he might be more intelligent than he had imagined. Maybe more cynical, too. He strode up to him, halted inches from his face and stared at him. Not too many people could withstand his stare. This one did. His eyes never wavered. The corners of his mouth were tilted into a tiny smile. His whole bearing irked him.

"When do you want to show us the place where he stays the night?" he asked him curtly.

"Any time," the other replied smoothly. Not a second's hesitation.

Obviously he was prepared for that question. Probably prepared for any question. Much too intelligent to be caught off guard.

"Why are you doing it? You're one of his disciples, aren't you?"

Judas ignored the question. "How much will you give me?" he drawled arrogantly.

"Thirty silver pieces."

"What? Only as much as for a slave?"

"That much is allotted."

"If the temple can't afford any more than that, then it will have to do. When do you want to know?"

"We'll tell you."

"Just don't wait until the last minute."

"It will probably be before the festival days, because afterward it might not matter any more."

Judas stood a moment longer, still smiling that peculiar smile, with his eyelids half closed, and then he left.

Annas waited several minutes to collect himself. He did not wish to return to that flock of priests in the next room right away. He had to admit: the meeting had given him nothing. He trusted his own intuition, his own perception, his own knowledge of men's minds. He was infallible at uncovering frauds and swindlers. Apart from the unexpected discovery that there were intelligent people among Jesus' disciples, he had gained nothing. But he could hardly admit that to the priests waiting next door. Let them enjoy themselves; they had not had much chance to do so lately He returned to the conference room, where the euphoria was now tempered, but expectant. They had to be told something.

"Thirty silver pieces," he announced in a loud voice, though no one had asked him. There was a brief pause, then the room burst into a flurry of comments and queries:

"What did he say to that?"

"Did he agree?"

"With luck, he won't change his mind. . . ."

Annas forced a weak smile. He said, "This way he won't think we're so very anxious about it."

He trudged back to his own chambers, trying to put the incident into proper perspective. The one question clamoring for an explanation was simply, why? Was it betrayal or connivance? Betrayal? That was too easy, and too inexplicable. To leave Jesus now, just when he was at the height of his success and popularity, when everything lay wide open to him? Judas must be aware of this. So then, a ruse? But at whose initiative, Jesus' or his disciple's? Was a breakup among them possible? What could they hope to gain? Discredit the temple before all Palestine that was streaming in for the holy days? They had had enough successes, they did not need that. He could not make it out. But there was one good thing in the whole affair, and that was the priests' euphoria. Not so very long ago it seemed at least half of them were followers of Jesus. How little was needed to get them back. One small, even superficial, setback had touched the master from Nazareth, and they were flocking back. He smiled to himself. Yes, yes, they weren't that eager to resign their posts or lose their jobs, or gamble on this new leader. They were afraid of an adventurer called Jesus, and as soon as they saw the possibility of maintaining the status quo, they declared for it boisterously and unequivocally. All that was needed were a few catchwords, a few banners, a few slogans, and the scent of victory, and you had faithful, devoted servants of the temple once more.

Caiaphas came in, rubbing his hands, swaying contentedly from side to side. "Well, and what do you have to say now, my dear father-in-law? How did you like Judas? We'll see who comes around next."

Caiaphas's familiar speech and manner astonished him.

"Do you really think that he wants to betray his master?"

Caiaphas froze in mid-gesture, then seemed suddenly to sag. "I beg your pardon, but what do you think?" He was stuttering again. "That he's in collusion with the Romans?"

For the second time in a minute he was surprised. Why the Romans? And then, while staring into Caiaphas's nervous face, a thought came to him, so suddenly, so unexpectedly that it took him completely by surprise. He was afraid to think of it, it was just too simple. Caiaphas's voice came to him as if from a great distance. He was no longer listening, so fascinated was he by this new idea: when Jesus seizes power and overthrows Herod, the Romans can be expected to defend Herod then, taking advantage of the revolution, they will seize Jerusalem and the whole Judean state. He repeated it in his mind several times, unsure of himself. How would the people react? For the present, they would simply wait and see what he did next. If he would only give them a couple more days, just a couple more days! He fidgeted around the room, automatically listening for sounds. He peered out into the courtyard: everything appeared normal. Then he realized Caiaphas was still there. Caiaphas realizing that he was not being heard, had long since fallen silent, waiting for Annas to notice him again.

"Who appointed Herod king?" Annas asked him abruptly.

Caiaphas followed him suspiciously with his eyes. "The Romans. But if I'm not mistaken, the Romans have had their fill of Herod; and, for that matter, they view Jesus and every-ing he does sympathetically."

"Yes, yes, you and I know that. But the people don't know that. The people only know that Herod is there by Roman appointment and, in order for Jesus to take over power, it would have to come to open warfare between his followers and Herod's army. Sooner or later the Romans would get involved. Then, taking advantage of civil war, and under the pretext of putting an end to the bloodshed, they would occupy the whole of Palestine."

Caiaphas stared at him wide-eyed, not comprehending.

"Think. Whom do our people fear most? The Romans. Whom do they hate most? The Romans. But the most sim-pleminded fisherman understands that the Romans cannot possibly allow someone to overthrow the order that they es-tablished. Jesus must die so that the Jewish nation and the remains of its independence may live. The people must believe this: that he is a terrible threat to them—to the entire nation; that as a consequence of his madness, the Romans will march in, destroy the temple, and cast the whole nation into the same kind of exile as the Babylonians did."

He saw Caiaphas' face slowly brighten. He went on. "But that news has to be circulated around Jerusalem with the speed of lightning, made to sound like a sensation, as if it were privileged information, to terrify both the residents of Jerusalem and the pilgrims. Then we'll be able to do whatever we please with Jesus. The news has to discredit him. People will understand better than you think that what freedom we have, at least we have it; that what Herod is, he is; but in the long run, everyone would rather have a bird in the hand than two in the bush."

He saw a doubtful look cross Caiaphas's face. He paused.

Very cautiously Caiaphas asked, "And then what, if I may be permitted to ask?"

"What do you mean, then what?"

"Please be so kind as to tell me what will happen to Jesus then."

"Why, we'll sentence him to death."

"We can sentence him ten times," Caiaphas began to shout hysterically. "I don't want to remind you how you did it the last time. On your own responsibility you sentenced several people to death, and because of that you lost your position as High Priest."

Annas was taken aback. Caiaphas was striking an open wound. He felt his rage bubbling to a boil—especially since he knew that Caiaphas would not stop there, but drag the whole business out into the open, like so much dirty laundry. And he did.

Caiaphas spoke rapidly, so rapidly that he did not stop for breath, as if he wanted to spill it out before he took fright, before he thought twice: "I'm not so terribly attached to this office that I occupy, but I have no intention of losing it, not even by the death of Jesus. They'll never appoint you a second time, not just because you have those other matters on your conscience, but because you're too old now."

It required superhuman control to keep himself from throwing Caiaphas bodily out of the door.

"And besides that," he went on, "I have to tell you . . . allow me to tell you"—he was flickering out, losing his impetus—"tell you that—"

"Pilate will sentence Jesus to death," Annas broke in.

"Excuse me, but before Pilate can sentence him to death, we have to judge him."

"That's what the information I just gave you is for. And that's why," he began slowly, very deliberately, "a day or two earlier, you'll convoke the Sanhedrin, and announce it as the latest piece of news. Knowing our worthy sages in the Sanhedrin, they'll instantly trumpet it all over Jerusalem. In addition tell the people in the temple to spread this disastrous news at every opportunity, everywhere, officially and unofficially, to residents and visitors as well."

Caiaphas stared at him as though transfixed. Must be thinking, Annas mused. Very intensively. Trying to grasp it all.

Finally Caiaphas stammered, "That's all very well and

good, but what if, in spite of everything, they don't believe it? Or, at least, if not everyone believes it?"

In his heart Annas agreed he might be right. Aloud he reassured him, "They'll believe, they'll believe. But quite right . . . just in case, we must try him very quickly."

"As far as I understand it, it is much more easily said than done."

Annas sensed fear in his words. Caiaphas did not want to take risks. Pretending not to have heard, Annas went on. "This is the way I see it: we'll arrest Jesus at night, and try him and sentence him to death at night—"

"I have absolutely no intention of violating the laws," Caiaphas broke in, on the verge of panic. "We are permitted to judge only during the day."

"No, not judge. Pass sentence," Annas corrected him. "We'll judge him at night, and pass sentence just before daybreak, and then we'll be in accordance with the Law."

"And then what?"

"Then quickly send him to Pilate."

"I beg your pardon, how will that work? At five o'clock in the morning to Pontius Pilate? He'll throw us out."

"No, not at five, at six," Annas conceded.

"Don't make jokes, please. Is that such a difference, five or six? That's not the time for official business. He won't receive us then either."

"He has to," Annas went on, oblivious. "And at seven, Jesus is hanging on a cross. Which of our people handles affairs relating to Pilate?" Without waiting for a reply, he went on, "Look over his last months, review everything about him, here in Palestine and in Rome, his family, his friends, how the situation looked after the execution of Sejanus, how the current Emperor feels about him."

"I truly marvel. I never dreamed you possessed so much imagination," Caiaphas said, without concealing his irony.

"All right," Annas snapped, "fine, we'll do what you want. You propose something. I don't have to bother myself with all this, I'm not the High Priest. Please, go ahead, do as you like."

He knew he was uttering gibberish. This was no time for

pride and ambition. He pulled himself together. "No, I apologize, I let my nerves get the better of me. Listen, if you have a better idea, go ahead. But you reproach me for taking risks. Don't you understand we have no other choice? We're in a situation in which we have to gamble. Delaying would be a hundred times riskier. We simply have no other alternative. The important thing now is to calculate everything very precisely, consider every angle, then push the plan through without glancing to left or right."

Caiaphas was listening intently; he at last seemed to have understood. When he finished, Caiaphas nodded. "You are right, thank you, I apologize. I'll try to make sure everything takes place as you said."

After that day, he rarely saw Caiaphas, and if he did, it was only fleetingly. Caiaphas failed to appear at meals—for that matter, he himself rarely came to eat at the common table. He did not feel well. He felt he had fulfilled his responsibilities and he wanted to give himself a respite. At night he had trouble sleeping, so he was usually drowsy during the day, often dropping off suddenly in his chair. He lived in virtual semiconsciousness. Voices reached him, but they were only so many sounds in the background; figures passed him by, greeted him, wished him well, stopped to chat with him, but he scarcely recognized them or knew what he was replying to them. He went about his everyday affairs automatically without conscious thought. Once he even asked Caiaphas abstractedly if the sentence had already been carried out. Caiaphas, preoccupied with his own affairs, had turned a perplexed face to him, unsure what he was talking about. Several days elapsed before his strength and vigor returned. Only then did he realize just how much the Jesus affair had enervated him. He was grateful that he had not been needed during his recuperation, that his presence had not been required. Even now he kept to the sidelines, satisfied that, when the need arose, they would notify him, they would come for him. But now he listened with an ear that was freshly tuned. He sensed an excitement in the air that surpassed anything the temple had ever experienced. But he kept his distance, he did not want to become involved in details, he wanted to keep his peace as long as possible. His instinct told him, however, that the moment of release was fast approaching.

It was Thursday evening. Annas was still at supper when Caiaphas rushed in.

"It's tonight," he said tersely. "If you can, try not to sleep. Or go ahead and sleep, and we'll wake you. We should be back around midnight." He turned abruptly and left.

Annas had said nothing. He had no mind for questions now; he had to conserve his strength for later, when he would need it most.

All evening he nervously tramped the floor of his chamber, waiting, wondering. Sleep was out of the question. Hours passed, still no word. An uneasy feeling began to take hold of him: something had gone wrong. He tried to dismiss it. After all, Caiaphas had said midnight; there was still time. He mumbled psalms to himself from memory, an old habit that always soothed his nerves. Every few minutes he paused to listen for footsteps. It was taking to long, something must have gone wrong. He was about to retire in despair, when Caiaphas burst through the door. His eyes were wide and apprehensive; he struggled to catch his breath.

Annas waited for him to speak. Finally, unable to control himself, he asked sharply, "What has happened? Did Jesus put you to flight?"

Caiaphas looked at him sourly. "They're bringing him now." He gulped and added, "Jesus," as if he thought there might still be some doubt in the other's mind.

"Then return to the Council. I'll be there shortly. What are you doing here? You could have sent someone for me."

Caiaphas made no move to leave. He stood panting for air. Finally he breathed, "Nothing is ready yet in the Council. They are not all there yet, and we still have no witnesses."

"Then what do you want me to do?" he shouted. He was angry. Everything should have been prepared.

"See him here first, and in that time I'll make all the necessary arrangements."

Annas was furious; but he said simply, "Very well, send him here to me."

The muscles in Caiaphas' faced relaxed. He hurried from the room.

Annas spluttered under his breath: "They had so much time to complete their preparations, there's no excuse. They should have worked out every last detail. I could understand if I hadn't told him, but I had told him. This is what happens when I don't take matters into my own hands. I should have prepared everything myself, and not relied on those idiots. I've told them how I detest surprises."

Still muttering to himself, he passed into the audience hall. Voices rumbled in the distance..Yes, they were on their way. He listened to the singing and cheering: sounds of enthusiasm, he thought; just like the day Jesus rode into Jerusalem.

He moved away from the door. Guards, attendants, priests, and Levites crowded into the hall. They were wet and flushed with excitement; their clothes and faces were splattered with mud and blackened from the torches they swung over their heads like banners. The hall filled with hoarse shouts and songs and the odor of smoke and sweat.

He stood off to one side. No one paid him any attention. He waited patiently, he was in no hurry. If anything, they wanted him to take his time. Minutes passed before a group of priests spotted him and rushed over with a flurry of reports. They all shouted at once, drowning each other. Each one wanted to impress Annas with the importance of his particular role in the capture. He did not listen; he was searching the room . . . for him. He moved toward the wall. The circle of priests followed him like screaming gulls. He stepped on to the dais and scanned the hall. There was a movement in the throng. It was him. The mob was pushing him, handing him forward very slowly, as if reluctant to let him out of their grasp.

Fragments of the priests' reports of the capture in Gethsemane reached him.

". . . . We found eight of his followers sleeping at the entrance. The rest were in the garden . . . took them by surprise . . . tried to defend themselves . . . Peter . . . Malchus. . . ." The name Malchus was mentioned several times.

". . . . But he didn't try to defend himself. He surrendered peacefully enough when we agreed to let his followers go. . . ."

". . . . Of course, we agreed, this way there was no bloodshed. . . ."

He watched as they pushed him roughly to the foot of the dais. His hands were tied. It surprised him to see that Jesus looked exactly the way he had last Sunday—Palm Sunday, they called it. The mob taunted him with raucous jokes, insults, and threatening gestures. Jesus stood silently before Annas, his eyes lowered to the floor. Gradually a hush fell over the room.

Annas knew he could not delay much longer. The priests were still vying for his attention. He could kill more time by pretending to take an interest in them: he threw in a question now and then, nodded approval, shook his head emphatically in disbelief. But how long could he continue the pretence? The mob expected him to do a job, but there was nothing for him to do. He could think of nothing to say. The Sanhedrin was supposed to interrogate Jesus first. Surely everyone in the room knew that. They were probably wondering what they were doing here in the first place—and waiting all the more expectantly for what he was going to say.

I'm in this mess because of that fool Caiaphas, he thought crossly to himself. Now I have to put on a convincing act.

He wondered if they were ready at the Sanhedrin yet; surely he had given them enough time by now. Perhaps he could just send Jesus over to them. Yet it behoved him to say something to the throng, to placate them. He could hardly dismiss them with nothing. He could ask Jesus about his teaching. Let him talk to his heart's content. That would pass the time. He could always cut him short if he went too far.

He began his questioning. The crowd strained to hear. Annas noticed that his band of men, which had arrested him, and which must have been carefully selected for the job as being impervious to Jesus' teachings, seemed almost awed by the master of Nazareth; they pressed forward anxiously to hear his words. But Jesus remained silent. The crowd was disappointed. The silence was unnerving; Annas felt uncomfortable. He was considering what to do next, when suddenly

Jesus lifted his head, and in a calm, clear voice said to him, "I have spoken openly to the world: I have always taught in the synagogue and in the temple where all Jews gather, and I have said nothing secretly."

Annas was not exactly sure what Jesus was driving at, but it was certainly not the response everyone was waiting for. Before he could pose another question, Jesus said, "Why do you question me? Question those who have heard what I said to them. They know what I have said."

Annas simmered in frustration. He thought that Jesus would take the initiative and talk, but now it looked as though he would have to continue on his own. A tremor passed through the crowd. He could feel their eyes focused questioningly on him. Yet he was still at a loss for words. What should he say? Out of the corner of his eye, he noticed one of the attendants suddenly leap from the crowd towards Jesus.

"Is that the way you answer the High Priest?" he shouted, and struck him a vicious blow to the face.

It happened so quickly and unexpectedly. Jesus reeled momentarily under the impact of the blow, but instantly regained his balance. Annas expected him to turn violently and curse his assailant, but to his amazement, he heard him quietly say, "If I have spoken ill, bear witness to the evil; but if well, why do you strike me?"

A confused roar rose from the crowd. Annas struck his staff angrily against the stone floor and shouted for order. He did not like what was happening. "Silence!" he bellowed over the tumult. Slowly the hall fell silent. By now he had regained his self-possession. He turned to Jesus and addressed him: "I wanted to give you a chance to speak, but you refused it. In that case, you will be judged by the Council. Take him before the Sanhedrin."

The mob cheered its approval. He breathed a sigh of relief. At least he had been able to extricate himself still holding the upper hand. He eyed the men excitedly leaving the hall with their captive. "Oh, yes," he murmured aloud when he was alone, "it's not enough simply to arrest Jesus. He still has to be sentenced to death. I never thought he was so strong. He certainly showed quality," he added in grudging admiration.

On the way to his chambers he thought about what had just transpired. He was lucky that that thug had taken matters into his own hands and relieved him of the responsibility of saying something. At that point, he had not known what to say. The Sanhedrin was certainly going to have its hands full with Jesus. But he had played his part. They had what they wanted; he must have given them enough time to get ready. He could still hear shouting in the distance. He was tempted to follow, but, he thought, why should he? He was too old to interfere. Besides, they had their own High Priest. Of course it would not hurt to see what was happening. . . .

A moment later Annas was heading across the courtyard to the wing occupied by Caiaphas. As he neared the Sanhedrin conference hall, he could tell things were already going badly. The room was in an uproar, everyone trying to make themselves heard at once. He tried to discover what had happened, but could not make himself heard over the deafening noise. He saw Jesus: he was standing very still and erect, his head held high. The throng seethed around him. He searched the room for Caiaphas. There he was, raving like a madman, desperately trying to quiet the mob. He saw him frantically pull someone from the crowd, then push him roughly out of his way again. The fool has completely lost his head, he thought to himself. He watched Caiaphas plunge through the crowd again, then seize another man and shake him violently, until the man began to stammer: "We heard him say, 'I will destroy this temple built by the hands of men, and after three days I will build another, not built by the hands of men'."

Instantly the words produced a thunderous outcry from the crowd. Caiaphas wrung his hands in exasperation. Yes, there was a problem involving witnesses. Apparently something was wrong, inconsistent, in the man's testimony. After this last outburst, the noise suddenly died. Men returned to their seats like confused, helpless children. It had suddenly become clear to everyone in the room that this was the end. The Sanhedrin had nothing left at its disposal.

That's right, that's right, he fumed to himself. Just as I feared. Jesus has probably not even uttered a word yet, and already the Sanhedrin has suffered a total defeat. And at its own hands. It's over. There is nothing left now but for the mob to disperse and return to their homes. Pack of idiots! Don't they understand the danger?

A disruption of the trial had to be prevented at all costs. Like a specter, the image of Judas passed through his mind. Had he foreseen this impasse? With his intelligence, what could be easier for him, with the help of his eleven friends and the other seventy-two allies, to circulate their propaganda tomorrow and stir up the masses, to tear the prisons apart. And in the meantime, we would still be assembling witnesses to set up a trial. If, in fact, Jesus is counting on that to happen, then he is indeed brilliant, and we are a pack of fools.

He scanned the room. The howling had subsided into an undertone of cautious murmurs and remarks uttered in hurried whispers: everyone realized that a deadlock had been reached that could only be resolved at a normal trial. He would have to act now.

His heart pounding violently, Annas propelled himself through the crowd. He could feel the tension mounting as the whispering suddenly stopped. Everyone watched him push forward. His knees trembled helplessly—he was sure they would buckle under him before he could reach the edge of the crowd. He could feel all eyes riveted on his back. As he drew closer to Jesus, complete silence enveloped the room. He strode up to him in his characteristic fashion, well known to everyone there, so close to his face that his nose almost touched Jesus black beard. Peering with upturned face straight into his eyes, he demanded, "Do you make no answer to the things that these men charge against you?"

The silence was so oppressive, he could hear the blood pulsing in his temples. It was a stupid question, and everyone there knew it. The room tensed all the more. But Annas was Annas, and everyone knew that, too.

Jesus withstood his insolent challenge with a quiet gaze. Yet Annas could read in his eyes that he already knew what would happen; he already guessed the blow he would be dealt.

When no answer was forthcoming, he took two backward

steps, and in the most ceremonious voice he could muster, intoned, "I adjure you by the living God to tell us whether you are the Christ, the Son of God!"

Jesus appeared to hold back long enough for the question to sink fully into the minds of everyone in the room, then he said quietly, "You have said it".

With a well-staged gesture, Annas seized his robes at his throat and tore them in two. The sound of ripping cloth echoed ominously in the stillness. "You have heard his blasphemy!" he shrieked in a theatrical voice. "What further need have we of witnesses?"

He wheeled about dramatically and made to leave. It was sufficient. Let them wrap up the details themselves. But at the last moment, he changed his mind. Caiaphas was infinitely capable of undoing everything at the last minute. He turned to the assembly and in a voice full of indignation cried out, "You have heard the blasphemy. What do you think?"

The priests were so dazed that not one of them answered. No reaction. He began to worry. Did these imbeciles not understand anything? Suddenly a voice croaked: "He is liable for death!" Then others joined in, weakly, uncertainly at first, as if still unsure of a victory so easily won. Within minutes the hall resounded with the tumultous cry, "He is liable for death!" They increased their volume, screaming more and more loudly, as if to ensure their victory with sheer sound.

As he shuffled wearily from the hall, unnoticed by the clamouring crowd, he heard the sound of a sharp blow. He turned, but Jesus was no longer in sight, crushed out of view by the frenzied throng. Sounds of beating and spitting reached him. Oxen, he thought to himself. Fools and oxen. He left the room.

He went to bed. He lay there a long time unable to sleep. Several times he rose and paced the floor, thoughts crowding his head: I should not have shouted so much, like a second-rate actor: I should have been more dignified. He was angry with himself. He was angry with Caiaphas. He was angry with the entire Sanhedrin. The fools had better leave early enough in the morning, or they might not make it on time. But why should he worry? Worry was keeping him awake.

He lay down again. "I'm old now," he mumbled, the way he mumbled every night to lull himself to sleep. "These matters are not my concern any more. They have their own High Priest—let him worry." It soothed his nerves, it always worked. "I'm old now, these matters are not my concern any more. They have their own High Priest. . . ."

Caiaphas shook him awake. He was kneeling beside his bed, pale as death, tugging at his arm, babbling rapidly about something.

"To think I can't even get some sleep. . . ." Annas mumbled. He did not want to listen. He mumbled his formula from the evening before. "Don't bother me, I'm old now. . . ."

Caiaphas refused to leave him alone. He talked louder and louder into his ear. Annas refused to listen, he did not understand the words, he did not want to understand them, though he pretended to, nodding his head in abstract agreement, anything, to catch one more minute of sleep. All he wanted was to sleep. Suddenly one word hooked into his consciousness: "Herod". It jogged him instantly to his senses.

"Herod what?"

"Why are you asking me 'Herod what'. I'm telling you, for the tenth time, Jesus is with Herod, and you don't answer."

"Where?" He sat up. Caiaphas came into focus: wild-eyed and rumpled, as if he had slept in his clothes all night.

"With Herod," Caiaphas repeated.

"Have you all gone mad?!" he shouted. "Why did you take him there?"

"It wasn't us," Caiaphas piped, close to tears. "Pilate sent him to Herod."

"For what?" He understood less and less.

"To judge him."

Annas was afraid to ask the next question, afraid to hear the answer. Finally he choked it out: "You mean, he didn't sentence him to death?"

"No."

Annas sat on the edge of the bed. His rib cage felt as if it would shatter from the thumping of his heart. He fluttered his eyelids rapidly, tried to draw some deep breaths. He stared into Caiaphas's face, nearly at eye level where he was still kneeling.

"On what grounds did he send him to Herod?"

"He said that since Jesus is a Galilean, he came under Herod's jurisdiction."

Annas had never taken such an eventuality into consideration. He was dumbstruck. Chance? Or Pilate's cunning? Once again the face of Judas loomed in his mind. And if the whole thing was one joint move against the temple, the priests and Pharisees?

"Herod is supposed to sentence Jesus to death?" He stared at Caiaphas as if he were mad. "Put that out of your head. He sentenced John to death, and that will last him for the rest of his life. He discovered only too well what it means to sentence a prophet to death. Besides, he's too smart to do anything so foolish. You know he never would have had John beheaded if he hadn't been drunk."

"I know. Why are you shouting at me?"

"Well then, what do you want?" He looked into Caiaphas' frantic eyes.

"What do I do if Herod gives him back to us? If he decides that he's not guilty? Do you want all the Galileans here to attack us? What shall we do with him? What a mess you have got us into! This was your idea!"

Annas was surprised that he managed to keep his composure. Well, somebody had to remain sane in this company—he repeated one of his old sayings to himself. He watched Caiaphas cooly. Hysteric!

"What's going to happen when I'm no longer around?" he sneered. "Lice will eat the lot of you, that's what!"

"I've had enough! I don't want any more of your wise sayings. Come along with me!"

Caiaphas had lost all control, raving and convulsing like a madman.

"Where?" Annas asked calmly.

"To Herod's palace."

"Are you crazy? You know very well what I think of Herod. And besides, what will happen if people see me standing in front of Herod's palace like some kind of menial? And maybe all I need is for Herod to see me waiting there in front of his palace? Tell me, can you picture that?"

"I don't care. And if—" Caiaphas suddenly stopped in mid sentence. "Then I'm going alone."

"Stay here." Annas tried to calm him. "They know where you are, I'm sure you left instructions to be notified if anything important happens."

"Yes, but I'm going anyway. I want to be there, not just wait for someone to bring me word about what's happening." He was almost pouting. "I want to see everything with my own eyes."

"All right, then go." At heart, Annas was relieved. He would rather not have that hysteric here grating on his nerves.

Caiaphas leaped up and fairly bounded out the door.

"Go, I said, don't run!" Annas shouted after him. "Can't you act with dignity? You'll do more that way than with all your jabbering."

He was alone. Now he was assailed by doubts. He tried to brush them off, stay calm, but it was not easy. The cynically grinning face of Judas haunted him.

If all this is no accident, he speculated, not a coincidence, but a ruse, then I have let myself be trapped like a child. If it's all planned and premeditated, then they're having a good laugh at my expense. But it's too late to think about all that now. Something has to be done. Time is against us. With every minute more people are awakening, the city is awakening, his followers are awakening.

He looked out the window; the street was still fairly deserted. Suddenly he saw a priest racing around a corner, his robes flapping and flowing in his own wind. "What are we coming to?" he spluttered indignantly. "Priests running around like adolescent girls. That was unthinkable years ago . . . but, if I'm not mistaken, he's running to see me." He moved away from the window, waited. Yes, to him. A charge of footsteps on the stairs, another few seconds, and a priest's face in the door. He bowed hastily and panted, "The High Priest Caiaphas has instructed me to inform you that Herod has sent Jesus to Pilate."

Now that was very good news, though he failed to understand it. So the game was still on. Time was flying by, yet they were passing Jesus around from hand to hand like a ball. It was just as well Caiaphas did not comprehend anything, because he would probably be losing his mind out of fright.

"Were you there?" he asked the priest.

The priest nodded his head, still panting.

"So what happened?"

"Pilate must have discovered accidentally that Jesus is from Galilee. I'm not sure, but it looked that way. Then he sent him to Herod."

"But didn't it strike you as odd, my good man"—Annas was surprised at his own sudden talkativeness—"that in his city, Pilate was suddenly, for no reason, permitting the Jewish king to judge his subjects?"

"I didn't think about that."

"A pity, a pity, because if you had thought, maybe you would have thought something out. What do you think, who is more fond of whom: Pilate of Herod, or Herod of Pilate?" He was practically taunting the helpless priest. "How was it over at Herod's palace? Come in, maybe we'll have something to eat, you probably have not eaten all morning."

"But Caiaphas requests that you come immediately before the Praetorium. He is waiting there for you."

The news that Jesus was back with Pilate put him into such a jaunty mood that he felt like bantering a while longer with the priest, delaying indefinitely the moment of departure.

"No, no, don't worry. They'll manage without us. Tell me about it. Herod was feasting? Is that right? But tell me this, it's important to me, was he expecting your arrival or not?"

"No, he was definitely not expecting us. He was surprised."

"He was surprised, you say? Then what? Go on."

"He said he wasn't going to judge Jesus because he was on territory governed by Pilate, and that he had no authority to do so. And besides that, he had come to Jerusalem as a pilgrim and guest for the sole purpose of taking part in the Passover and not to judge people."

"There, you see! You people are always talking about how godless he is. And look how pious he's become—at least recently, isn't that right? Haven't you noticed? You say he didn't want to judge him? And you, what do you think, why?"

"I don't know."

"Now then, tell me how it was at Herod's, go on." He flashed him a genial smile. The priest was visibly astonished by such kindliness and good humor on the part of Annas.

What he was really after in the priest's report were details that might prove useful later. He was anxious to determine whether or not Herod was in league with Pilate, or if Judas might have his finger in the pie somewhere. He did not want to reveal to the priest what he was looking for. He was afraid of influencing his account.

"We were all very agitated," the priest went on.

"Furious, you were going to say."

"Yes, furious," the priest repeated, throwing him an uncertain look. "We weren't sure if it was simply a coincidence or a trick of some kind. It looked as though Pilate had accidentally stumbled on the idea of sending us to Herod, but who can say with him? One thing we did know—there was little chance of Herod being inclined to sentence Jesus to death."

"Miracles are few and far between, you were going to say, right?" Annas smiled.

The priest laughed. "Yes, Herod's one miracle, which he still can't get over, was the execution of John. But that miracle could have repeated itself. There was a chance if Herod was drunk enough. And we all knew he was having a feast."

"I think that, on past experience, you should have expected him to turn over half his kingdom rather than condemn Jesus," Annas noted skeptically.

"No, some felt Herod might risk it again. If he was very drunk."

"But go on, what happened next?"

"We wanted to get to Herod undetected. We were afraid of arousing the curiosity of people in the streets—it was still very early but the first passersby were already staring at us. We took Jesus in the middle of our group so that no one would see him, and we walked that way to Herod's palace. But am I talking too much?"

"No, no, we have time. Tell me everything exactly as it happened. I'm very curious."

"Well, even from a distance we could tell that a feast was in progress–we could hear the screams and shouts of his party guests. We stopped a moment outside the palace, because some of us wanted to ask Herod to come out to us, and others wanted to enter the palace, in spite of the revelry, and confer with him there. That was finally what we did—we went in. As we did not want to arouse any curiosity, we felt it would be safer inside. But it wasn't that easy to get in—drunken people everywhere, lying, sitting, staggering all over the palace."

"But they didn't bother you, surely?"

"Ha! They wouldn't leave us alone. They kept harassing us, weaving up to us and laughing at us that we were late. But luckily no one recognized Jesus. Finally we managed to reach the hall where the feast was being held. It was dark, and the stench of the night's wine was stifling. There was music and noise. We stood against the wall a moment, trying to adjust our eyes to the dimness. Finally I saw Herod. He was seated at the opposite end of the hall, bellowing to the man next to him—who was just as drunk as he was. He still had not seen us. I was instructed to go and announce to him our arrival. It took some doing to get over all the bodies and obstacles. I told him briefly why we were there. He did not understand a word I was saying. For that matter he made not the slightest effort to listen. He pulled me by the arm—I almost fell on him—and kept telling me to pour the wine and drink with him. I didn't want to. I kept on trying to explain about our group. Finally something penetrated: he understood that we wanted him to judge somebody. He looked at me as if I were mad—I don't blame him, a trial in that context! But we had no choice. He gestured around the room—but there's a feast going on! Finally he caught sight of our group huddled over by the wall. He started waving to them to come on over, to make themselves at home, and amuse and enjoy themselves with him. He said there would be time for judging later, that now we should drink. He sobered, though, when he heard the name Jesus. He didn't believe at first that we actually had him with us."

"Maybe he was just pretending not to believe you," Annas broke in, trying to sound casual.

"No, I should know, I was right there next to him," the priest exclaimed.

"Go on."

"He decided to see for himself. He could barely get to his feet. He finally did so with my help. Then he leaned on me— I thought I wouldn't be able to hold him up; I mean, I'm not that strong—and he went over to our group. H wasn't so much incredulous, I can assure you, as deeply disturbed. He inspected Jesus almost reverently. I heard him muttering to himself, 'And I wanted so many times to meet you.' He eyed us, too. He kept shaking his head in wonder, as if he could not believe we had managed to arrest him. He started sobering up very quickly." The priest paused, as if he were fascinated by that picture of Herod.

"Go on, what happened next?" Annas was impatient; the story absorbed him totally.

"Finally he asked us why we had brought Jesus to him. He asked—as if I hadn't already explained it to him ten times. We explained again. Then he burst out laughing, he wouldn't stop, he was convulsed like a madman. He almost fell over. When he finished, he said, 'Fine'. We were a bit surprised that he agreed so readily, when he had refused at first. We still did not know what it was supposed to mean, but we were about to find out. He clapped his hands for the servants. Still in high spirits, he ordered them to call all the guests wandering around the palace into the hall for a trial. We were perplexed—what did he need his guests for? I was personally afraid there was a trick, and I wasn't wrong. Somebody from our group tried to explain to him that his guests weren't necessary, that we would rather the affair didn't go beyond him and us. But he wouldn't hear of it. He must have been drunker than we thought."

"Are you sure about that?" Annas interrupted, unable to contain himself.

The priest stared at him, puzzled, not at all sure what he meant.

"Never mind, don't interrupt yourself, keep talking."

The priest was silent for a moment, having lost his train of thought.

Annas prompted him: "You were saying Herod was very drunk."

"Yes," the priest went on hesitantly, "Herod simply didn't register what we were saying to him. He started to play the fool, running around, setting up his guests who were straying in now, posting them around the room. The more lucid ones asked what was going on. Herod lead them up to Jesus, pointed at him, explained about the trial. His guests sobered up swiftly. For many of them it was a shock to meet the teacher from Nazareth. And on trial, no less. But we still did not know what Herod intended to do. It was unbearable. There were people climbing all over us, pawing us, breathing on us, asking stupid questions. Most of them refused to believe it was really Jesus. They did not even believe we were priests. They thought it was an elaborate joke of Herod's. They tugged us and fingered us. They tugged and handled Jesus, asking him all kinds of questions, demanding he prove that he really was that self-same Jesus everyone was talking about. They wouldn't give up until he gave them a sign, a miracle of some kind. They were absolutely impossible."

"Why didn't you leave? You could have seen it was getting you nowhere."

"By this time there was really no way of getting out. They wouldn't have let us go. And anyway, there was still just a chance, we might get what we came for."

"Continue."

"Herod was still running around, trying to bring the place to order, calling for quiet and dignified conduct at the hearing. Unsuccessfully, of course. He set up the witnesses, the judges, the accused. Then the hearing was opened."

"You mean the parody of a hearing," Annas corrected him.

"No, not entirely. That was the strangest thing about the whole affair. Herod began to question Jesus seriously, exactly as it's normally done at a hearing, about his name, place of birth, descent."

"And Jesus answered?" Annas asked curiously.

"No, not a word. He was silent."

"Well, then, how did Herod cope?"

"We had to answer the questions as witnesses."

"Imbeciles. You're all such imbeciles. Go on."

"After that, Herod asked us what the charge was against him."

"And you told him, right?"

"Yes, we told him that he claims to be the king of Israel."

"Then?"

"Herod had a toga pulled off one of his guests who was asleep in a corner, and he dressed Jesus in it."

"That's pure comedy."

"Then he stepped back and stood before Jesus and declared, 'Well, now, there are two of us kings. How can I judge him, when he can judge me just as well?' Then he turned to us and said, 'You tell me, who is the King of the Jews? Judge for yourselves.' In dead earnest, without the shade of a smile, he said to everyone, 'You choose. Into your hands we put our fate, Jesus and I both'. Not only was he serious, but the whole room suddenly grew very somber. He asked again, 'Who is worthiest to stand at the head of the chosen nation? Jesus or Herod?' I thought I was losing my mind. It seemed as though the whole future of the world depended on our decision, not just to me, but to everyone there."

"So what happened?" he spurred him on.

"So we picked Jesus."

"Sheer madness!"

"Exactly. But then Herod burst into a fit of laughter. The spell was broken. Everyone started to laugh."

"And then what?"

"Then he simply shoved us out the door and said for Pilate to judge Jesus, because he was the master around here."

"And now you have brought him back to Pilate?"

"Yes, but I haven't been there yet. I hurried straight here with Caiaphas's request that you go there at once."

"Yes, of course, we'll go, but we needn't hurry. Pilate will either agree immediately, in which case we won't be required there at all, or the matter will get complicated, and then it will take some time. But all right, all right, we'll go now."

He snatched up his staff, took the abashed priest firmly by the arm and, leaning on him heavily, shuffled stiffly out of the door. The streets were still largely deserted. Annas chatted idly with his companion, but all the while his eyes carefully scanned the streets for signs of activity. Finally they neared the Praetorium. Annas was startled to see the street leading directly to the square jammed with people. Where had they all come from. He grew apprehensive—they must have found out about Jesus after all, and come to demand his release. The smiling face of Judas flashed through his mind. So, he had made it after all. The crowds were spilling into the adjoining narrow streets.

"Who are all these people?" he whispered anxiously to the priest. "Where had they all come from?"

The priest smiled comfortably. "A few sightseers, but the rest are our people from the temple. That was the High Priest's order. This morning, on his way to Pilate with Jesus, he ordered everyone, starting with the priests, right down to the cleaning menials, to accompany him."

Annas had to admit he had never thought Caiaphas capable of such foresight.

"First we all went to Pilate," the priest droned on. "Then later, when it became necessary, to Herod, and now back again to Pilate. Those who couldn't come at once were ordered to join as soon as possible. Some busybodies swelled our ranks along the way—there was nothing we could do about those who followed our procession out of curiosity, to see what was happening."

"Where is Caiaphas now? I don't see him." He glanced around nervously.

"We're going to him now," the priest reassured him.

They made their way fairly easily through the crowd.

"He's there, by the wall." The priest pointed to a group of chief priests.

Annas hurried toward him. People respectfully moved

aside. Caiaphas, when he saw him, left his circle of priests to greet him.

"Well," Annas whispered to him, "I didn't give you credit for so much sense. That was a stroke of genius, taking so many people along with you."

Caiaphas' face brightened, then he added candidly "I have to admit I did it because I was afraid to go to Pilate with Jesus by myself. It's always safer in a crowd."

"One way or the other, the idea was excellent," he praised him again.

"If you will allow, let's go higher up," Caiaphas proposed. "You can see better from up there."

He almost feels like the host here, Annas thought to himself. Aloud he asked, "But aren't you speaking to Pilate?"

"No, I preferred to observe from a distance. But the ones who went in to him know exactly what to say."

"What's happening there now? Where is Jesus?"

"In the Praetorium."

"Why?" He did not understand what was happening.

"Pilate sentenced Jesus to be scourged."

Annas' heart leaped to his throat. "Why? That's all we need. How could you have allowed it? He has to be sentenced to death!" And as he said it, he suddenly knew the answer to his own question: Caiaphas did not wish Jesus to die. The thought came out of nowhere and suddenly seemed to answer a lot of questions. Now he understood the entire burden was shifting back to his own shoulders and no one was going to help him with it. He could count on no one. He was surrounded by traitors.

". . . It's not up to me. . . . How can I help it . . . ?"

He listened skeptically to Caiaphas's halting excuses.

". . . . It's Pilate who wants to release him at all costs. He announced that he would scourge him and then let him go—"

"Out of the question."

"But what can we do?"

"We won't leave here until he passes the death sentence. Has he had him in there long?"

"Oh, a while. He's in no hurry."

Caiaphas's words brought back to him what he had told himself earlier: time was working against them. He peered around. From where they stood, they had an unobstructed view of everything. The square adjoining the Praetorium was not as densely packed as he had first thought. People filled the area, but rather loosely. New arrivals were streaming in constantly from the side streets leading to the square.

"Are those still our people arriving?" he asked.

Caiaphas scanned the flow. "Some Jerusalem people, some pilgrims," he said after a moment.

"So they're not our people any more?"

"No, no, everyone who could come is already here."

"Don't you think it might be good if no one else came on to this square?"

"I don't think it really matters, to be honest. And, anyway, what can we do about it?"

Annas, however, was increasingly worried by the influx. He was also irritated by Caiaphas' nonchalant attitude, his total lack of concern, which was becoming more obvious to him every minute. "Can you tell if there are any disciples of Jesus on the square?" he asked uneasily.

"I don't think so. If there were, I'm sure I would have been informed."

Annas wasn't satisfied with the answer. It only served to increase his uneasiness. At length he said, "Have you reckoned with the possibility of his disciples coming to the square?"

"Oh, no. They scurried off yesterday in panic, only too happy we let them go."

Annas knew what he should do. "Post guards and close off the square," he said suddenly.

Caiaphas was silent, visibly reluctant.

That irritated Annas still more. "I don't like surprises," he growled. "Don't let anyone else into the square."

"Forgive me, but we have no right—"

"Close off the square," he snapped.

"All right, all right. If it means so much to you, I'll give the order." He left. In a moment he was back. Instinctively Annas sensed that he had not done it. He was about to say something, when a movement on the Praetorium terrace caught his eye.

"They're bringing Jesus out," Caiaphas said.

In his time, Annas had seen quite a few shocking sights, but what he saw now stunned even him. A frightful, unrecognizable mass of blood. He squinted hard to make it out more distinctly. "What's that on his head?"

Caiaphas stood staring at the ground, apparently unable to look. Now he lifted his eyes timidly and took a quick look at Jesus. "Some kind of hat they made of thorns. That's why he looks so streaked with blood."

The crowd on the square grew very quiet. Pilate emerged. The hush deepened, as if the onlookers were all holding their breaths at once. Pilate waited a long moment in the stillness. Then facing the square, he pointed dramatically to the figure of Jesus and said simply, "Behold the man."

Annas felt the whole square freeze. The sight of him had stunned the entire assembly. Not he, not anyone had expected that grisly spectacle. The silence lengthened in confusion. He could feel Caiaphas's frightened eyes on him. He heard him whisper, "What now?"

It seemed there would be no end to the silence. Annas stood still, as if paralysed. He had to say something. Say something. Now. Immediately. With delay. Because in another instant it might be too late. Say something decisive. Then the necessary words came to him, automatically tore out of his throat and lungs: "Crucify him!"

His cry bounced between the stone walls of the square in a roll of echoes. It seemed to hang in the stillness. Clearly no one had expected to hear that kind of response. But only for a moment. Suddenly the group of Chief Priests nearby took up the cry. Others followed suit, then more, until the whole square resounded with the chanting rhythm of "Cru-ci-fy him! Cru-ci-fy him!"

Annas fell back against the wall, throwing out his arms to keep his balance, reeling from emotion, hardly able to keep his feet. Red spots sparkled and flashed before his eyes. He grabbed at his chest where his heart pounded dangerously.

"I'm too old for this sort of excitement. This shouldn't even concern me," he gasped.

He grabbed Caiaphas by the arm, squeezed it to indicate he was leaving. Caiaphas held him back. He leaned over and said in his ear, "I beg you, stay. It's just another moment. Lean against me. You'll regret later you didn't stay till the end. Lean against me." The square still shook with shouting. "Look at Pilate, it's worth it," Caiaphas urged him.

Annas squinted, trying to discern the expression on Pilate's face. The throng's reaction appeared to have taken him totally by surprise—the Procurator was searching the crowd left and right, as if he were trying to make sense of them, trying to locate a clue to their reaction.

"Why is he looking around like that?" Caiaphas's whispering hissed in his hear. "What does he want to do now?"

"He's a democrat, and wants to talk to the Jewish people, not with us."

Annas saw him suddenly whirl around and disappear inside the Praetorium. A moment later a soldier pulled Jesus in from the terrace. That disturbed him. What was Pilate planning to do next? He didn't want to meet the crowd's demand. Slowly the square was becoming quieter. What could be done? His misgivings swelled until they hurt. He came to an abrupt decision.

"Come, we'll go to Pilate together." He seized Caiaphas roughly by the arm. "Come on, because in another minute it might be too late!" He pushed forward, nearly dragging Caiaphas behind him. "He might do something foolish. We'll try to help him resolve his dilemma."

Caiaphas balked. "No, please, I appeal to you, don't risk it. You don't know Pilate? He's capable of anything. He could throw us out or have us arrested, or order his soldiers to disperse the people to the four winds of heaven."

"We have no other alternative," Annas growled. "Come on, before it's too late."

He made his laborious way through the crowd, with Caiaphas reluctantly in tow.

"Please, he's a madman, I appeal to you—"

"I'll try to be gentle with him."

"Maybe we should take more people with us. Listen to me at least this once. Please."

"No. This time it will be better without witnesses."

They were at the Praetorium entrance and spoke to a soldier on guard.

"Ask the Procurator if we may have a few words with him," Annas said.

The soldier disappeared inside. All conversation on the square died. The crowd sensed a new development.

The sentry returned. "You may enter." He stood aside for them. They went in. Pilate was staring out his window, and even with his back to them he looked very angry. He did not bother to turn around at their entry. Jesus stood against a wall.

"We humbly beg your pardon," Annas began as he entered. "But we feel obliged to present to you our point of view regarding the prisoner." He spoke haltingly, as if he were trying to overcome his diffidence in the presence of the Procurator.

"We have come to you because we are deeply aware of the grave danger hanging over our unfortunate nation because of this man." He pointed to Jesus. He lowered his eyes, he shuffled his feet, and put on an air of intense embarrassment, as if to apologize for having made so bold as to enter and disrupt the Procurator's hearing.

"He has consistently aimed at seizing power over our nation and proclaiming himself King of the Jews, and in so doing, usurping the throne of the lawful Jewish king whom our Roman Emperor was pleased to appoint. The accused has many followers and could precipitate an outbreak of civil war and even the overthrow of Herod, the rightful king, who is the guarantor of peace with Rome and our friendship with the great Roman nation." He spoke cautiously, on the alert for a reaction from Pilate. But the Procurator stood impassively at the window.

"In that event, the Roman Emperor will be forced to intervene," he continued, "and will march into our country with his army. In this way, a war will result between Rome and Jesus' fanatical followers. We beg your pardon but it seems to us that it is better to act now, even to overreact, than be sorry later. If, and God forbid such a thing should happen, it resulted in such anger on the part of Rome, the fate of the whole Jewish nation would be endangered. And it would all be caused by the madness of this man. We, as loyal and devoted subjects of the Emperor, for whom the fate of our nation is no trifle, cannot allow this to happen. We are only priests whose function is offering sacrifices to the Lord God, we have no interest in politics—'' He broke off because at that moment Pilate turned around and faced him, as if he wanted to take a good look at him or determine if he was joking or serious.

Annas went on quickly, "The Sanhedrin, which convened yesterday, sentenced him to death. But in reality, it was neither we who sentenced him to death, nor you.'' He knew he may have gone too far, suggesting too bluntly to Pilate what he should do, but Pilate appeared not to have noticed. He listened with a look of indifference on his face.

He hurried on, "But he has condemned himself to death by proclaiming himself the King of the Jews. He is a rebel against the Emperor and against Rome, and for that reason, we cannot release him, nor can you.''

Now he steered more sharply and pointedly in his intended direction: "We know that if we release him we would lose the Emperor's trust and would cease to be his friends. And so will you, if you release this man, cease to be the friend of Caesar.''

He paused deliberately to allow his words to sink in. He was only too well aware that what he said bordered on insolence, but it had to be said. Now he began a hasty retreat: "Forgive us that we had to speak these things so plainly to you, but this is a very important matter, and if it results in a disaster, then we would have to explain our position in this matter to Rome. We would have to show how we did everything to avert a catastrophe, and how we warned you, as well, that he is a rebel and ought to be sentenced to death.''

Now, he thought, pausing for breath, we have to show our teeth a little, scare him. "You know, of course,'' he went on, "that we inform Caesar directly of every important matter that occurs here, since we consider him the father of the entire Empire, and as such, the guardian of our nation." He broke off abruptly. "We will go now. Remain in peace."

Unobtrusively, he squeezed Caiaphas's arm, and bowing deeply in a series of rapid movements he pulled him out after him. He did not wait to give Pilate a chance to answer, not even a chance to formulate a response. They left the Praetorium barely concealing their haste. Another moment and they were on the terrace, past the sentry, then very slowly, with solemn dignity and modestly lowered eyes as befitted two servants of the altar, they returned to their places.

Annas collapsed against the wall. His knees quaked fearfully, he wrung his hands to stop their trembling, he shut his eyes. Caiaphas's whisper was in his ear: "You were brilliant". The square buzzed evenly. Annas thought rapidly to himself: it was all that could be done, there was nothing more I could do. It must have worked well. He must be going wild in there—just so long as he doesn't do anything foolish. He should be coming out by now, why doesn't he come out? What is he doing taking so long?

Finally the curtain in the entrance rippled: a soldier led Jesus back out on the terrace. A moment later Pilate appeared.

"Look," Caiaphas whispered.

Pilate looked cool, calm, confident—he must have arrived at a decision. They watched him seat himself comfortably in the tribunal and wait, as if he were satisfying himself with the hush in the square. Finally he pointed to Jesus. "Behold your King," he cried out.

Annas could feel the worried gaze of Caiaphas on him. He did not look at him; he did not understand himself what was happening. The throng in the square seemed to freeze momentarily, then suddenly recover. This time without prompting it roared in unison: "Cru-ci-fy him!" Annas held his breath for what would come next: a mass slaughter on the square, or compliance with the will of the people.

When the noise died down, Pilate raised his hand and asked with a malicious smile, "Shall I crucify your king?"

What did he want? what was he trying to do? Annas fumed.

Suddenly an outburst rattled his senses from right alongside him: "We have no king but Caesar!"

It was Caiaphas shouting at the top of his voice. Now where did he summon up that from? he wondered. Meanwhile he noticed Pilate examining the palm of his hand and then turn to one of his servants with an order. What was he up to now? The servant returned moments later with a bowl and a pitcher of water. Pilate leaned over the arm of his chair to wash his hands. What was he doing? Had he gone mad? As he was wiping his hands, Pilate turned abruptly to the closely-bunched priests and addressed them: "I am innocent of the blood of this just man".

Annas felt as if a millstone had suddenly dropped from around his neck. So, it was to be the death sentence. And now, in front of all the people, Pilate wanted to demonstrate that he was not to blame, but they, the priests; that he was not accepting the death of Jesus on his conscience. "Very bad actor," he muttered.

One of the priests in front—he could not see which—cried out, "His blood is upon us and upon our children!"

Our priests have become very talkative of late, he said to himself sarcastically. Especially now, when we are winning.

The crowd seized wildly on the words. They cried out with a vengeance: "His blood is upon us and upon our children!" They understood that they had won. They laughed, roared, cheered, spun around on their feet, threw their arms in the air, and swayed to and fro as if they were affected by a collective madness. They had won what they wanted. The sweet taste of victory: they had defeated the Roman. The Procurator of eternal Rome had to yield to them. Israel had triumphed once more.

Annas smiled smugly, leaned over to Caiaphas. "I'm not needed here any more. I'm going back. Get rid of the people. Have them return to the temple." He liked order.

He plodded off slowly in the direction of his house, to the accompaniment of the frenzied crowd still insisting that, "His blood is upon us and upon our children!"

His bones and muscles ached from weariness; his head and shoulders sagged; his hands felt swollen. He dragged his feet

one heavy step at a time, stopping every few moments to
support himself against a wall. The city was awake: number-
less pilgrims streamed by on donkey and on foot. Today was
Passover. He had lost all sense of time; it seemed as if whole
years had flown by. The closer he drew to the temple, the
tighter the streets became with stalls and portable kitchens,
donkeys, sheep, and cages of doves. He squeezed in and out
laboriously. Every few minutes someone recognized him and
greeted him or stopped him to inquire about this priest or
that priest or someone else working in the temple. To every
question, he answered simply, "They'll be here shortly. Just
wait patiently."

He gave up his plan of returning home as he had originally
thought to do—someone had to mind the temple. Finally he
arrived within its cool walls. He felt at home; it was his temple
once more. It was quiet and empty within, as if completely
deserted. He made his way to the conference hall, where he
sank into a chair with a heavy sigh. He closed his eyes and
felt the blood coursing through his veins and the throb of his
pulse in his temples. The distant hum of the city lulled him.
It was good here, this was home.

He was roused from a deep sleep by a voice in the room.
It was hard to tell how long he had been dozing. An attendant
stood before him.

"What are you doing here?" he asked him. "Are you back
from Pilate already?"

"No, I wasn't there. A few priests were told to stay behind
to watch the temple, including, unfortunately, me."

"What do you want? A man can't even take a nap in
peace," he grumbled, already dropping off to sleep again.

"One of the disciples of Jesus wishes to speak with you."

"Whose disciple?" The name jolted him awake.

"That master of Nazareth who was arrested during the
night—I was there, I saw it."

Annas sat up suddenly in his chair. I must be an idiot, he
thought to himself. Sitting here like this in an empty temple—
they could have murdered me right here, and no one would
ever know who did it.

"Are you armed?" he asked the priest.

"Yes. I have a sword—left over from the night."

"Come with me. And be prepared."

Which one could it be? he wondered, following behind the priest. Peter? That one was capable of anything. . . . He could kill me the way he tried to finish off Malchus.

He entered the hall, peered around uncertainly. He could not see anyone.

"That's him." The servant pointed to a figure pressed closely against the wall. In the dusky light he saw an indistinct form. He took a few steps forward, balancing himself against the servant's left side. Now he thought he recognized him. Judas? Even were it light in the room he would scarcely have recognized him. There was the same reddish hair and beard, but this was another, a different man: clothes soiled and rumpled; ashen, empty face and eyes; a crushed drooping figure propped unsteadily against the wall. Annas felt a quiver of fear shake him. what did it mean?

"What do you want?" he demanded harshly.

He saw the other's face twitch, saw the parched lips move.

"I have betrayed innocent blood."

For an instant he thought he saw that other, ironic smile flicker across those lips, and then die. He watched him with a rising feeling of contempt and triumph—the unkempt garments, the fallen arms, the sagging figure barely keeping to its feet.

"What has that to do with me? That's your affair." He turned without another word.

He was almost at the door when he heard a heavy metallic thud. He spun around instantly and saw an object fallen at Judas's feet. He waited while he groped his way out of the room. "Go and see what it is," he told the servant.

The servant went over, stooped, picked up a leather pouch and tossed it several times in the air. "Money."

"Count it."

"He spilled the contents on the floor and a moment later announced, "Exactly thirty silver pieces".

What did I expect? he thought irately to himself. Of course there could not be any less or any more. He returned to his chair in the conference hall, feeling exhausted to the point of collapse. He mumbled aloud in the vacant room: "I don't understand it. What was that supposed to mean? What function did Judas have in all this? Something must not have worked out for him, something must have gone wrong. But what was supposed to have succeeded? Was it as I suspected? By whose orders was he operating? Jesus'? Pilate's? Herod's? The other disciples'? His own? But he is a real threat to us now—if he starts repeating to the masses what he just said to me, if he starts telling them that for money he turned Jesus over to us, the priests. Humm. . . . Who knows if he might not have to be dispensed with. . .?" His thoughts began to scramble . . . fade. . . . He fell asleep again.

For some unknown reason he awoke with a start. He thought someone had entered the room, but it was empty. A deathly silence pressed on his ears. He felt cold and alien in the room. A chilling shiver ran through his body. "Let's get out of here and see what's happening at Golgotha," he said out loud. "If a man doesn't attend to everything himself, then he's likely to regret it later." But he knew he was justifying his eagerness to flee that room.

Outside in the gallery a blast of warm air struck him. He looked around with pleasure: everywhere life was back to normal, all things were as they should be—and that was the way it would be until the end of the world. A moving, bobbing sea of pilgrims filled his field of vision. And scattered in their midst were priests, Levites, and temple attendants. He accosted a passing Levite. "Are you free?"

"Always at your disposal."

"Then come with me. We'll walk a bit."

He took him by the arm and chatted with him for several minutes. Then: "Were you at Golgotha?"

"Yes."

"When did you return?"

"When they raised Jesus on a cross."

"So he's hanging."

"Yes, for the last couple of hours, along with two companions."

"Two of his disciples?" he asked in surprise.

"No, criminals. So he would be in good company."

"But surely he hasn't killed anyone," he said deliberately.

"No, but he would have led the nation into civil war. Between his fanatics and Herod's army. Then the Romans would have intervened and occupied the whole country. That makes him worse than a murderer who kills only one man."

Annas listened half amused, half surprised to hear his own words being uttered from the mouth of this fool. He could hardly suppress a laugh.

"What are the people saying about all this?" he inquired cautiously.

"The same as me. It's the truth, isn't it? Of course, there are still some who think differently, but they're fanatics."

They reached the city walls and found themselves in a procession of people headed toward Golgotha. Through the opening of the gates, they could see three crosses sticking out of the top of the hill against the sky. Annas stopped. "Which one is he?"

"The one in the middle."

They climbed the path to the hill. Distrusting his own legs, Annas leaned heavily against the Levite's arm. "Let's go higher," he said. "I want to see Caiaphas."

The Levite made a way for them in the slow-moving column. At the top they came upon a large group of priests.

"Call Caiaphas over for me," Annas said.

The Levite disappeared. Annas glanced around the hill: people were already densely assembled. He surveyed the two condemned men on either side of Jesus—those two would last a while yet. He shifted his gaze back to him.

Jesus hung in immobile exhaustion with his head sunk on his chest. Annas shrank inside at the sight. It was a long time since he had seen a man so tortured. Dark dried clots of blood from wounds received during his scourging speckled his entire body. Some still oozed stubbornly. But his head with that thing of thorns—that was the most ghastly sight. Clouds of flies circled insanely around it. Flies everywhere, crawling all over his body and especially his face. Those flies must be causing him the most misery, Annas thought to himself. Jesus seemed somehow small now, insignificant, not at all like the man of Palm Sunday. He spoke to him in his mind as he watched him on the cross: not much was lacking and you would have won. You would have become the King of the Jews. It's another thing altogether if you ever wanted to be king. A few more minutes and I'll start believing myself what I dreamed up about you. But I fulfilled my responsibility to save the Covenant and the temple. I am responsible, I guard the Holy of Holies, I did my duty. And I saved them. Or perhaps I only saved my own power over the temple? Somehow the feeling of victory eluded him. There was no sense of satisfaction. Only an emptiness. He wanted to get away. Now, immediately. He could not wait for Caiaphas. He had to get away. But where to? Back to his normal everyday existence. Somehow he could not picture himself in the temple now, among his people. He would go away. Yes, that would be best, if he went away somewhere.

Caiaphas came up from behind him. "It's good that you came," he mumbled, just to say something. His face was gray.

"What is it?" Annas asked curtly. "Is everything in order?" He tried to pull Caiaphas together with the harsh tones of his voice.

"Yes, in order."

"There were no disturbances?"

"None."

Annas noticed that Caiaphas wouldn't even turn his eyes in the direction of the crosses. "Are Jesus' disciples here?"

"There was practically no one here at first, now they're beginning to mass," he answered vaguely.

Annas thought to himself, he's already reporting to me like a soldier on duty. He'll probably start believing in me again. I just hope I can believe in myself, too.

"Whom have you seen?" he asked sharply.

"I know few of them. There's Lazarus, Joseph of Arimathea, and Nicodemus. I don't know the others. A lot of women. His mother and Magdalene. Oh, of the Twelve there's only John."

"It would be good if we could finish with this whole business as quickly as possible."

Caiaphas looked at him with clouded eyes. "But how? Crucified men sometimes linger for days."

He is ready to start crying on me, Annas thought sarcastically. I'm no nursemaid.

"I know that, but we can't allow it. We have made too many stupid mistakes. We can't make any more. Send someone to Pilate, let him give his permission to have the condemned men finished off. Tell him that tomorrow is the Sabbath or something like that. I'm going down again. I'll be watching the temple. I'm tired, and I've had enough."

He turned away from Caiaphas, clamped a hand on the Levite's arm for support, and slowly made his way down the hill. An endless stream of men and women climbed processionlike to the top of Golgotha. He barely dragged himself back to the conference hall, where he sank into his seat.

"Don't let anyone in." He gave the order and fell instantly to sleep.

A crash of thunder jerked him to his feet. The room was in total darkness. Rain pelted the flagstones in the courtyard. He peered through the window. Water flooded the gallery. A cloudburst or what? It had cleared away all the people—not a soul in sight. Another clap of thunder, then another—the storm was right over the city. Suddenly a bolt of lightning blinded his eyes, and a deafening crash exploded in his ears. For an instant he thought lightning had struck him. He sprang away from the window and fell against a wall. He glanced around, shaken. No, it must have hit somewhere close by. From deep in the interior of the temple, he heard a faint cry. The sound suddenly rose in volume—not one man, not dozens, but now hundreds of voices shouting in panic. His hair tingled and stood on end. He crouched paralyzed against the wall. Something dreadful had happened, he knew, but he couldn't tear himself away. His legs were weak, they refused to hold him. What could have happened? He heard a sound, closer, louder—running footsteps. Dozens of terrified faces appeared in the door. He heard one of them stammer: "Lightning has torn the veil before the Holy of Holies from top to bottom!"

MARY MAGDALENE

After her parents' death, it was as if all restraints and inhibitions had suddenly fallen away from her—gone were all the checks, the pressures, pleas, naggings, and their hopes for her. But there was no one left either on whom to rely in planning her future, or in making simple, everyday decisions. Lazarus, on whose slender shoulders had suddenly fallen the whole burden of administering the estate, had little time to give her. For that matter, always kind and easygoing, he would never have been able to bridle her whims or impose his will and judgment on her the way their parents had. Martha, her older and less outgoing sister, alienated her with her unrelieved sternness and often groundless reprimands. Martha had never had any real influence on her. Her sole weapon—"because I'll tell Father", or worse, "because I'll tell Mother"—was no longer effective. Now Mary did things to spite Martha, to annoy her, flaunt her independence and superiority. In her sister's severity, she thought she detected jealousy, and probably not without reason. Mary knew she was witty and sharp, and that she easily attracted other people, especially men. It was always Mary who attracted the interest of visitors to their home, instantly becoming the focus of attention. Martha, with her gruff and stubborn ways, attracted no one. But now even Martha had no time for her. The house had suddenly become empty. Mary felt keenly not only the absence of her parents, but of their friends who used to converge at the house as well. For a time, she looked for diversion among the vinedressers on the estate, but quickly tired of their company. She took to visiting her girl friends in Jerusalem, at first under the pretext of attending their various family celebrations, then under no pretext at all. She quickly came to enjoy a life filled with evernew faces, adventures, parties, trips. A whole new world opened up before her among a whole new society of friends: the rich and carefree, whose lives were equally remote from the toil of the village and the frenzy of the big city, who spent their time partying, strolling, and entertaining. Mary discovered places hitherto unknown to her: Tiberias, Capernaum, Magdala. Especially Magdala. Set on the side of a hill sloping gently toward the shimmering edge of the Lake of Gennesaret and dotted with lovely villas half hidden among lush gardens, Magdala became the object of her dreams.

Why shouldn't she, like those rich owners, lie on the terrace of her own villa and admire the sunsets over the lake, watch the fishermen sail in from their morning catch, and dance and entertain in her own garden amid hanging lanterns? She could not put up with the atmosphere at home much longer, the work and the days of sweltering drudgery among the workers in the fields and vineyards. Less and less of her was seen at home, until she disappeared from it altogether. She rented rooms in Jerusalem and vowed never to return home. None of her brother's or sister's appeals would move her; too late they discovered what had happened. By now she could not imagine herself back in the village, where each day was as tedious as the last. Now she enjoyed the diverse company of rich young people and older men—many of whom would readily take her for a wife. Their proposals of marriage amused her; she laughed at their attempts to win her favor. She was attracted to far too many men, she told them, to dream of marrying any single one. She stayed with each as long as it pleased her, for as long as she felt good, then dropped him capriciously, on an impulse, the instant she was bored or caught sight of something else. She toyed with people, winning them over for the game, only to discard them once she had won, never taking any further interest in them. She passed from hand to hand, but voluntarily, because it was what she wanted, because this one or that one appealed to her at that moment.

Jerusalem was only a steppingstone. She did not enjoy life

under the squeeze of the Pharisees and doctors of the Law. All the rules and regimentation that the people blindly and unquestioningly obeyed gained her unqualified contempt. She loathed the shadow of the temple that hung over Jerusalem. Nor could she stand the political pressures and intrigues. She had her own ideas about how she wanted to live, and those ideas centered largely around her dreams of settling in Magdala.

Any excuse found her there. Very cautiously she asked around about the prospects of purchasing, or at least renting, some kind of villa. It wasn't easy to find something decent; the prices were exorbitant. The salubrious climate and beautiful surroundings attracted the rich of Jerusalem—those with a desire for quiet and relaxation, and those on the lookout for pleasure and amusement. Finally an opportunity arose. A villa, perfectly situated, like the dream she had sketched, was for sale. Without a moment's hesitation, she decided to buy it. She demanded from Lazarus her share of her parents' estate. Despite Martha's very vocal protests, Lazarus paid out her rightful part. The money was enough to buy the villa, but not enough to furnish and repair it. So she borrowed large sums at soaring rates of interest. She was confident she could pay back her debts; she knew herself, she knew how to calculate. She was extravagant, to be sure, but only when her instincts told her it would pay off. And when people laughed at her, that she was throwing money out of the window, in her heart she told herself that it had to come back in through the door. And it did. Her neighbors very quickly discovered who she was and what she was looking for in Magdala.

Her reputation often spread as far as Jerusalem. Mary of Magdala—beautiful, well-born, keeping an open house; whose friends and benefactors counted among the richest people of Jerusalem. But her benefactors very quickly came to know her as well. They learned how expensive her friendship could be, more expensive than any other woman to date. They paid for everything, sometimes surprised at their own lavish concessions, and sometimes indignant at her careless, extravagant attitude. Sometimes they rebelled; they protested, they quarreled, they threatened to break off, they left in a huff. She laughed. You'll be back, she told them. And usually they were: they came back. She was in fashion. It was considered prestigious, uppercrust, to find oneself in Mary's villa, to become one of her benefactors, or at the very least, a frequent guest. And so they came back and kept on paying, and Mary accumulated evernew clothes, jewelry, furniture, rugs, and exotic plants. She bought up her neighbors' land and enlarged her gardens—at wondrous expense. And she hired very reliable servants—known for their discretion.

Though she rarely went to Jerusalem now, she kept her rooms there. This way, when she did arrive, she was independent of anyone's largesse. It was not long before she was recognized on the streets of Jerusalem: at once the object of awe and envy, or outrage and venom. There were those who couldn't take their eyes off her, and there were those who spat vehemently behind her. "Adulteress"—and the most dangerous one Jerusalem had ever possessed. She didn't concern herself with either. She laughed, confident of her looks, her charm, her money, her connections, her youth, her intelligence. Nor did she worry that she had made herself the object of hatred of one of the Scribes whose attentions she had once flippantly spurned. But she was unaware of his plan for revenge.

During one of her visits to Jerusalem, a scribe called on her, and explained at length how it was they had met. For the life of her, she couldn't remember, but anyway, it wasn't important. Finally he came to the point of his visit: with a few of his friends, he was giving a feast that evening in a very close and private group, and they would be greatly flattered by her presence. He added: she would meet someone close to her there. Though she was free that evening, she didn't really feel like going. When she finally accepted, it was against her better judgment—but precisely because of the aura of the mystery and danger she sensed. She couldn't quite put her finger on it, but she was certain of one thing: nothing had been said to indicate the real purpose of their meeting. The address was suspicious. She knew that section of the city well: a squeeze of tenements in the dingiest alleys near the temple. Certainly not the residence of the type of company to which her visitor subscribed. She was intrigued; she couldn't wait for the appointed hour.

A litter came for her punctually. She must have been the last to arrive, because the place was full: some women of easy virtue, very elegant, but "imported," not from Jerusalem; the men: doctors of the Law. She knew a few of them by sight. The flat was drab, uninteresting, obviously borrowed and equipped for the evening, just as she had suspected. A lavishly laid table, with painstakingly selected foods. For the moment, nothing was amiss. She was sure there was a surprise in store for her, but she couldn't tell if it was to be good or bad. For most of the evening the seat next to her at the table was vacant. The answer to the riddle was sure to come from there, from the person who would appear next to her. Finally, when the last course was being served, he entered, the man they had all been awaiting. Ah, yes. She almost sighed aloud. It was him, "her doctor," as she often referred to him disparagingly among her girl friends. Rejected by her with a laugh and a toss of her head. Suddenly she felt in grave danger. She wanted to get up and leave, but she pulled herself together and determined to stay and fight. The next minutes, however, proved her suspicions were groundless; no attack was forthcoming. Her "enemy" behaved as if there had never been anything between them. Again she felt unsure of herself— what was the point? Until it happened. It was after drinking the next serving of wine. The funny taste struck her—but only after she realized that something strange was happening to her: the room was beginning to spin; pictures, objects, people began to shift and merge; double, triple images blurring; her tongue rolling; she couldn't hear herself speak, though she knew she was speaking; voices in the room coming to her as if from another place and time. She felt herself sinking into an abyss. As she slumped down against the table, for an instant she caught the knowing looks shot across the table at her menacing neighbor. She understood: she had been poisoned.

A piercing scream awakened her. She opened her eyes. She couldn't tell where she was or what was happening. She tried to lift her head; it felt like so much lead. Every movement sent stabs of pain that felt as if they would split her skull. She was nauseated and racked with pain in her whole body. Slowly she lifted herself from the bed on which she lay. She realized now that she was half naked. With an effort she turned and focused on the woman standing in the door with her finger pointing at her, shrieking over and over as if she were crazed: "Adulteress!"

In a daze she watched the room suddenly fill with excited men shouting and pointing at her. Two young men rushed up and seized her roughly by the arms and dragged her from the bed toward the door. She cried out in pain and struggled to free herself, but they held her tightly. They pulled her almost tumbling down the stairs, even though a little crowd that had collected in the hall at the sound of the commotion, and into the street. She screamed desperately, hoping to attract help in the street. Several young men ran up— they were coming to her assistance, she thought. But a moment later she saw that they, too, were part of the conspiracy. Her assailants quickened their steps, fairly ran with her, half dragging, half carrying her in the air. She fought them furiously, tearing, biting, kicking, screaming for help. A heavy fist stuffed a gag in her mouth. With a superhuman effort, she tore free—but only for an instant. Hands, countless hands, beat down on her, grabbing at her clothing, her arms, her hair. She resisted like a wild animal. In vain. Her bare feet kicking, stumbling against the stones, splitting her toes and nails; her arms twisted brutally in their sockets; her hair pulled savagely—she thought she would go mad from pain. With a snared animal's instinct, she knew she was being carried to slaughter. Any second now, she expected the lethal blow. Then the thought raced through her mind: if they had wanted to kill her, they could have done it at night. Where were they taking her? She looked around at the faces; who were these men who had abducted her? Not one was familiar. Then she glimpsed a man hurrying alongside the group dragging her thought the street. It was him, "her doctor." This was his revenge.

Abruptly her attackers slowed and began to force their way through a large silent crowd of people. She could hear people in the crowd sharply telling the intruders to be quiet. Suddenly she was heaved like a sack and flung violently to the ground. She lay there a long moment, bathed in the bright uncompromising sunlight, half wild and dazed with fear and pain. Hesitantly, she pulled herself into a crouching position and looked around.

She had been thrust into the open space at the front of a sombre crowd. She had no idea where she was—and that silence! How could it be so quiet with so many people there? She brushed away her hair and rubbed her eyes with her tattered sleeve, then stared around. She suddenly realized that no one was watching her, that all eyes were fixed above her head. She turned, and on the steps behind her saw the master of Nazareth. Though she had never met him, she knew who he was. She had heard about him and his teachings, but never took an interest—their paths were very different indeed. He was just another one of those prophets. Except, perhaps, insofar as he was detested by the priests, whom she herself held in contempt; or perhaps insofar as he lived among the common people and—as the Pharisees put it—ate with sinners and publicans. She had heard that there were even publicans among his closest companions.

She could not see his face. He stood with his hands folded and his head bowed. He was not looking at her, nor did he appear to be paying attention either to her or the men who had dragged her there. It took a moment before it suddenly dawned on her, that it was quiet because he had been asked a question and now everyone was poised and waiting for his answer. What was the question? She had only half heard it. Why didn't he answer? And then they asked it again, mouthing the words as if he were hard-of-hearing, or as if they wanted to make sure that every last man and woman in the crowd heard it more distinctly: "We have just now caught her in the act of adultery. Moses commanded us to stone such a one. What do you say?"

She froze. No, it was impossible, it was nonsense. Frantically, she searched the faces of the doctors of the Law. No, she wouldn't find any mercy there. But why hadn't they stoned her right away? Why didn't they just stone her now?

Why were they asking his opinion? The answer came in a flash: she wasn't important here at all; it was he, the teacher of Nazareth, who was under scrutiny, it was his fate that was hanging in the balance. He didn't want to say "yes"—the one who lived among sinners. But now he couldn't say "no," because Moses himself commanded the stoning of such as she. Her gaze froze on his lips: what would he say? And if his answer was "yes," she knew it would be the last moment of her life. They would kill her without the least compunction. And yet he couldn't say "no," because then he himself would be stoned to death. "Moses commanded us to stone such a one, and what do you say?" they repeated. Why doesn't he answer? A teacher posed a question must answer if he wants to continue teaching. Why doesn't he say something? His silence was unbearable.

Then, when she thought she would never awaken from that suspension in time, she saw him lift his head and calmly gaze at the doctors of the Law who were waiting in smug confidence and simmering with spite and anger. She closed her eyes. She heard his voice: "He that is without sin among you, let him cast the first stone at her."

He spoke softly, but the silence was such that his every word resounded. She saw the confusion on the faces of the crowd and the doctors of the Law. And the surprise—he had extricated himself and from the attacked had become the attacker. Now he was waiting for their answer, and not just an oral reply but an action, a deed. Slowly the eyes of the throng shifted from him to the group of doctors of the Law. What would they do now? No, no one was reaching for a stone. They stood in their places, confounded, undecided. No one moved. Finally he started toward them. What was he doing? Leaving? The people in front shuffled about to make way for him to pass, but he stopped in front of the group of doctors, directly in front of the first of them. Without a word, he bent down and began to write with his finger in the sand. The doctor wouldn't look, wouldn't condescend to read what the hated Nazarene was writing. Finally he shot a furtive glance at the ground, then suddenly bent very low over the writing and stared. He straightened up very stiffly, and trying

to conceal his agitation, hurried away. With his hand Jesus
smoothed what he had written and began to write again in
the sand at the feet of the next man. And in that way, one by
one, they left, as many as had come. Mary still lay in the
same crouching position, dazed and not quite believing that
they had really gone, the men who only minutes before had
hauled her here with intent to kill. She saw Jesus rise to his
feet and move towards her, as if he had just noticed her. He
came up very close to her. She cringed, afraid the fatal blow
would fall now. He must have sensed her fear. Very gently
he bent over her. She saw his quiet eyes on her. He raised
her up from the ground and asked, "Has no one condemned
you?"

Numb with fear, bewildered, and now gazing into those
eyes, all she could say was, "No one, Lord".

He placed his hands gently on her head and said, "Then
neither will I condemn you". And after a moment, as he was
already turning to leave, he said, "Go, and sin no more".

The crowd, mute witnesses to the scene, slowly trailed
along after him. She was left alone on the square. Now reaction set in: she felt herself shivering all over; she threw
herself against the steps and burst into uncontrollable weeping. When she finally stopped, she lifted her head and looked
around. It was still the same morning. She was sitting on the
steps of the temple. Its walls gleamed brilliantly in the sun.
A few people were wandering in the square. Life was going
on around her as usual. It could almost have been a dream—
were it not for her scraped hands, bleeding feet and cut,
bruised skin. Every muscle in her body ached, and the cuts
and abrasions burned. She struggled to her feet. She fixed her
hair mechanically, and without thinking began to limp painfully in the direction in which Jesus had disappeared. He had
defended her. Just like that, as if it were his duty, as if were
the most natural thing for him to do. And then he had left.
The look in his eyes came back to her. She felt sobs welling
up inside her again. What did he say? "Sin no more." So
many times she had heard that word, "sin." Among her
friends it was an unfailing cue for vulgar jokes and buffoonery.
Now it suddenly stood before her in all its gravity. She hob-

bled through the streets, drawing the startled and curious
stares of passersby. She did not notice. First she had to meet
him again. If only to thank him. After all, she owed him her
life, she belonged to him now, yet she could not define the
feeling that was beginning to awaken in her.

She made her way to her flat. At the door she was greeted
with the screams of her servant girls at the sight of her. Crying
over her all the while, they prepared a bath, then helped her
into her bed, where they tended to her injuries. Lying in her
bed, she was thoughtful a long time, then suddenly she asked
them, "Who is Jesus of Nazareth?"

"Is he to blame for what happened to you?" one of them
asked hesitantly.

"No," she said curtly.

They understood that she did not wish to discuss what had
happened. After a few moments, they began to express surprise that she knew nothing about Jesus, and since she made
no objection, they began to tell her about him: how he had
been moving around Palestine for the last two years, teaching,
healing, helping and feeding the poor, distributing money to
them given him by the rich, how once he even multiplied
wine at a wedding feast.

Mary listened attentively. She was especially struck by
their tone of voice, the way they spoke about him. She could
not help wondering, did anyone ever talk about her with such
fondness and affection, the way they talked about him? Would
anyone ever remember her with such warmth? She closed her
eyes and listened to the girls' stories as though she were
listening to some children's tale about Goodness, Understanding, Patience, Mercy, Unselfishness—the legend of a good
man, a hero who helped others. Minute by minute her rescuer
ceased to be an unknown benefactor; her servant girls
sketched a clear, detailed portrait of the man who had saved
her life.

"What does he teach?" she interrupted.

"That the greatest sin is hatred, and that the only commandment is love."

Suddenly the girls broke off in an embarrassed silence.
Mary guessed: to them the word "love" rang strangely in

that house. She smiled. Almost audily they breathed sighs of relief and rushed to chatter, all at once, as if to crowd out that moment of awkwardness.

"He teaches that if someone needs something, you should give it to him—"

"And if you lend something, you needn't claim it back—"

"That you can't serve God and money—"

"That you shouldn't worry about what you will eat, or what you will wear—"

"And once he told a parable about a rich man who. . . ."

Mary was no longer listening. Out of her own memory, parables and sayings came back that had reached her over the last few years, and that she had dismissed contemptuously. Yes, it was he who taught people not to be anxious about food or clothing, because that was what pagans concerned themselves with. Yes, those were his comparisons with the birds of the air, and the lilies of the field. Back then she had laughed, refused to accept them; they interfered with her plans, her dreams. Yet now when she thought about it, wasn't everything he said true? Really, what did she need all those things for? What did she need all that money for? She suddenly saw her life at Magdala as if it were not her own, as if through a macabre dream. Maybe Magdala itself was a dream? Maybe the villa, the parties, the drunken, rowdy orgies were all just a dream? And that crowd of depraved, smug, loathsome cranks and perverts and debauchers she put up with and played up to. Had she lost her reason? The decision suddenly exploded in her mind: she would never go back to Magdala. She shook herself out of her reverie. The girls had not noticed; they were still chattering.

". . . . But the most amazing things happen with people possessed by evil spirits. As soon as he goes near them, the devils flee them shrieking, and the people return to normal."

Mary smiled to herself. I'm sure it doesn't always happen that way, she thought. In my case it was a little different. The devil that fled me was not shrieking—maybe because he was not alone; there had to be at least seven of them.

"Many of the sinners he converted now follow him." The girls went on eagerly, sensing her interest.

"There are even some among the famed Twelve."

"What do they do when they're with him?" Mary asked.

"They teach, they help him, they help those in need."

Instantly Mary fired to the idea—she, too, would follow him. But a moment later the flame died. She would only compromise him by her presence. At least she could see him one more time, she had to thank him. But first she had to find him.

She sent her girls out with instructions to find out where he was. They were a long time in coming back. Finally one returned with the information: he had been invited to dinner at the house of Simon the Pharisee. A wave of alarm swept her: was he one of the men who had abducted her? No, of course not; he was a Pharisee, he would not know anything about the schemes of the doctors of the Law. She dressed quickly and, as she was about to leave, she glanced around the room to see if there might be something she could take with her. Her eyes fell on a flask of spikenard oil—her favorite fragrance. She picked it up and took it with her.

It was rich and spacious and on the outskirts of the city— the house of Simon, one of the most eminent of Pharisees, a scion of ancient stock. Mary ignored the looks of the servants on seeing her enter. With her usual self-assurance, she asked where the dinner was being held. She went in. The room was in subdued half-light. She could barely distinguish the figures at first. From the sudden hush that fell over the room, she guessed the impact that her appearance had made: everyone there knew exactly who she was. All heads gestured in puzzlement to Simon. Out of the corner of her eye, she saw his bewildered shrugs and gestures—obviously giving his guests to understand that he had absolutely nothing to do with her coming. But she didn't care, she had already spotted Jesus. Without a word she walked up to him, sank to her knees at his feet and clasped them to her face. Her whole ordeal of just a few hours ago surged to her mind in all its horror—the panic, the humiliation, the pain. And the gratitude for her rescue. She was swept on a wave of boundless trust in him, a sweet surrender to his goodness, wisdom. The flask of oil was in her hand. She opened it, poured it over his feet, and simply clung to them long and tightly in a gesture of deepest humility.

The strain in the room started to lessen. She sensed the shift from surprise to indignation. It suddenly occurred to her what they must all be thinking—to the detriment of the master of Nazareth.

. . . . There we have it, another one of his admirers, and not of the best virtue either. Let us call her by her proper name—a loose, wanton woman. And how impertinent, how sure of herself, that she brazenly marches into the house of a stranger to display publicly her affection for her master. And he should know exactly the kind of shameless woman she is, even if he does only rarely come to Jerusalem. He should know she is a sinner. Or perhaps he knows and is pleased to receive her expressions of admiration. . . . She had not stopped to think that she may have unwittingly caused Jesus offense by her coming.

"Simon, I have something to say to you."

It was him. Now he was going to explain to them what had happened a few hours ago and excuse himself that way.

"Master, say it," Simon answered.

"A certain creditor had two debtors. One owed him five hundred pence, and the other fifty. And when they did not have the means to pay, he forgave them both. What do you think, which of the two loved him most?"

She had no idea what he was talking about. She did not dare lift her eyes.

Simon answered vaguely, "I suppose he to whom he forgave most."

From the uncertainty in his voice, Mary guessed he was somewhat surprised by the sudden question.

"You have judged rightly," Jesus said to him.

Then turning to her, he said to Simon, "Do you see this woman? I entered your house and you gave me no water for my feet. But she, with her tears, has washed my feet, and with her hair has wiped them. You gave me no kiss. But she, since she came in, has not ceased to kiss my feet. You did not anoint my head with oil. But she has anointed my feet with ointment."

Mary was dumbstruck. No, never had she expected him—about whom it was said that he cared nothing for honors and tribute and scoffed at the Pharisees' love of titles and at the way they vied for favors—never had she expected him to react in such a way to her actions.

With his next words he stunned the entire assembly: "That is why I say to you: many sins are forgiven her, because she has loved much. But to whom less is forgiven, he loves less."

She could not believe her ears. He was talking about her! She pressed her face more tightly to his feet. She was not quite sure what he meant; all she knew was that he had not scorned her and thrust her away. Apparently the others did not understand either, because in a strong voice, so there was no doubt left in anyone's mind, Jesus repeated, "Your sins are forgiven you".

A buzz of indignant murmuring rose around the table. "Who is this that he even forgives sins?"

Then she heard that same even voice speak to her again: "Your faith has saved you. Go in peace."

She rose unsteadily, the tears streaming down her face, misting her eyes. Blindly she groped toward the door and left. With her heart bursting, crying with this strange new happiness, she determined to return to Bethany. Until this moment, the idea of returning home had never occurred to her. Now it came as the most natural, the only, thing to do. She would return to the days of her childhood; she would begin all over again.

She settled accounts with her surprised servants and distributed her clothing and other personal effects among them. By the following morning very early she was tramping the road to Bethany with Jerusalem at her back. She limped along slowly, sorely, wincing at every step. The sun rose lazily; the air over the fields was cool. She turned joyous eyes on the sleeping world. She had eaten nothing all that morning and only now stopped for water at a roadside well, where she paused a moment to rest before continuing on her way. Soon she found herself on the outlying grounds of the family estate.

The lush, luxuriant wheat was ripe and high; the vines of grapes scrambled irresistibly toward the sun. Already several vinedressers were working around them. Suddenly one of the women workers spied her. She gave a start and a little help of surprise, clapped her hand over her mouth and stared. Then she darted over to her companions, and they all huddled together watching her and whispering, until one of them tore away from the rest and ran down the road in the direction of the house, kicking up clouds of dust with her feet and skirts and flushing the droves of sparrows out of the road as she ran.

Mary watched the whole scene with a smile. It was not far to the house now. One more rise in the road, and the dark grove of trees near the house loomed ahead. She slackened her pace, suddenly confronted by doubts: she had not stopped to think how she would be received. Now she vacillated. But no, she had no other choice. If they rejected her, she would simply go off and lose herself in the world somewhere. She walked very slowly now, grappling with her pride: would it not be better to depart now? She had no right to this house, she had renounced it, she had taken her share. They might not accept her. But really, who might not? Not Lazarus. At most, Martha.

Closer now, she could see the white belt of wall girdling the garden, and the black hollow that was the gate. A figure stood against the opening, his hand cupped over his eyes. He started to move toward her. She knew him at once. Lazarus, her brother. Moving closer, no longer walking, breaking into a run. The same tall figure, the long hair tossed back from his face, the tanned skin, the bright smile of a kind man. He looked the way he had when she still lived at home. Except for those lines on his face, and those graying hairs. Caused by cares, afflictions, worries that she had multiplied. Her vision began to blur, she felt the tears creep into her eyes, the tightening around her heart—and she sank to the ground just as Lazarus rushed up to her. "Forgive me," she sobbed, burying her face in her hands.

He picked her up, gathered her into his arms, and led her to the gate, in front of which the servants had all clustered to

watch. Through a haze she heard his orders. He led her up
the stairs to her old room. He stayed with her a moment,
hugging her, soothing her, drying her tears. She mumbled
tearfully, she did not know what she was saying, or what her
brother was saying. The world was spinning in her head for
joy. Finally he left her to wash and dress. She looked around
the room: everything was at it had been then; nothing was
changed. She found her clothes clean and ready. She smiled
to herself. So, they had been waiting for her all this time. The
tears welled up in her eyes again.

When she finally ventured down the stairs, she found the
whole house bustling with excitement. The servants greeted
her in turn, smiling. She noticed that a feast was in preparation. "For whom?" she asked Lazarus. "Are you expecting
guests?"

"For you, for your welcome."

She blushed with shame and with joy.

"Where is Martha?" She still had not seen her sister.

"She hasn't come in from the fields yet. She's looking after
the harvest. Let's go to her, if you're not feeling too tired."

They left the house together and headed through the fields.

"She works very hard," Lazarus said.

Mary spied Martha from a distance. She was returning
with the reapers.

"Stay here," Lazarus said to her. "I'll go to her first and
prepare her for the surprise."

She followed very slowly behind him. Now she realized
again that it hadn't been Lazarus she feared, but Martha.
She was unsure of her sister's reaction. She stopped at a
distance, she did not want to get any closer. She could not
hear them, but Lazarus was speaking earnestly and with
evident joy, pointing in her direction. Martha did not turn
her head. Apparently she already knew about her sister's
arrival. She raised her voice—it sounded harsh and full of
reproach. She made a move as if she wanted to leave. Lazarus
held her back, put his arm around her, steered her gently
back with him. Mary stood cowed and rooted to the ground;
she saw the stern eyes, the tightly pressed lips.

"Greet her, Mary," Lazarus urged.

Mary pushed herself forward timidly, extended her arms to her, caught the hard look in Martha's eyes directed at Lazarus, then threw herself into her sister's arms, which after some resistance, slowly closed around her in an embrace.

Later there was supper in the garden with music and hanging lanterns and neighbors who dropped in to welcome her home. She recognized the older ones among them, but few of the younger. It was as if she had returned from a long and distant journey. She was happy. There was only one person missing, who, to make her happiness complete should have been seated there in the place of honor.

The following morning, Mary was awakened by the stillness in the house. the others had already gone out to work. Martha was gone, and only Lazarus was waiting for her. At breakfast, she asked him abruptly: would he go with her to Jesus to thank him personally? Lazarus agreed in an instant.

"When do you want to go?" he asked her.

"Right away. He might leave."

They dressed for the road and left. En route, she asked her brother one more favor: would he try to invite Jesus to Bethany, even if for only a brief visit. He would try, he said.

In the city, they lost considerable time trying to locate Jesus. Finally they found him, or rather, they found an immense multitude in the midst of which Jesus was supposed to be. They squeezed through to the centre. He was there. She saw him bending over someone, explaining something to him. He saw them. Mary's heart fluttered to her throat. She grabbed her brother's arm. Lazarus hailed him and began to speak. Jesus listened, his eyes resting on Lazarus' face. She was surprised by how beautifully Lazarus thanked Jesus for returning his sister to her home. At the end he extended a sincere invitation for Jesus to come and stay with them in Bethany. Jesus promised—he would be pleased to spend a night with them, since he would be in Jerusalem several days. They bid farewell. They turned and left. A tide of people closed around him. The two started back to Bethany. Mary's heart was heavy; she didn't know when she would ever see him again.

She waited. She prepared a room for him, arranging and

rearranging it endlessly, setting and resetting furniture and objects in every possible combination, in anticipation of every need and eventuality. She had the feeling Lazarus was observing her. Often she went and stood at the gate to see if Jesus was coming. And finally he came.

It was an odd affair, his coming. First two plain rustics appeared, claiming to be his disciples and announcing his arrival. Then came a swarm of people of every imaginable type. Suddenly their peaceful home was deluged by men calling themselves the chosen disciples, women, convalescents, the cured, and those out of whom—so they said—Jesus had cast devils. They crowded into every inch of the house, clamoring and insisting and demanding something or other, always in the name of Jesus, always because the master so pleased, always because these were his instructions. They ate, they drank, they cooked, they did their laundry. Martha was furious. Lazarus, as usual when guests were involved, was accommodating to a fault, trying to meet every demand and need, and disconcerted when he could not do so, acting as if it was not even his house they were in. Mary felt ashamed. This was not the way she had dreamed about his visit to Bethany. In the confusion she could not even find him. Finally she bolted away from the intruders and went to look for him. There he was in the garden, sitting under a tree with his head against the trunk. He heard the rustle of her steps and looked up. He smiled. She greeted him. She asked: Could she serve him? Bring him something? Was he hungry, or thirsty? No, he did not want anything. She sat down on the grass beside him. After a moment, he began to speak to her, slowly, in an undertone, only to her. She listened raptly, hardly breathing so as not to lose a single word. The world she so longed for was opening before her again. Martha's impatient voice suddenly jerked her out of her absorption—she had not even seen her sister approach.

"Lord, don't you care that my sister has left me alone to serve all these people? Tell her, then, to help me."

Martha's face was flushed and severe. Mary sprang to her feet; she was sorry. But as she hastened toward the house, the thought: she could not leave Jesus. He was the guest here, he was the one who mattered. It was not important that everyone ate and drank and was satisfied; what *was* important was to be able to converse quietly with him, hear him. Why, that was what Jesus had come for, that was why she had waited for him. Just as she was about to return to him, she heard his voice: "Martha, Martha, you are anxious and troubled about many things, but one thing is necessary. Mary has chosen the best part, which shall not be taken from her."

The next morning Jesus departed, along with his crowd of hangers-on. Lazarus accompanied him to the gate. He begged him to consider their home his home, to feel free to visit whenever he wished. Mary was so grateful to her brother for saying that. They returned to the house, where the servants were hurriedly tidying up after their strange, noisy, bumptious guests.

In truth, Mary did not think Jesus would ever avail himself of their invitation. So when she saw him again that very same evening in the garden, she almost rubbed her eyes in disbelief. Only the twelve were with him, but how had he managed to get away from the rest? He came every day for the next few days as well. In her entire life, she had never been so happy. She was also delighted to see how friendship had grown in that short time between him and Lazarus. They were together constantly, often discussing late into the night.

Then the time came for Jesus' departure to Galilee. The house became unbearably empty. For the second time in her life she had that gnawing feeling of restlessness; she did not seem able to settle to anything. Mostly she sat in the garden where she had listened to him the first time. And it was there that Lazarus found her and asked her simply: "Do you want to follow him?"

It was in that instant that she realized how much she desired it, but she had never allowed herself to think it, because she wished to remain faithful to her decision to stay at home. She threw her arms around his neck and wept in gratitude. Lazarus held her in his arms a moment, then gently pushed her away and gazed deeply into her eyes.

"You saw those people who follow around after him?" he asked her.

"Yes."

"And you want to be part of them?"

"Yes."

"I ask only one thing. If you change your mind, if you don't like it, return home immediately."

She went to Jesus simply because she wanted to be near him. She wanted to hear what he said, watch what he did, go where he went. She thought she might even be useful to him, maybe prepare his meals, or his lodgings, or maybe wash his robe or mend it.

But she had one other motive as well. She wanted to protect Jesus from that swarm that dogged him day and night, guard him against their rapacity, their exploitation of him for their own selfish interests. She wanted to shield him from the people who flocked to him by the hundreds, the thousands, like locusts, always asking, begging, wanting, demanding, insisting. And finally, she wanted to save him from himself: make him understand that he could not go on living like that, that he could not be constantly at the disposal of who came to him, or be at the beck and call of everyone who needed him, or give everyone what they wanted for the asking, or listen to everyone who had anything at all to say, or go wherever he was pulled and pushed. A man could only do so much! She could not stand the parasites who wasted his time, ruined his schedules, disrupted his plans. She could not stand their selfish indifference to his weariness, or their callous interruption of his sleeping hours which were already pared down to the minimum. She cried at night to see how exhausted and overworked he was, how concerned for every person, large or small, who came to him, every matter brought to him. He simply could not manage, there would not be enough of him to go around, he would burn himself out in that fire of concern, in that pushing and jostling to reach everyone.

Seeing all these things, Mary instantly revised her own dreams and ambitions, especially since she, too, had thought

to secure a place for herself at his side. She had counted on
his being able to devote some of his free time to her, for
discussions with her, for her own purely personal affairs. She
very quickly gave up that idea. Seeing him so terribly de-
pleted, she made every effort to put herself entirely at his
disposal, without asking or expecting anything in return, not
even a word or gesture of notice or appreciation, without
complaint or grudge. But she still wanted to protect him from
the crush of sheer numbers, so unasked, uninvited, she started
to take over management of that perpetual bazaar that tagged
along everywhere after him. She drove away the hordes of
professional beggars, cheats, and frauds. The instant she detected any trickery or dishonesty, she exposed it mercilessly
and sent the perpetrator packing. Yet it hardly made an
impression on the numbers. So she began scrupulously to
screen and sift through even those supplicants who came to
Jesus with genuine needs and problems. By every possible
means, she refused to let them near him, and she took their
problems and troubles upon herself, or divided them up
among the disciples and the other women accompanying
them. It worked to an extent. She could say with some satisfaction that she had managed to take the strain off Jesus—
at least a little; at least a little, she had managed to spare
him. But it was still not enough. The numbers of petitioners
and supplicants and their problems grew by leaps and
bounds, because it was rare for someone who had been cured,
or saved, or reconciled, or comforted not to reappear a second
time, now often seeking a closer place in his friend's life. And
every "friendship," every bond, required time, attention, patience, care.

The longer she stayed, the less Mary was able to reconcile
herself to what she saw: to see him live that way, keeping
nothing for himself, without regard for his own future, heed-
less of fame or other people's opinions; to have absolutely
nothing for himself. He had no home, no place of his own—
the way he himself had once put it: "The foxes have holes,
and the birds of the air nests, but the Son of Man has no
place to lay his head". He did not even have time during the
day to sit down quietly and eat. Though there was one ex-

ception: the evening meal with his closest followers, which he
took pains to attend, at which he never rushed, and over
which he presided like the head of a family. Yet even that
supposed respite was not for himself, but flowed out of his
love for his closest companions: he simply wanted to assure
them a little time to converse with him, share their problems
and anxieties with him, confident that he would listen, that
he would advise, praise, reprimand, that it was their time,
reserved especially for them.

Herself overworked, harassed, and at her wit's end with
the constant scrambling and squabbling, Mary made every
effort even so to stop and listen whenever he preached. More
and more she came to understand that his boundless devotion
to the affairs of other men was not some kind of spontaneous
burst of natural kindness, nor the weakness of a good and
spiritually deep man unable to refuse or ward off the supplicants begging his help. This was in fact his very concept of
life.

She became particularly sensitive on that issue which was
best illustrated in his parable of the last judgment, though
she did not discover it right away. Yes, it was a beautiful
analogy, but in the end it repeated what Jesus had emphasized so many times before about the necessity of doing good:
"I was hungry and you gave me to eat; I was thirsty and you
gave me to drink". It was analogous, because here the judge
identified himself with the man in need. But its essential
theme eluded her for a long time, until in fact she stumbled
upon it on another occasion. It was while listening to him
speak about love of one's enemies. ". . . . Because if you love
those who love you, what reward will you have? Do not the
pagans do the same?" And then she had rediscovered the
words from that other parable: "Whatever you do to the least
of my brethren, you do to me." That was what she had not
been able to fathom, that "least of my brethren". Now she
understood: it was supposed to signify complete unselfishness.
Do good to the one who will never return the kindness, never
compensate, never repay, never even show his gratitude, because he cannot or because he does not have the means. In
other words, to help and serve simply because someone needs

it; to give one's possessions, time, and life only because it is what should be done.

Mary began to understand more and more clearly—and that was precisely what frightened her. The prospects of a life of such utter self-denial were unthinkable. He was handing them a model of a life that they, too, were supposed to accept. She could not believe it was possible ever to live in that way, without any basis in justice. She was afraid that such behavior would lead to the elimination of self, of her individuality. She rebelled against such selflessness, afraid of being exploited, used by other people. But he kept on returning to the same theme:

"Take care that you do not do your justice before men, to be seen by them: otherwise, you shall not have a reward of your Father, who is in heaven. And when you pray, do not be like the hypocrites, who love to stand and pray in the synagogues and on street corners that they may be seen by men: Amen I say to you, they have received their reward. But when you pray, enter into your chamber, and having shut the door, pray to your Father in secret. And your Father, who sees in secret, will repay you. And when you fast, do not be like the hypocrites. For they disfigure their faces to show to men that they are fasting. Amen I say to you, they have received their reward. But you, when you fast, anoint your head and wash your face that you will not appear to men to be fasting, but to your Father who is in secret. And your Father, who sees in secret, will repay you."

At first, Mary was unsure whether she had heard or understood correctly. But no she had not been wrong: Jesus repeated the same message over and over, though in a wealth of different contexts.

". . . . Therefore, when you give alms, do not sound a trumpet before you like the hypocrites in the synagogues and in the streets, that they may be praised by men. Amen I say to you, they have received their reward. But when you do give alms, let not your left hand know what your right hand does, so that your alms may be in secret. And your Father, who sees in secret, will repay you."

She still could not reconcile herself to it: nothing for the sake of gaining something from others. No compensation, no balancing of losses, not from the recipient, and not from anyone else, even those who would see it.

And what was stranger still—people actually listened to him. People accustomed to trying always to gain or to make a profit on everything—if not money, then at least indebtedness or favor or popularity—were suddenly hearing a condemnation of such motives. The misers from Capernaum, the crude commoners from Tiberias, and especially those people from Bethsaida, who, one would think, would not be moved even by an angel from heaven. And Jesus went right on telling them things that no teacher in the whole of Israel would dare teach.

". . . . And if someone strikes you on the right cheek, turn to him also the other. And if a man wants to contend with you in judgment and take away your coat, give him also your cloak. And whosoever forces you to walk one mile, walk two with him. Give to him that asks something of you, and do not turn away from him who would borrow from you. Love your enemies, do good to those who hate you, and pray for those who persecute you, so that you may be the children of your Father who is in heaven. For He makes his sun rise upon the good and bad, and rain upon the just and the unjust. For if you love those who love you, what reward will you have? Or if you salute your brethren only, what do you do more? Do not the heathens also do this?"

Here was a concept of living that was absolutely unheard of, and yet, more realistic than any other. Not to live only for the sake of collecting, assembling, building, accumulating, storing up—like the householder who filled up his barn and died the next day. In spite of outward appearance, this was no carefree youthful lightheartedness, but a carefully considered trust in the boundless goodness of God.

". . . . Are not two sparrows sold for a farthing? And not one of them shall fall to the ground without the will of your Father. But the very hairs on your head are all numbered. Do not fear, therefore; you are better than many sparrows. And why are you solicitous for raiment? Consider the lilies of the field, how they grow: they labor not, neither do they spin, but not even Solomon in all his glory was arrayed as one of these. And if the grass of the field, which is today, and tomorrow is cast into the oven, God so clothes: how much more you, O you of little faith?''

From his disciples and those he sent out on apostolic work, he expected nothing less, commanding them: "Do not take with you a purse for your journey, nor two coats, nor shoes. Freely have you received, freely give."

While that was all very well and good, what Mary really found in Jesus' immediate circle was tragic. People of every ilk fastened themselves to him like leeches: people who were somehow betting on him in their private schemes, and who jealously resented the admission of any new faces into their group. They had accepted her very grudgingly—another one with whom they would have to divide the spoils. She was stunned to find that many of them never bothered to listen to the master teach, never made an effort to understand his meaning, and did not really care. They had not joined for that purpose at all, to listen to him. Through his help, on the crest of the waves he always made, they were going to ride to riches and glory: the smalltown politicians, who saw in him a chance to realize some of their wildest and often ludicrous schemes; then there were the fortune hunters, who were going to get rich quickly with his help, or attain power—though none were really quite sure how they were going to achieve this. There were many who were captivated by his person and appeal—and many who only pretended to be. There were his zealous followers, but there were also spies sent by the Pharisees, Sadducees, priests, and doctors of the Law. Hence the constant tension—the endless verbal fencing, in which every word was snatched up and analyzed, in which every sentence had to be perfectly weighed, so that it would not supply a pretext for charges that it offended the Law and the Prophets, or the Pharisees, or the Sadducees, or the priests, or the doctors bf the Law, or the masses. And finally, there were the myriad troubled, sick, injured, broken, and unfortunate people who far outnumbered all the rest. They wanted him to hear them, give his advice, supply remedies for their problems, tell them what to do and for how long—give them

miraculous solutions to the hopeless situations and problems
in which they had found themselves. An endless treadmill of
human problems.

Apart from all that, Mary found unbearable the state of
constant excitation in which all these people lived, their incessant waiting for evernew miracles; and the lamenting
atmosphere created by the army of sick people wanting at
least to touch him, or pleading to be healed. These last were
supplemented by the men and women begging for the cure of
their loved ones back home—could he please come, only for
a moment, look at them, touch them. And that delirious
watching and waiting for the creation of the new Jewish
kingdom. The very idea frightened her—she had had enough
of the politics of Jerusalem, always sighing for a great and
powerful Jewish state. But the more she listened to Jesus, the
more she understood that all the gossip circulated about his
great plan to build a new Jewish kingdom had materialized
out of thin air; that these people understood the words "Messiah" and "Son of David" to mean him who will return the
nation to its former grandeur, bring it independence, and
liberate it from under the Roman yoke. No one asked how he
was going to do it. They never even asked the most essential
thing: did Jesus even want that? Mary understood that he
was talking about a kingdom of people able to serve God in
spirit and in truth—for God himself, and not for personal
interest or gain, and that was the sole sense of his kingdom.
This was the most frightening thing, the misunderstanding:
he was talking about one thing, and his listeners were inter-
preting quite another. Two worlds, two ways of thinking that
could not converge. They could not converge even though
Jesus did everything to make himself clearly understood.

But the most saddening thing of all was when she saw that
even his closest disciples did not understand him. That
famous Twelve. The ones he himself had chosen from among
the legions around him. And so, the best ones. Wtih her own
ears she heard them arguing about who was going to be
greater in the Kingdom of Heaven. If someone had told her,
she would never have believed it, but with her own eyes she
saw Peter, that kindhearted colossus, go up to Jesus—prob-

ably at the others' instigation, because she would never suspect him of doing something like that on his own initiative—
and say to him: "Lord, behold we have cast aside everything
and followed you. What will we receive for it?"

Mary felt she could tear him to pieces for that. So that was
the extent of his love, his friendship. They were following him
in the expectation of reward, only they did not know exactly
what, and now they were trying to find out. And he kept
telling them, over and over again, day and night, about love
and unselfishness—and that was how much they understood
about unselfishness. In his place, she would have dumped the
whole pack of them. She wanted him do so, too. But he
replied to Peter (she could not tell if he really meant it, or if
he was being ironic, though there was never any irony in
him): "You, who have left everything and followed me, at the
end of the world will sit on twelve seats and judge the twelve
tribes of Israel". But later she could not control herself, and
she upbraided every last one of them, especially Peter. She
had to admit—he sat there listening to her like a whipped
dog.

It was no better among the women, either. Beneath a show
of concern and kindness and attention towards Jesus, they
were constantly after advantages and favors for themselves
and their families. And it was not just her imagination. Once,
as she was bringing something to Jesus, she arrived just as
the mother of John and James—who was always pushing her
services on him anyway–came up to him with her sons and
said: "Command that these two sons of mine may sit one at
your right and other at your left in your kingdom." That
must have been the first time Mary ever saw him—who
handled so deftly the more subtle, unexpected questions
tossed at him by the Pharisees, Sadducees, und priests—now,
in the face of this request, suddenly at a loss. Apparently—at
least this was the impression she got—he never expected to
hear anything like that from John, on whom he had lavished
a special affection. He said to them: "Can you drink the cup
that I drink?" And when the two of them, like schoolboys,
gushed out with, "Yes, we can!" without even asking him
what he meant by it, he said to them: "Ah well, then you

shall drink the chalice that I drink, but as to sitting at my right and at my left, it does not belong to me to grant it; that is for those to whom my Father has destined it."

One of the Twelve—she did not notice which—could contain himself no longer and sidled over to hear what they were talking about, then immediately ran back and told the others. They flew over like a flock of sparrows. She had to laugh at the sight of them, complaining loudly all at once, and shouting out indignantly. And the way they turned on the duo! For a minute it looked as if they were going to thrash them. As it turned out, they were not concerned that anyone had tried to ask Jesus a thing like that– they were just angry because those two asked him first. Until Jesus, disturbed by all the noise, called them over. They went still shaking and muttering about the injury done them. And he, with the tenderness of an understanding father, said to them: "You know that among the Gentiles the rulers govern imperiously, amd that the great of the earth make their rule press heavily. Let it not be this way among you. Whoever among you wishes to become great will make himself your servant, and whoever wishes to be the first will be the servant of all. Even as the Son of Man has not come to be served, but to serve." How ashamed she felt for them.

Definitely the most intelligent among the Twelve, she decided, was Judas. But he could not be depended opon; quite the contrary. In her opinion, he was the most dangerous because of his obsessive political ambitions. She was frightened by his dreams and fantasies about a powerful Jewish nation state that would play an extraordinary role among nations—they were a conglomerate of personal and national myths and superstitions. Judas buttressed his dreams with texts from the Scriptures, which he read as if in a distorting mirror, or through the eyes of a sick mind. He was very reluctant to discuss his beliefs, views, plans, with the others. He seldom betrayed his thoughts or gave his opinions. He listened, he said nothing, he smiled in his peculiar fashion. He probably regarded them all with some contempt. No one knew what he was really thinking. But he trusted her. She managed to draw him into discussions about topics that occupied his mind. Whenever she listened to him talk about the need to rebuild the Jewish nation, she agreed: of course, he was right; she could not stomach the Romans either; or the puppet Jewish king, Herod, for that matter. But that was not Jesus' role. She explained to him in elementary terms, as if to a child: Jesus and king were two entirely different things. Yes, it was true, he spoke of a kingdom, but it was a differently conceived kingdom, one that had to do with people living differently, not solely for themselves. But Judas stuck to his preconceptions: Jesus was the Messiah, and the Messiah was going to restore the Kingdom of Israel.

Of all the disciples, she was closest to John. But he was still such a child and had to be lead around by the hand. And she could not forgive him that "sitting at the right side of Jesus in his kingdom"—which he was very much ashamed of later and tried to explain by telling her that his mother had made him do it.

But all her worries fell away like so much water whenever she was close to Jesus. Somehow she always discovered herself in his teachings: she was the merchants who sought after beautiful pearls until he found the one of greatest price; it was she sho had found treasure in the field; and she was the woman who had recovered her lost drachma.

She was still not sure what she was going to do in the future, and she did not much concern herself about it. After all, Jesus had distinctly said: "Do not be concerned". For the present she wanted to be with Jesus, especially since she thought he needed her: she tried to be helpful to him in everything, listen to and discharge his instructions, sense his every need and wish. She wanted to stay with him for all time, though realistically she knew it could not always be this way. She was happy because she thought she understood him a little—she understood what he meant in his teachings. Listening to him, she sometimes had the impression that she herself had said the very same thing, or had heard it somewhere before, or as if he had put her very thoughts into words. But more often, it was the other way around: some of the things he said came as a complete surprise or as outright shock, which often took a long time before they came to be seen as natural. Perhaps the hardest incident for her to understand was that which involved his mother.

They were at the house of one of the Pharisees—the place was packed with disciples, Pharisees, bystanders, and gossips. The atmosphere was extremely tense. Jesus was being bombarded with questions, criticisms, caustic remarks, ironic asides. Mary could not even remember what the whole thing was about. As usual, she was afraid that the wrong word might be uttered, that they might make him lose his patience, or use a word or phrase taken out of context against him. Suddenly someone came in and shouted to him above the din: "Your mother and brethren have come and are waiting outside for you." Mary sprang up, expecting him to do the same. He did not even move, however, and all he said was: "Who is my mother, and who are my brethren? Whoever does the will of my Father is my brother and sister and mother."

Mary froze, she could not believe her ears. Her first impulse was to rush up to him and demand an explanation, but she saw the messenger hesitate a moment and then turn back toward the door. She hurried through the people to get there first. Outside, a little group of people—strangers—were standing in a circle. Among them, his mother. Though she had never seen her, there was no doubt in Mary's mind that it was she, and she rushed up to greet her. His mother was a bit startled—it was not for her she was waiting.

She introduced herself: "I am the Mary from whom your son cast out seven devils." Then she simply threw herself into her arms, talking rapidly: "I wanted so much to meet you, I'm so grateful to you for your son. He forgave me my sins, took me to himself, but you know better than I how he is. He can't come out to you right now."

She felt his mother stiffen slightly and gently move her away.

"He won't come out to me? He knows I'm waiting for him?"

"Yes."

"What did he say?"

She repeated his words. His mother grew thoughtful, bowed her head, and without another word, began to walk away.

She walked with her a moment in silence, then heard her say: "Return to him. Please give him this robe I wove for him." She handed her a parcel and left.

Mary went back to Jesus with the package from his mother. He took it without a word. He asked nothing, and she said nothing. Many times she returned to that incident in her mind, and always she arrived at the same conclusion: if I want to be close to him, like a sister, then I must be like him in unselfishness and self-sacrifice.

Mary's sojourn with Jesus was interrupted sooner than she expected. A servant arrived with news from Martha that Lazarus was gravely ill.

"What's wrong with him?"

The servant did not know exactly. "He's very sick."

It turned out that several days had elapsed since the servant had left their house—he had been unable to locate her right away. She mounted the led-donkey he had brought for her and quickly rode to Bethany.

A muted fear hung heavily over the house. Everywhere she went, she ran into strangers: doctors, quacks, medical and pseudomedical advisers. Lazarus lay in the dark in his room with the curtains tightly drawn. His breathing was faint. She knelt at his bedside and touched his hand. His eyes fluttered open; for a moment they searched in lost, confused circles. Finally he recognized her. He smiled.

"You came? Has something happened to Jesus?" A worried look crossed his face. "Is he in danger?"

"No. Everything is all right."

"Then why are you back?"

"Martha sent word that you were ill."

"Does Jesus know?"

"He knows."

Lazarus hesitated. "Did he . . . say if he was coming to me—to us?" He corrected himself.

"No. He told his disciples that your illness was not to the death."

Lazaruss closed his eyes. He seemed to lapse into sleep. He was smiling—probably trying to picture Jesus saying that. She rose and tiptoed from the room. After some searching, she finally found Martha. Her sister practically pounced on her.

"Where's Jesus?"

"He isn't here."

"You came alone?"

"Yes."

"Why didn't he come?"

"I don't know."

"Did you tell him Lazarus is ill?"

"Yes."

"Did you ask him to come?"

"No."

"Why not?"

"I didn't want to ask. Everyone is always asking him for something. And anyway—"

"What anyway?" Martha exploded. "Don't you see what's happening? That he's dying? Don't you even care about him any more?! I'm sending a messenger this minute with a letter telling Jesus to come at once. If he doesn't, then he has nothing to show himself around here for any more."

Mary started. "No, don't, I don't want that. I don't want to take advantage of his friendship. I don't want that. He knows Lazarus is ill. He spoke very plainly. Let him do what he thinks is best. Leave him.'

She took Martha's hand. Martha pulled away and stalked out. A few moments later she heard the fast pounding of a horse's hooves on the road. So, Martha had gone ahead with her plan anyway.

Lazarus never regained consciousness. Mary spent the entire night at his side. His breathing came in increasingly difficult gasps. He mumbled incoherently in his sleep. A few times she thought she heard him call the name "Jesus." As if he were summoning him from a distance. She prayed feverishly for his recovery. She cried out to Jesus, begging him the favor of her brother's life. Just before daybreak, she was

semi-conscious with exhaustion, and Martha hauled her off
to bed.

It must have been noon when she woke. The unusual
activity in the house made her apprehensive. She rushed into
the hall, and in dread of the answer, asked a passing servant
about her brother's condition.

"He died a short time ago," came the answer.

She reeled and fell heavily against the wall. Jesus had not
made it after all was all she could think. In her brother's
room, under Martha's supervision, several women were com-
pleting the preparation of Lazarus's body for burial. Mary
shuffled around the room, trying to help. After a few moments, she heard Martha's voice: "Leave off now. We'll finish
it ourselves."

She stood off to one side, helplessly watching the women
bustle about the room in silence. She was surprised at her
own calm—Lazarus was the dearest and closest to her; she
could not imagine life without him, without his kindness, his
tenderness, his wisdom. What was it Jesus once said?
"Whoever keeps my word will not see death forever." What
did he mean by that?

The house swiftly filled with mourners. It was then that
Mary saw for the first time how many true and sincere friends
Lazarus had, both among men of his own class and among
poor and simple people as well.

The following day Lazarus's body was laid in a tomb in a
corner of the garden. In the stir and activity following his
death, during which time all eyes in the household were
turned to Martha for direction, Mary realized that now there
was no place for her here. But she did not feel homeless; she
knew her place was with Jesus. She could not leave right
away; the funeral observances were still going on. She spent
whole hours at the tomb, often in the company of mourners.
But they respected her pain and fell silent when they found
her sitting near the grave.

On the fourth day after the burial, fairly early in the morning, Martha came into her room. "The master is here," she
said. "He's calling for you. He's outside the village."

Her heart leaped: so he had come after all. She sprang up

and rushed from the room. Downstairs she ran into a group of mourners who still occupied the house. They scattered to let her pass, then began to stream out behind her, apparently thinking she was heading for the tomb and wishing to comfort her once more.

She raced through the garden. Where could he be? Probably in the palm grove. She dashed through the empty village streets. There they were: a large group of people resting in the grass in the shade of the palms. She spotted him. He was seated against the trunk of a tree, and must have just finished speaking to them, because now he was silent. He watched her approach. Every head turned in her direction. She stepped over, around, and between the people until she finally reached him. Another instant, and she thought she would burst out sobbing. She wanted to hide with her sorrow somewhere— she fell at his feet. She felt the touch of his hand on her hair. She tried to collect herself.

"Lord, if you had been here, my brother would not have died." Her voice broke with emotion.

She waited for his words. He said nothing. His long silence worried her, she looked up. She saw the master with his head bowed and tears flowing down his face. She was even more deeply moved by the sight—how he must have loved Lazarus she thought. No, never had she seen him weep. But it was only for an instant; he wiped his eyes with his sleeve and asked her quickly, "Where have you laid him?"

"Come and see."

He rose to his feet with some difficulty. Only now did she notice how extremely weak he was: the journey had worn him to exhaustion.

Martha came hurrying up, and together they led him back through the village and into the garden. The crowd followed at their heels. As they neared the sepulcher, Mary heard someone behind her remark: "He who opened the eyes of a man born blind, couldn't he have prevented this man from dying?"

"It's here," she pointed. And for the second time she noticed the tears in his eyes and then the same swift motion to brush them away.

"Take away the stone," he commanded a group of bystanders.

They looked at him incredulously but, accustomed by now to his often peculiar instructions, they went and began to lift away the heavy slab.

Martha tried to stop them. "Lord," she cried, "by this time his body will stink. He has been in the tomb four days."

"Have I not told you," he said, "that if you believe, you shall see the glory of God?"

He stepped closer to the open tomb. Nobody moved. The only sound in the air was the incongruous lively chirping of birds filling the nearby branches. Jesus raised his eyes to heaven. Mary heard him speak aloud: "Father, I give you thanks that you have heard me. I know that you hear me always, but because of those that stand around me, I have said this, that they may believe that you have sent me."

She stared; she did not understand. Jesus peered closely into the dark of the tomb and suddenly called out loudly, as if to someone at a distance, "Lazarus, come forth!"

She stiffened, aghast. A rustling sound reached her from the interior of the tomb. Her hair prickled across her scalp. In the black opening of the vault, a white figure materialized like a specter. She stood rooted to the ground. The squeals of the women finally jolted her out of her paralysis. She heard Jesus urging them, "Unbind him and let him go."

Mary rushed up to her brother and tore away the napkin from his head. He squinted, blinked his eyes at her, confused, unawares, as if he had been rudely awakened from a sound sleep. He did not appear to recognize her. With her hands shaking uncontrollably, she unwound the bandages that several days earlier they had bound around his limp, lifeless body. Then she heard his thick cry like a moan: "Jesus".

She looked up. Lazarus was staring at his friend. His eyes said that he had suddenly grasped everything. Another moment, and he threw himself into his arms.

His movement suddenly released the tension among Jesus' followers: they burst into joy; they screamed, they laughed, they cried, they threw themselves at Lazarus, touching him, hugging him, kissing him. Off to one side, Jesus finally said to them smiling, "Let him leave now". Mary clasped her beloved brother to her side and helped him make his unsteady way back to the house.

Then came the deluge, as she called it. Rivers of people, endlessly flooding the inside and outside of their home—relatives, friends, neighbors, strangers, enemies, observers sent by the Pharisees, Sadducees, priests. Mary wandered through the house in a daze of emotion. She felt most sorry for poor Lazarus, having to tell and retell without respite how he had died and then been reawakened. Every few minutes he had to escort someone to the sepulcher and point out the bench where he had lain—where his body had lain. Actually, Lazarus had very little to tell. He sent the most persistent enquiries to his sisters, and since Martha was especially expert at getting rid of nuisances, she was hemmed in by the largest crowd. Nonstop, a thousand times or more, she recited the whole story.

But the interrogations by the priests were frightening and disturbing. After talking to them Mary almost believed that her brother had never come back from the dead, had never even died. It was at times like these that she most regretted she was not like Martha, who laughed in their faces or, if they irritated her, threw them out of the house. Now for the first time she saw just how much these people hated Jesus. It was incredible the way they managed to misinterpret everything, literally everything, he said and did to his detriment; the way they saw the most subversive, cunning design in his most unselfish acts; he damage to the Jewish nation that they read in his every activity; the way they refused to see any of the faults and shortcomings he pointed out in them, but explained them away as his "spitefulness." She was not even surprised to hear that the raising of Lazarus from the dead had created such a stir in Jerusalem that the priests were planning to murder her brother.

On hearing of the project to kill Jesus, Lazarus, always one to avoid pomp and ceremony, decided to hold a lavish feast in honor of Jesus. All the officials of Jerusalem were invited. Every prominent Pharisee, scribe, and especially priest was included on the list of guests. Mary wondered how her brother invited into his house people he disavowed, and with whom he had no social contact.

"It's not for me, it's for him," he explained. "Let them come and by their presence give honor to Jesus. And if they don't come, then let them know officially from me that I'm alive and to whom I owe my life."

"Will you allow me to honor him in my own way?" she asked.

He smiled broadly. "What do you have in mind?"

"Shall I tell you?"

"Yes, please do."

"I'll buy some spikenard oil and at the end of the feast anoint his feet with it."

"I might have guessed," he laughed. "Perfumes are your speciality."

Just as they expected, many of the guests did not appear, but the number that did was still impressive. It seemed as if there wouldn't be space enough to accommodate them, though the entire house and garden were thrown open for the feast, and everything that could have been borrowed from neighbors, was. The atmosphere was one of rejoicing. Lazarus seated Jesus at his side in the place of honor. His Twelve disciples positioned themselves close by. Mary moved among the guests trying to help Martha as best she could, checking that nothing was in short supply, that everyone was content. She was happy, so happy in fact that she was afraid something might happen to mar her happiness. It was very hot. Jesus, though in good spirits, appeared very tired to her. Toward the end of the feast, exactly as she had planned, she went to her room and returned with an alabaster flacon containing nearly a pound of spikenard. She hurried up to Jesus with it.

"May I?" she asked him.

Jesus saw the open flask of oil, smiled, nodded his head. She knelt at his feet and carefully poured the contents over them. The pungent scent of the perfume instantly penetrated the entire room. All eyes turned to Jesus. Suddenly he appeared to grow sad and thoughtful. Someone was speaking out loud, one of the Twelve (later they said it was Judas, but she was not sure): "Why all that useless expenditure? Why wasn't the perfume sold for three hundred denarii, and the money distributed to the poor?"

She realized that Jesus had heard the remark. He looked up and said, "Let her alone. Why do you distress her? She has done me a good turn. The poor you will always have with you, and whenever you wish, you can do them good. But me, you will not have always. She has done this for my burial."

Mary gave a start. The flask fell out of her hands and shattered against the floor. She felt faint. She sat on the floor at his feet a moment, afraid to rise, then unobtrusively crept to her room where she burst into tears.

Yes, she had sensed it correctly. Jesus was well aware of the danger and was walking consciously into death. When she tried to consider the possibilities open to him, she had to admit that he had no way out. At best, a flight from the country. But not just outside the borders of Palestine, outside the whole Jewish nation. Even if he escaped to some little town in Asia Minor or Macedonia, they would still get to him, everywhere they would get to him—all Jewish groups were subject to Jerusalem. She tried to put her finger on the mistakes he might have made that now had brought him to the brink of disaster: what he had neglected, what he should have avoided, what and where he had said too much, what he had done needlessly or improperly, what he should have resisted in order to prevent the sentence that hung over him now. But the conclusion was always the same: it was inevitable. And he had been aware of it from the very beginning and had never wavered in the face of danger. He had said everything he ought to have said to show the masses what it meant to serve God.

But she wanted to prevent his death. She would shield him against it in anyway she could.

On the following day, as Jesus was leaving for Jerusalem, Lazarus detained him at the gate and urged him to come and spend the nights with them in Bethany for as long as he was in the city. "It's only an hour's journey," he argued.

How grateful she was for those words! When the two of them headed back to the house alone, she sensed Lazarus was thinking the same as she was: he understood the danger that threatened Jesus and wanted to safeguard him against an attack. Although she did not really believe Jesus would heed their request, to her surprise he came that very same evening. He came the second and third nights as well.

On Thursday he told her not to wait with supper for him; he wanted to eat the Passover feast that night with his disciples in Jerusalem. Mary did not like those nights in Jerusalem, in strange places and strange houses, and she especially did not like them the closer they got to the festival days, during which—according to the Pharisees—Jesus was going to take over the city. She lived in constant fear of betrayal, that they were going to find out where he spent the night and capture him while he slept. She felt she could defend him in their house in Bethany—she, together with the servants and his disciples, whom she eagerly took in for precisely that reason.

It was a punishing night. She tossed for hours unable to sleep. Several times she went outside to listen. If she could, she would have run all the way to Jerusalem. She lay down again, persuading herself that everything was all right, that Jesus would chide her for worrying and order her straight to sleep. But she could not put his words out of her mind: "She has done it for my burial". Nightmares tormented her as she half dozed: she thought she heard them marching to seize him; she had to defend him, alert his people, but her legs refused to respond, her feet sunk like rocks in the ground, she could not summon help. The sound of barking dogs roused her—that was no dream. Nor was the rattling at the gate. Someone was desperately trying to get in. She threw on a coat and ran downstairs and right into Lazarus, who apparently had not been to bed at all, or at least had not undressed. He was still fully clothed. Without a word they ran toward the gate. A rumble of voices carried through the night air— the servants on guard were talking to somebody. In the torchlight Mary recognized him—James, the brother of John. She saw the agitated look on his face, his tousled hair, his disheveled, mud-splattered garments, and dried blood on his beard and chin, apparently from his nose. Before he said a word, she knew.

"They seized Jesus," he groaned.

She stayed—at least she thought she stayed—absolutely calm, though when she tried to speak, she could not find her voice. Lazarus put his arm tightly around her. "Come, let's go inside," he said to them.

They returned to the house, where they sat down in heavy silence. Mary's heart pounded so violently it hurt.

"They seized Jesus," James repeated in a choked voice.

"Who?" Lazarus asked.

"The chief priests."

"How did it happen?"

"First we had the Passover supper—"

"In whose house?" Martha broke in.

No one had noticed Martha come in. As always, she was exact, to the point, impatient with inaccuracy.

"Don't interrupt," Lazarus said. "What happened next?"

"At the very start, he washed our feet. Then he told us one of us will betray him. Then Judas got up and left."

So, it was Judas, after all, Mary thought to herself.

James took a long shuddering breath and went on: "After eating the supper, we went to the Garden of Olives. He left eight of us at the gate to watch the entrance. He entered the garden with Peter, John, and myself. Then a group of men assaulted us, and they bound Jesus."

"Who were they?"

"Attendants from the temple and some other men, but they were lead by priests."

"Did you defend yourselves?"

James hesitated a moment. "Peter tried to, but Jesus forbade him," he said weakly.

"Where is Jesus?"

"I don't know. John told me to hurry here to you, and he went to follow them."

"First we have to find out where they took him," Lazarus said. "The most important thing is that they didn't kill him. If there were priests among them, it means they'll want to judge him for violating the Law and the Prophets. A trial will have to last a few days. Just gathering and hearing the witnesses alone will take them a considerable amount of time.

Then they'll pass sentence. If they condemn him to death, the sentence will have to be sanctioned by Pilate. We'll begin our efforts in the morning. Now let's try to get some sleep. There are still a few hours to daybreak."

"That's out of the question," Mary protested vehemently. "We'll leave for Jerusalem immediately."

"For what? Everyone is sleeping. Whom do you want to wake up at this time of night?"

She thought feverishly. Joseph at Arimathea. He was the only one.

"We'll go to Joseph of Arimathea," she said. "You know that he's in Jerusalem. He'll help us."

"You're right, we should go to him. But it's still too early."

"It will be light by the time we get to Jerusalem," she insisted.

"All right," Lazarus conceded, though reluctantly. "But at least allow James to wash and have something to eat. In fact, we all ought to eat and drink something before we start."

Mary did not want anything, she could not think about eating. At Lazarus's insistence she took a cup in her hands, but could scarcely hold on to it, they shook so badly. Lazarus calmed her, reassured her—they would not dare to raise a hand against Jesus while the city was so full of pilgrims.

"Why, the vast majority are from among those he healed, fed, comforted—people who trust him," he assured her. "The priests would never dare make a foolhardy move like that. They have to reckon with the possibility of rioting, or even rebellion against them."

She disagreed. "You heard how they spread the rumor that Jesus wants to proclaim himself king during the festival days."

Lazarus was unconvinced. "Don't listen to that nonsense. They don't believe it, and neither does anyone else."

The city was still fast asleep as they entered the gates. They headed directly to the house of Joseph of Arimathea and roused him. No, he knew nothing about it, but he was far more alarmed by the news than they had expected. After hearing them, he determined to go straight to the palace of Caiaphas and make inquiries there. Meanwhile, he told them, they should remain at his house, make themselves at home.

They declined; they preferred to accompany him. By now the city was slowly beginning to come alive. In the streets they passed stalls already spread with fish and fruit and vegetables.

The gates of Caiaphas's palace were swung wide open, with people scurrying in and out. Joseph stopped and appeared to be undecided. Mary saw his growing uneasiness. She saw him glance around nervously, looking for someone to speak to. A figure emerged from the gate—Joseph hurried up to him. The two men slipped into an alley and spoke together for a moment. Joseph ran back to them with a tightened look on his face.

"He's already with Pilate," he said.

"Who? Caiaphas?" Lazarus cried.

"Jesus."

"How can that be?" Mary could hardly barely choke out the words. "What about the trial?"

"They have already judged him. They passed sentence at daybreak and took him to Pilate, demanding that he sentence him to death."

Mary felt as if she were slipping into a hazy trance. This is impossible, she repeated to herself. She heard Lazarus' voice asking Joseph: "You know Pilate well. Will you go to him?"

"Yes, of course. I only hope it's not too late. They left with him almost two hours ago."

At the mouth of the street opening on to the square before the Procurator's palace, they encountered a group of people. They pushed past them, trying to reach the square, and suddenly found their way obstructed by large numbers of armed temple attendants. Joseph forced his way toward one of them. The man recognized him at once and saluted him, but would not let him through.

It was the first time Mary ever saw Joseph enraged. He ordered the man to summon a priest at once. One of the guards shuffled off reluctantly. They waited for what seemed like hours. Sounds from the square reached them: muffled shouts and chants. Mary strained to listen, trying to single out the words. Incredulous, she thought she distinguished the words, "Crucify him!". Then again, and again, "Crucify him!" Chills rippled down her spine at the sound. Several others joined the group, asking what was happening on the square. A voice responded: "Jesus is being tried by Pilate." "Jesus of Nazareth? Why would he be there? Why, only yesterday he was preaching in the temple."

At last the guard returned with one of the priests. He saluted Joseph. The two moved a few steps away. Mary saw Joseph tremble with indignation. His raised voice reached her: "Why didn't I know anything about this? Why wasn't I informed about a special session of the Sanhedrin?"

The priest listened to his outburst with a thin smile on his lips. Mary heard the irony in his bland reply: "And what do you think, why?"

"I want to speak to Pilate," Joseph said emphatically.

With an exaggerated look of regret, the priest said, "No, unfortunately you can't. It is the wish of our High Priest that in order to avoid needless confusion and misunderstandings, no one be permitted to see Pilate. Anyway, it wouldn't do any good. Sentence has been passed."

"What is it?"

The priest dropped his eyes. "Death by crucifixion."

Mary's knees buckled under her. She felt herself sinking to the ground.

The clap of the sandals of the Roman soldiers awakened her. She looked up and saw the face of Lazarus bending over her.

"Are you feeling better?"

He helped her to her feet. Over the heads of the crowd she saw a moving file of Roman eagles. She stood on her toes, trying desperately to see what was happening beyond the heads blocking her view. She saw what looked like a serried detachment of armed soldiers, followed by a cordon—she could see the gleam of their helmets. The cordon was lapped on all sides by the excited mob. For a fleeting instant she caught a glimpse of him through the crowds, and in the same moment collapsed again in a dead faint.

When she revived, Mary found herself lying on a stone bench attached to a wall running the length of the street. Her brother's face hovered over her again. It took her a full minute to remember where she was. Jerusalem, this was Jerusalem, and she had fainted at the sight of Jesus.

"Was that him?" Her voice was hoarse with disbelief.

"Yes."

"What did they do to him?" A sob ruptured her voice.

"Calm yourself."

"No, let's go and follow him."

She tried to pull herself up, but fell back again. Her head ached, she must have struck it when she fell.

"Stay here a moment, because you'll faint again. We'll go in a few minutes." He held something out for her to drink.

"Why did he look like that?"

"Pilate ordered him scourged."

"But that thing on his head. . . ."

She closed her eyes, almost wishing she could faint again and not have to think, not have to see, not have to hear, just die. She felt a light touch on her face. She opened her eyes. Lazarus. He thought she had swooned again. How fortunate that Lazarus was alive. She got to her feet and grabbed hold of her brother's shoulder for support—she never thought a fainting spell would so weaken her. Or was it only weakness. She dreaded another glimpse of Jesus; she thought she could never bear the horror of it. Lazarus sensed it. He walked slowly. "Maybe you would rather return home?" he asked gently.

She shook her head. Not even at home—nowhere—would she be able to stand it for a moment, as long as he was hanging there on a cross. Her place was at his side.

As she stepped shakily over the stones, she noticed drops of blood scattered at intervals in the hollows. Fresh, untrampled by the masses, they glistened like little crimson beads.

Slowly they ascended the streets to the gates of the city. The horizon gradually opened before them. She knew it, though she did not see it: she kept her eyes pinned to the ground, afraid to lift them—he would be there. But she had to get used to the sight; crucified men sometimes hung for days.

The thought staggered her. Resolutely she raised her eyes. Yes, three crosses in a row on Golgotha. His in the middle.

It was enough. She dropped her eyes. They climbed higher. How had he managed to climb the slope in his condition? she wondered. They reached the loose fringe of bystanders on the hill and some clusters of priests and Pharisees.

The ring of space directly under the cross was largely empty. There was only John, Jesus' mother, and her sister Mary of Cleophas. Mary hesitated a moment, then broke away from Lazarus and joined their group. If only to be closer to the cross, closer to him. She could still not bring herself to lift her eyes. She stared at the ground, at the slowly widening puddle of blood. Her whole being shook with dread and aching grief. Slowly she moved her eyes along the pillar of the cross, along the trickling strings of blood, until they found his feet, punctured and abnormally distended by jutting nails. She shuddered and fled with her gaze to his face. That was better, that was how she wanted to stay, looking at his face . . . . if only there was not that horrible tangle of thorns. He was unconscious. He breathed strenuously, his chest rising and falling in violent spasms. His head hung limply on his breast—it almost seemed as if he were watching someone intently on the ground, except his eyes were closed. At intervals his whole body quivered violently, or his breathing stopped altogether—and her heart sank each time in the fear that he would never open his eyes again, never speak again. A long time she stood, slowly, numbly beginning to accept the situation. Now she began to register the howling and whooping and laughing going on around her; the epithets, the taunts, the jeers; the coarse, abusive vulgarity. Never had she felt such abasement; whatever pierced him, pierced her as well. A voice bellowed above the tumult: "Come down from the cross".

A spate of shouts instantly followed interspersed with peals of laughter.

"He saved others, now let him save himself!"

"Hey you, the one who destroys the temple of God and in three days rebuilds it, save your own self!"

"If you are the Son of God, come down from the cross!"

"If he is the King of Israel, let him now come down from the cross and we will believe him!"

"He trusted in God; let him now deliver him if he wants him!"

"After all, he said, 'I am the Son of God!' "

The chorus of insults swept over Mary like so many stabs of a knife. Louder and closer they came.

"He saved others, but he cannot save himself. Christ, King of Israel. Let him come down from the cross now, so we can see and believe."

One of the soldiers jeered, "If you are the King of the Jews, save yourself."

Unexpectedly, she heard a voice from over her head: "If you are the Christ, save yourself and us!"

It was one of the condemned men hanging at one side of Jesus, speaking to him.

Immediately she heard the other condemned man answer the first: "Don't you even fear God, seeing that you are under the same judgment? And justly for us, for we are receiving the due reward for our deeds. But this man has done no evil."

Mary listened to his words in wonder. One man alone in this ocean of hatred. His next words took her breath away: "Lord remember me when you come into your kingdom."

He must have met Jesus somewhere, she thought, or heard him, or at least heard about him. Then she saw Jesus slightly lift his head, turn it in the man's direction, and slowly, with a painful effort, say to him: "Amen I say to you, this day you will be with me in Paradise."

So he heard, he was conscious, he knew what was going on around him! Everyone fell silent when it was seen that he was beginning to speak. But only those standing closest could hear, and now they began to relay it back to the others who were craning to find out what it was he said.

"He promised Paradise to a criminal condemned to death for murder!" They were scandalized.

Mary's heart leaped for joy—Jesus was still himself. He had not surrendered, he had not changed. Even now he was attesting the importance of a man's conscience; what was important was that he was contrite. She had distinctly heard the criminal say: "We justly suffer our punishment". And so, what the Pharisees taught was false: that he who dies on a cross as a criminal is a sinner, condemned to eternal damnation. Her flood of thoughts was interrupted by words from directly above her: "Behold your son".

She looked up and saw his open eyes directed towards his mother. After a moment, he shifted his gaze to John. Perhaps to take advantage of the lull in the noise, or perhaps for fear that he might lose consciousness again, he was now expressing his last wish. She waited hopefully; maybe he would say something else. His eyes were still open. He stared fixedly at John. Maybe he would notice her, maybe he would utter a word to her. But without taking his eyes off John, after a long pause in which he gasped heavily for air, he heaved out the words: "Behold your mother".

The effort surpassed his strength, his head sank to his breast. He appeared to have lapsed back into unconsciousness.

She had not noticed when a black cover of clouds rolled across the sky; suddenly it was dark. A cold wind whipped her garments. The first scattered drops of rain spattered the ground. Swiftly the hill began to empty. The storm broke loose with all its fury. She clasped his mother tightly to herself. Lightning hurled across the sky with a volley of thunderclaps. As if awakened by the noise, Jesus shifted his head slightly and groaned, "I thirst."

A soldier idling nearby rose, stuck a sponge on his lance, dipped it into a dish, and raised it to his lips. Mary watched anxiously. He could not drag up his head, he did not open his lips—he must have lapsed again. It was nearly the end, she could feel it. And she wanted it. So that he would stop suffering, so that he would stop moaning, so that he would stop gasping horribly for air, so that he would stop hurting. She could not bear to watch his agony much longer. She could not stand to hear his wheezing breaths. Then, when she thought it was over, and he had surely expired, he suddenly threw up his head and cried out: "*Eloi*, Eloi, *lamma sabachtani!*"

A voice behind her murmured: "Listen, he's calling Elijah."

Jesus gave out one more anguished groan, and it was over.

His head slumped, his body shuddered, sagged, then froze on the cross. Mary felt her heart constrict with a sickening pang. She felt herself reeling, sinking; she threw out her arms, grabbed the post of the cross for support, and slid to her knees. She would have knelt that way, numbly clinging to the cross indefinitely, but a hand was on her shoulder. It was Joseph of Arimathea. She had completely forgotten that he and Lazarus were there. She rose shakily.

He was speaking to her. ". . . I'll go to Pilate now and ask permission to bury his body."

"Very well, go." Mary breathed between clenched teeth. She shivered from the cold and the heaviness in her heart. Her wet clothing clung awkwardly to her body.

"But I have a favor to ask. I'll need to buy bandages and balsam and spices."

"I'll go," Lazarus volunteered.

"No," Joseph said, shaking his head. "I would rather you stayed here."

The sudden talk and activity seemed to revive her. Perhaps it was better this way, she thought. It might be easier to bear if her mind were occupied.

"I'll go," she said.

"Do you feel strong enough?"

She forced a smile. Joseph handed her a pouch of money. "Take this. It should be enough."

As she headed down the hill, she glanced over her shoulder and saw a group of other women standing near the foot of the cross. Among them she recognized the mother of James the less and Joseph, and Salome, the mother of the sons of Zebedee. She carefully picked her way over the wet rocks slippery with mud. At the bottom she saw a group of men approaching from the opposite direction. She recognized one of them at once—Nicodemus. He used to visit Jesus on occasion for discussions, though at odd hours, always at night.

He saw her. "Is he then . . . dead?"

"Yes."

"Where are you going?"

"For bandages and burial sheets. I also want to buy aloes and myrrh."

"Buy only the sheets and binding. We have the rest."

The servants with him had sacks of spices slung over their shoulders.

On her way down, she shook her head in wonder: how peculiar Nicodemus was, that he could anticipate things like that. She could never do that.

In the city, the stalls were already folded away for the day. Apparently the storm had scared off the merchants. But the shops were shut as well. She should have expected it: it was nearing the Sabbath. She raced from shop to shop, but everything was locked for the holy day. She could not buy anything. Finally she ran into an old friend who agreed to sell her what she needed. She hurried back up the hill against a tide of men and women descending.

At the top she found the situation changed: his two companions were also dead. The contorted shapes of arms and thighs did not escape her notice. She shuddered, she knew what it meant. Involuntarily her eyes sped to the body of Jesus, searching it—had they broken his bones as well. No, she breathed a sigh of relief, there were no signs, though blood streamed from a narrow slit in his side where there had been none before. She ran up to Lazarus and Joseph.

"Did you buy everything?" Lazarus asked her.

"Yes."

"You were gone a long time. I was getting worried."

"What happened?"

"The priests went to Pilate and asked to have their legs broken, so they wouldn't hang through the Sabbath. We didn't expect that."

"What about Jesus?"

"No—thanks to the centurion. He forbade the soldiers to break his bones. But they ruptured his side with a lance."

She turned to Joseph. "How did you fare with Pilate. Did you see him?"

"Yes. Pilate has permitted me to bury him."

"Where do you want to lay him?"

"It's very near here. A new tomb, only recently completed. Perhaps you didn't know—my gardens reach right to this hill. But we have to hurry, it's getting late. We must finish before sunset.

Mary was hard pressed to find a clean spot on which to lay his body for washing. Mud was everywhere. Finally she found a clean piece of rock. With some of the other women, she carried over the pitchers of water, which someone had already prepared for them. She spread the sheet on the ground and waited. And tried not to watch Joseph and John and Nicodemus taking down the body. Then, together with his mother, she arranged him on the sheet. It is so heavy, his body, she thought to herself; the way it falls over so limply and helplessly. Like Lazarus' body.

She dipped a cloth in water and tried to wash off some of the brittle crusts of blood. Now she saw just how badly beaten he had been. She shrank in horror every time she caught a piece of torn flesh or muscle on the cloth. Now, to get those horrible thorns from his head. Gently she pulled out each thorn embedded deeply in his scalp and entangled in his hair—every pull made her wince in fright, as if he could still feel the pain.

"Hurry, hurry, or we won't make it," Lazarus rushed her gently.

"But we can't bury him like this," she cried. "He can't have a worse burial than any other man."

"You can come back and finish after the Sabbath."

Yes, it was true, she hadn't thought of that. She finished quickly. They arranged the body on another linen sheet and sprinkled it with aloes and myrrh.

"Without anointing?" she protested.

"We don't have time. Everything else later."

She helped them bind the body with bandages. Then another sheet, a cloth around the head, and they carried the body of Jesus down into the garden. Just as Joseph had said, the tomb was very close by. The sun was slowly setting behind the horizon when the men emerged from inside the cave. With the gardener's help, they slowly rolled a heavy stone across the entrance to the tomb. They had finished before sundown. They wiped their brows, brushed and straightened their robes, and breathed with relief: it was over.

Lazarus came up to her. He said, "I'm returning to Bethany. I'll be back after the Sabbath. Are you coming with me?"

"No, I want to stay." She threw Joseph a look of entreaty.

"But of course." He had anticipated her request. "My home is at your disposal," he said, gracious as always. Then he and Lazarus left.

Mary sat down wearily before the tomb. A few other women joined her, then they, too, disappeared. She was alone. A wave of acute grief swept over her. The image of Jesus grotesquely stretched on the cross tormented her. She buried her head between her knees and abandoned herself to the flood of despair.

Without realizing it, she began to speak to him aloud between sobs: ". . . . What good did that kind of life do you? Overtaxed, overworked, always in a hurry, morning to night. You never had any time for yourself. Nothing but people exploiting, taking advantage of you. And where are they now, those people? Don't tell me you don't know. By now everyone knows what happened and they didn't come, not to your cross and not here to your grave. Who rose up in your defense? They tagged along after you as long as you multiplied bread and fish for them. And they knew where to find you when they got ill. They took what they wanted and now they've gone back again to their unscrupulous lives. You didn't inspire anyone to follow you, you didn't convert anyone to your kind of life. Who has stayed with you? Lazarus? Nicodemus? Joseph? John? But even without you they were still good men. Oh, and a few pious women. That's all. And me. At least you had one success. But is even that one complete? If it were, I wouldn't be complaining about you now. . . . "

Her monologue dwindled into a soft whimpering in a half-dreaming state in which scenes from the past crowded her mind. She saw him again against the dazzling white of the temple walls, bending over her; and his odd question: "Has no one condemned you?" She heard her own faint, "No one, Lord". And those most beautiful of words anyone had ever spoken to her: "Then neither will I condemn you". The bittersweet moments at his feet in Bethany poured over her now like balm. She began to weep again, rocking back and forth in time to her words: "You could now be walking through the fields of Galilee, the way you used to, or sailing out with the fishermen, or enjoying the sunset". She burst into wrenching sobs. "And what's left after you? A few more years, and no one will even have heard of you."

Grief, sympathy, despair, anger, every emotion washed over her in turn, tearing the grief from her soul. She sat wailing like a weeper before the tomb, mourning for her Jesus.

Evening set in but she did not notice. Nor did she hear Joseph's footsteps behind her.

"Come home now. It's late, you'll catch a chill. You must eat something."

He helped her to her feet. Her legs were numb from having sat on the rocks so long. Joseph walked beside her in silence, not wishing to intrude upon her sorrow. He led her to a guest room in his house.

"Tomorrow is the Sabbath," he said before taking his leave. "If you think you can, be so kind as to prepare the aromatic ointments and sweet spices for Sunday. I have asked Mary, the mother of James, and Salome to help you. It would be best to get to the tomb as early in the morning as possible. There will probably be people there later."

How kind he was, Mary thought. He wanted to occupy her mind so that she would not brood.

When she finally finished mixing the ointments and spices and returned to her room, she was exhausted to the point of collapse. She just managed to slip out of her clothes and fall on to the bed, and instantly she was asleep.

The next day she awoke feeling sore and with an aching head. The room was very warm: the sun was already high. She dressed and went into the garden feeling dull and listless. The sight of Roman soldiers milling about the tomb quickly sobered her. What was it supposed to mean? She hurried back to the house and found Joseph confessing with a group of priests. Shaken, anxious, she could scarcely wait for them to finish to find out what was happening.

Joseph seethed. "They didn't expect me to take the body of Jesus to my own tomb. If he had been buried in a common grave, there would be no problem. But now they're afraid of a sensation. They say someone could steal his body and then spread the rumor that he has been resurrected from the dead. That, of course, is supposed to mean his disciples. They remembered what he had said so many times about how after his death he would rise again."

"Yes, but where did the Roman soldiers come from?"

"The priests went to Pilate and told him this, threatening that if it should happen, rioting would erupt. They demanded that he post guards."

"Now I understand."

"I can't help wondering," Joseph added bitterly, "who exactly is supposed to steal his body, which of the disciples? They scattered like leaves in the wind afraid for their own skins."

"What did you say to the priests?"

"What was I supposed to say? Was there anything I could say to that? I had to agree to having a Roman guard in my garden."

"But I was supposed to go early tomorrow morning to anoint his body."

"I know. And it has to be done—it will be the third day, and the days are warm."

"Yes, but what about the soldiers? Will they let me through?"

"Yes, of course. I'll talk to them about it."

She sat the entire day in the garden near the sepulcher. People came and went, she did not bother to see who. The soldiers respected her mourning, left her alone, and did not accost or harass her. In the evening she saw Mary and Salome and promised to wake them in the morning on her way to the tomb. Right after sundown she returned to her room, still aching and spent. Several times in the night she started up, thinking she had overslept. Finally she awoke again, and it was nearly daybreak. She dressed and crept down to the room where the other women were sleeping. She roused Salome and Mary. Another of the women, Joanna, awoke and begged to accompany them. They left the house quietly, carrying the vessels of spices and ointments.

The morning was cool and dark, but already a narrow strip of dawn glowed along the horizon. They entered the garden. The women walked in silence, their skirts rustling softly. Mary trembled inside; she could barely hold the dish of ointment in her hands. She was cold, but she shivered more at the thought of seeing his body again. She was frightened of touching his wounds, especially those horrible yawning puncture wounds from the nails and lance.

The white sepulcher loomed ahead in the darkness. But what was that black spot near it? She felt a chill run down her spine. Could that be the entrance? She ran ahead, leaving the other women behind. She ran faster, trying to pierce the dark with her eyes, her heart pounding like thunder in her ears. Where were the soldiers? Her uneasiness turned to terror—it *was* the opening. The stone had been moved away. Who did it? The soldiers or someone else? Then the thought struck her like a fireball—they stole the body of Jesus. Maybe they were still inside. She did not stop to think, but raced up to the tomb and fell against the rock. She peered inside. In the gloom she saw the faint white outlines of scattered sheets and bandages. The body was gone. They had taken it. She fought back rising despair. She had to do something. But by herself she could do little. Lazarus had gone, but Peter was here, and John and Joseph. They could search while there was still time. It must have happened just a short time ago. She raced back to the house. All the men were sleeping in the first room—Peter and John would be in there. She located their two sleeping forms, started whispering, "They have taken the Lord". She could not wake them. She shook them gently. "They have taken the Lord," she repeated.

They started up. "Who? What did they take?"

"Get up. They have taken the body of Jesus. We don't know where they have laid him."

Finally her words registered "They took Jesus?" They sprang up and all three ran to the tomb.

The two men raced ahead. She stopped for breath and watched them from a distance. She saw John reach the tomb first and wait outside for Peter. Was he afraid? Peter went in, then John followed. They stood in the entrance a moment

and stared at each other in confusion. She heard one of them
say: "Let's go and call Joseph."

They bounded toward the house. She was alone at the
tomb again. All she could think of was that another injury
had been meted out to her, though she did not know why, or
by whom. Tears streamed down her face. She stood with her
hands hanging helplessly at her sides, staring into the black
of the empty tomb. But she could not just stand there crying,
she had to do something, search for him. She turned and
through her tears saw a white figure in the twilight. The
gardener. But what was he doing here? Maybe he had done
it, maybe he hid the body? Or perhaps he knew something
abut it? Why else would he be at the tomb so early in the
morning? She started toward him.

"Woman," she heard, "why are you weeping? Whom do
you seek?"

Between her tears and sobs she stammered, "Sir, if you
have taken him, then tell me where you have laid him, and
I will take him away."

Then, trembling fearfully to hear a word that might give
her even some small hope, she heard her name spoken in a
voice she would know among thousands:

"Mary."

SIMON PETER

They headed back at dawn. The night fog still clung to the lake, although overhead the sun spread slow gold over a blueing sky. His men were worn to drowsiness. He watched their sluggish, sleeplike movements, their shiftless fumbling. He, too, was exhausted: sand grating under his eyelids, muscles tightening like knotted ropes, shoulders aching and sagging. All he could think of was sleep, though he knew he did not deserve a rest. He had waited much too long. He should have quit hours earlier. He had known they would not catch any fish; his fisherman's instinct told him as much. It was a bad time for fishing: the lake like a slab of slate; thick unmoving air stifling it. But he had been counting on a quirk of luck. When he finally gave the word, "We're going back," his companions all heaved a sigh of relief.

The boat drifted lazily. A barely perceptible breeze lightly puffed out the sail. He did not have the heart to order his men to take up the oars. One by one, they dropped off to sleep, propped up against the sides of the boat, confident that he was keeping watch and would steer the boat safely to shore. And he did, he kept watch.

The shore was still shrouded in low mist, but he knew it was there, straight ahead. From the stillness beyond the fog, voices carried over the water. He listened. No . . . one voice. The words were unclear, but . . . yes, he recognized that sound. It was the voice of that teacher from Nazareth. He knew it only too well, ever since they day Andrew charged through the door, shouting to him, "Come, we have found the Messiah!" He followed his brother outside, where he came upon a large crowd assembled by the shore, and in the center of it, him, Jesus of Nazareth. He would not quickly forget that first meeting, the way Jesus had looked at him, and his words: "You are Simon, son of John. You will be called Peter." Just like that! A stranger, suddenly changing his name from Simon to Peter! He did not like that, he was not used to anyone telling him what to do. Around here he gave the orders, he made the decisions. From that day forward, he felt an uncomfortable antipathy toward Jesus—and he hated the idea of Andrew following Jesus around like a puppy. Every time his brother tried to persuade him to go—"just this once"—and listen to him, his gruff answer was the same: he had work to do and did not have time to listen to some carpenter; his business was catching fish, drying nets, and taking care of the house. "You ought to look to fishing yourself," he growled, "and not tag along after some preacher."

To hear his brother rave endlessly about Jesus every time he came back from one of his gatherings irritated him. He did not want to listen. Maybe he was a little afraid of that young teacher. He did not want change. Everything was fine now the way it was. His life had stabilized: he had a wife and a house, he was slowly, comfortably beginning to settle down. Fishing was a good business. It was hard work, certainly, but he did not lack the strength. He knew where to find good, prosperous clients, he knew how to bargain, he knew how to sell. He had earned the respect and leadership of the local fishermen: they came to him for advice, mediation, redress. True, fishing had its ups and downs. Sometimes they came back empty-handed, like today. But tomorrow was another day.

Through the soft lap of water against the sides of the boat, he listened to the voice that was the source of so much of his disquiet. Why did that carpenter from Nazareth have to anchor himself here, he thought angrily. He disturbs the peace. He ruins business. Galilee is long and wide, why could he not have gone somewhere else.

The fog had begun to thin along the shore. He was surprised to see a considerable crowd lining it—where had they all come from at such an early hour? There he was, that was him, the master, with his back to the lake, addressing them.

He felt like changing direction so that he would not have to meet him when he pulled into the the shore. But to his men he would appear to be running away.

Simon's animosity toward the teacher had sharpened considerably since his mother-in-law had been taken ill. The woman was more than a mother to him; she treated him better than she did her own sons. She had been suffering a debilitating fever for a long time. He spent hours at her bedside. He did everything, brought everything he could to help. Nothing did. Finally Andrew suggested asking Jesus over—maybe he could cure her. Simon rejected it categorically, and they quarrelled. Simon called Jesus a charlatan, or something like that. Andrew took offense. In the meantime, the woman's condition steadily worsened. Finally Andrew brought Jesus over without Simon's permission.

He spotted them when they were walking up to the house. He was furious. He stalked out of the room ostentatiously, practically colliding in the doorway with the teacher. He had not gone very far when he turned back, out of genuine concern for his mother-in-law—and not a little curiosity. The door to the room was ajar. He saw Jesus walk over to the bed without a word, bend over her, and take her by the hand. He saw her smile and pull herself up as if in greeting. Then, without the least bit of fuss, she pushed aside the sheet she had over her, got up, threw on a robe, and went to the kitchen to make him a meal. It was all so quick, simple, and natural that it hardly even made an impression on him. He distinctly remembered the whole incident, because later he argued about it with Andrew, who insisted it was a miracle. Well, he did not see anything at all miraculous in the whole affair. He explained to Andrew that she was simply overwhelmed by the master's visit. When she saw him, she overcame herself and got up to serve him in spite of the fever. Or maybe the illness had simply run its course. "She recovered out of sheer concern," he repeated. "Things like that happen sometimes."

But after that, he felt an even more intense dislike for Jesus, especially since now the whole household was thoroughly enchanted by him. They followed him with delighted, entranced eyes; he had become the subject of greatest interest, of conversation, of expectation—a constantly awaited guest. And he, Simon, the head of the family, retired into the background.

The boat lay close to the shore. Everyone aboard was wide awake now and listening to the master from Nazareth preach. Simon felt that familiar pang in his heart again. They were not his men any more, but the Nazarene's. If they could, they could follow him just the way Andrew did. He pretended not to notice their absorption; he busied himself with maneuvering the boat to shore. It scraped the bottom gently and slid with its momentum on to the sandbank. He hopped over the side into the water. It was warm. He strained to heave the boat higher aground. Seeing him, his men remembered themselves and quickly scrambled over the sides to help him push. They began to unload their nets, heavy with water and weeds. The second and third boats slid to shore. In the middle of all the commotion of frustrated fishermen shouting, and wading, and hauling in their boats and nets, Simon suddenly heard his new name.

"Peter."

He gave a start. The teacher was calling to him from the distance. He looked up and saw Jesus heading toward him. What can he want from me? he grumbled to himself. Not without some satisfaction, he saw that the master looked very tired. His face glistened with perspiration. Simon was surprised: he never thought preaching could be so tiring.

It took him several moments to understand what Jesus was trying to say: too many people had massed and he could not reach them all with his voice, and so could he speak from Simon's boat? Teach from his boat? Simon could not see how it would make much difference, unless he were higher on shore. But with a motion of his arm, Jesus indicated where he would like Simon to anchor the boat in the water.

Simon was completely taken aback. How could Jesus ask such a thing? Could he not see how exhausted they were? If he were by himself, he would never agree, but he felt constrained in front of his men, who had clustered around and were listening. He knew their esteem for Jesus only too well. He looked questioningly at them; they nodded their heads. In spite of himself, he gave in.

They shoved off again and drifted close to shore until they were directly across from the multitude. They dropped anchor there. The fog had lifted almost entirely, unscreening a full blue sky. The sun beat down on them hotly. His men sprawled out around the bottom of the boat, or sat back against its sides and instantly fell asleep. Simon did not sleep. He found himself listening to the teacher. He was observing for the first time at such close range the man whose fame had risen so suddenly and dramatically, the man who had emerged as the foremost personality in Galilee. He was speaking to the multitude about poverty.

". . . . Do not be solicitous for your life, what you will eat, nor for your body, what you will put on. Is not the life more than the meat, and the body more than the raiment? Behold the birds of the air, for they neither sow, nor do they reap, nor gather into barns, and your heavenly Father feeds them. Are not you of much more value than they? And which of you by thinking can add one cubit to his stature? And for raiment why are you solicitous? Consider the lilies of the field, how they grow: they labor not, neither do they spin. But I say to you, that not even Solomon in all his glory was arrayed as one of these. . . ."

Simon was too tired even to bristle at the words. He just looked down at his cracked, calloused hands, and at his broken fingernails. Jesus talked about the birds of the air that neither sewed nor reaped nor gathered into barns, while he had to scramble and wear down his hands, and break his back to make a living, hauling fish to Capernaum, and to Magdala just to get a better price, drudging from morning to night like a mule to provide food and support for the whole household. Everyone looked to him. The kind of life that the teacher preached might be good for birds of the air like himself, or maybe like Andrew—that one was still free. He did not have a mother-in-law, or a father-in-law, or a wife, or a house on his shoulders. Yes, and he was free thanks to people like himself. Not for him that kind of life. He was no bird of the air or lily of the field. He did not look like Solomon, and he had to catch a lot of fish to clothe himself and his household. Weariness spread over him with a wave of numbness; he felt himself drifting into sleep.

He awoke with a start, or rather, he was awakened. The face of the Nazarene was over him. He stared around in confusion, not yet fully conscious. The boat floating on the water, the crowd lining the shore—he remembered where he was now. People were removing food from their bundles. A break in the sermon, he thought to himself. He looked up at the teacher. What did he want now?

"Launch out into the deep and let down your nets for a draught."

Simon pulled himself to his feet. He could not believe what he had just heard. Jesus knew perfectly well they had just returned from a whole night's work and had not caught a single fish. Could he not see it was useless? He looked at him doubtfully, but was struck again by how exhausted Jesus looked. He thought, perhaps he should do him that one favor and get him away from the throng who were clamoring for more sermons and cures, and give him at least a moment's respite. He weakened; he heard himself: "Master, we labored all night and caught nothing. But at your word, I will let down the net."

He roused his men. They took up the oars in a daze, not quite believing they were really going out again. They did not even bother to hoist the sail; it would not have made the slightest difference. The warm air hung still over the glassy water. With each slap of the oars against the surface, the whole expedition looked more and more preposterous. Simon was angry with himself for giving in so easily. If Jesus was tired, he had only himself to blame. So many times had he promised himself never to do anything against his better judgment. It was too late now. He would look fool in front of his men and the crowd waiting on the bank. "How could I have agreed to something like this," he muttered testily. "If he has no conception of fishing, that's his prerogative, he's a carpenter. But I'm a fisherman, I should know better." He was so furious he would not even look at the teacher.

The men tugged uncertainly at the oars. They were far from shore. How long was this folly going to continue? Finally he stole a glance at Jesus: he lay quietly in the prow of the boat. Simon smiled ironically to himself. What will the master do when they throw the empty nets on shore? What will the crowd say to that? He looked around. It was a shame to tire himself and his men out, there was no sense in going any farther. He turned to Jesus: could they start fishing now? The master's eyes were closed, but he was not asleep; he heard him. Without opening them, he said, "Yes."

Simon gave the order, and together with his men began to spread the net over the lake. It had hardly sunk below the surface when it happened. It must have been a whole immense school of fish that suddenly filled the net so densely; they were powerless to pull the weight of it into the boat. Simon shouted and waved to the fishermen on shore to come and help. They hurried out in their boats, amazed.

He went about his work as usual—pulling in the draught, steadying the boat, directing his men, as if it were just an ordinary everyday catch. But in his heart, Simon was as frightened as a small child. Why did he do it? What did he want? It was obvious Jesus wanted to win him over to himself. That meant that he, Simon the fisherman, was somehow important to him. And so, he knew about everything, about the animosity, the antagonism. And that was why he had asked if he could teach from his boat. It had nothing to do with the people being unable to hear him. Or at least, not entirely. Simon wanted to overcome his enmity. He glanced furtively over at Jesus, who was sitting up now and watching them feverishly loading the fish. First their boat, then the boats of the other fishermen. It seemed as if all their boats together could not accommodate the haul, as if they had taken every last fish in the lake, emptied the waters for all time.

Why did he do it? With a crushing clarity Simon began to see his own obstinacy, narrow-mindedness, jealousy, and on the other hand, Jesus' goodness, gentleness, tolerance. They came back to him, all the master's earlier attempts to approach him—the shy reaching out to him with his hand, the smiles in passing, from the first moment they set eyes on each other, all of which he had sullenly ignored. The master's brightness shone glaringly beside his own darkness. He felt overwhelmed with shame and remorse. He made his way to the bow of the boat where Jesus was sitting, and fell down before him. "Depart from me, Lord, for I am a sinful man," he cried.

As if his outburst had come as no surprise, as if he had been waiting for it, Jesus answered him softly. "Do not be afraid. Henceforth you will catch, not fish, but men."

He joined Jesus. He travelled Palestine with him, length and breadth. From the start he assumed the managerial position among the growing troop of disciples—he was genuinely convinced that Jesus had recruited him, with his hard hand accustomed to directing people, for just that purpose. He did not completely sever ties with his home, however. Occasionally he dropped by to cast a paternal eye on things, and each time he found that, while it was certainly not easy for them without him, they were somehow managing for themselves and were finally able to get by without him. Obviously they were hoping he would return to them—they complained, they showered him with news, enticed him with gossip. But they did not ask him to stay. They had too much regard for Jesus. They believed that if he took Simon from them, then they surely would not perish. And after every visit he was forced to conclude: Jesus needed him more than they did.

And that was how Simon Peter became a bird of the air and a lily of the field. Not that he had no worries on his mind. Apart from keeping Jesus' train of followers under control, his biggest concern was the master himself. An odd relationship formed between them. He adored Jesus, he was devoted to him as deeply and as thoroughly as any man could be to another, but at the same time he took solicitous, almost paternal care of him, advised him, counseled him, scolded him; and Jesus listened, smiled, submitted to his care, and gave him free rein at the head of their group. He disliked being away from him. A day without Jesus was a day lost. He was blindly obedient to his every instruction, attentive to even the simplest query or request, real or imagined. Yet there were times when he could not help wondering why Jesus had gathered them around himself. For what purpose had he chosen them? Just to follow him? So what if they followed him?

The answer came one day very simply and unexpectedly. It was evening; they were huddled around the camp fire. It was Jesus' custom after supper and after prayers to discuss their plans and instructions for the following day. This time he spoke to them very slowly and deliberately. He appeared unusually tired, drained. He told them he wished to remain there a few days alone. Peter jumped to the alarming conclusion: the master was ill, he wanted to be left alone. Jesus went on, however: he would like them to go before him, preferably in pairs, to the villages and settlements to which he would shortly journey, and prepare the people for his coming. The announcement produced a surprised hush around the fire.

He went on, "Do not go in the direction of the Gentiles, nor into the towns of the Samaritans. Go rather to the lost sheep of the house of Israel. And going, preach the message, 'The Kingdom of Heaven is at hand.' Do not take gold, nor silver, nor money in your purses. Nor scrip for your journey, nor two coats, nor sandals, nor a staff; for the laborer deserves his living."

He paused, as if anticipating questions or protests. The disciples glanced around at each other in confusion. Their questions were too numerous to be asked.

Jesus went on, "Into whatever city or town you enter, inquire who in it is worthy, and abide there until your departure. And when you come into the house, salute it, saying: 'Peace be to this house.' If that house is worthy, your peace shall come upon it; but if it is not worthy, your peace shall return to you. And whoever shall not receive you, nor hear your words, going forth out of that house or city, shake off the dust from your feet."

Peter had to agree it was not such a bad idea. How many times had they arrived at a town or village and had to start all over again with the same naive questions and hostilities and misunderstandings? Their advance arrival could spare

Jesus tremendously. Especially since the demands made on
his time and strength were sweeping him along with alarming
momentum and taking their ravaging toll. It was no longer
a question of simply giving a sermon or two here and there;
these were movements of human masses—towns, villages,
hamlets affected by his teachings—and everyone in that human tide wanting to meet him personally, touch him, talk to
him. In truth Peter could not quite imagine his fellows in the
role of speechmakers. They were fishermen for the most part,
who did not know how to speak decently, let alone publicly.
He was not even sure about himself, whether he could acquit
himself intelligently or not. Maybe he would not have to;
Jesus would probably order him to stay behind with him.
The master needed him at his side. He asked, "Everyone,
Lord? And I, too?"

Jesus nodded.

Peter winced at the unexpected prick to his pride. Jesus
had put him on the same footing as the others, sending him
away as if he were dispensable. He set his jaw and said
nothing. He was not going to beg to stay. If that was what he
wanted, so be it. He threw himself down sullenly to sleep.
But he could not sleep. He sulked. The stones irritated him.
He tossed and turned. He could not find a comfortable position. But after the first stab of wounded pride wore off, he
began to turn the idea over in his mind. What exactly did
"prepare the people" mean? Which people? The elders of the
synagogues? What would they say to them? Where? In the
synagogues? In the squares? Somehow he just could not picture it. And who should he take with him? John? He liked
John best, though it sometimes irked him to have a youngster
under his feet. Probably Jesus would keep John with him; it
would be funny to see a stripling like him preaching. What
about Matthew? No, too shrewd. Judas? Too much of a pol-
itician. Thomas? Too much philosophizing. Then who . . .?
It must have been nearly daybreak when he finally dropped
off to sleep.

He rose that morning feeling tired and irritable. Either it
was his imagination or the atmosphere was unusually
strained. The other disciples all appeared pensive, uncom-

municative. There were none of the usual jokes or laughter. They probably all felt the way he did. In a few minutes they would have to go. He had still not made up his mind whom to take with him. He scanned them furtively, making selections. Finally he decided. He walked over to John. "You'll go with me," he grunted. He pretended not to notice the surprised look on the boy's face.

They took their leave of Jesus and the others and set out. Neither spoke for a long time. Finally Peter turned to John and said, "Just remember, you're going to do the talking."

"Me?"

"You."

The two fell silent again. Peter felt his inadequacy with words keenly. Boats and fish were what he knew. Why did he have to go and leave his trade to play at itinerant preacher? For the first time since he had joined Jesus, he regrettted the old days.

Around noon they saw a village ahead. Instinctively they slowed their steps. They reached the first houses. They looked deserted. The sound of women's voices carried from a distance. They rounded a corner and came upon a group of women washing clothes at a spring. Peter felt awkward that he, a man, should address a covey of women. No, he told himself, if he was going to be a disciple of Jesus, then he must be like him. He walked briskly toward the women. They stopped washing and eyed them curiously.

"Peace be to you," Peter greeted them.

"Peace, peace," they chimed readily.

"Are you looking for someone?" one of them inquired. "One of our people?"

"No, we . . . well . . . yes, where are they?"

"At work. What do you want?"

"We want to tell you that in a few days Jesus of Nazareth will come to you."

Without his even noticing it, the problem that had looked so insurmountable—discourse with strangers—began to solve itself. The few distrustful looks quickly disappeared, the strangeness dissolved, and in no time they were chatting together like neighbors.

John amazed him—the boy began to speak with so much charm and enthusiasm that he almost envied his youthful loquacity. The women focused their attention on John, especially since the John they had heard so much about was the Baptist, and he told them he had been one of his disciples. That news transported the women. They bombarded him with questions about the rumors of his death at the hands of Herod, and he responded with thrilling details. Their eyes wide, their faces flushed, they listened.

"It had to do with his having his brother's wife," he recounted. "The Baptist started to talk about it in public, and then went to Herod himself and told him to his face: 'It is not lawful for you to have her'. Herod imprisoned him. He wanted to put him to death, but he feared the people, because everyone considered the Baptist a prophet."

Peter smiled as he heard the childlike manner in which John told his story. But the important thing was that the women were interested.

". . . . And on the day of Herod's birthday, the daughter of Herodias danced before the guests and greatly pleased Herod. He swore he would give her anything she asked of him. Her mother persuaded her to ask for the head of the Baptist. The king was greatly upset, but in view of his oath and those who had heard it, he had him beheaded in prison. And his head was brought on a dish and given to the girl, and she brought it to her mother. Then his disciples took his body and buried it. Afterward they came and told it all to Jesus."

As he concluded this speech he stared around at the women.

"You say that Jesus is the one whose coming he announced?" one of them asked.

"Yes, I witnessed it," he exclaimed with pride. "I was there when he Baptist said of him, 'Behold the lamb of God, who takes away the sins of the world'. I heard him tell the Pharisees when they came to him, that he was announcing the coming of one greater than himself—the latchet of whose sandal he is not worthy to loose."

That evening, when the men returned to their homes, John

had to repeat almost word for word everything he had related to the women. Nor did the women seem to mind.

The two disciples remained among these people several days, assisting them in their work but, primarily, speaking. Their listeners enjoyed most the stories of what they had seen with their own eyes, such as the time Jesus rescued an adulteress from stoning, or cured a Roman centurion's servant. They liked the parables, too, especially the ones about the Samaritan who tended the wounded Jew, and the ungrateful people invited to a wedding. The two disciples were received hospitably everywhere in the village. They ate and worked and slept in a variety of homes, telling and retelling their stories, preparing the way for Jesus.

Peter and John were among the first to return to Jesus. They watched the other disciples come back as thoroughly delighted and contented as themselves. When Jesus was out of earshot they boasted about their successes and traded experiences and information for future missions, confident that this was only the first of many. In almost every instance, the disciples brought back news of similar reactions: nearly everyone was asking about John the Baptist. His fame was established all over Palestine. His name aroused great and joyous expectation. The disciples had all discovered that John the Baptist was their best passage to discussing Jesus himself.

Peter was no longer sorry he had decided on his "apostleship", as they began to call it among themselves. The discovery that he could speak publicly—and not just speak, but speak convincingly, grab and hold the attention of his listeners—was a turning point in his life, even though he had to admit that he lifted words, phrases and stories from Jesus' sermons and private conversations. But he used them successfully.

Their absence had only further exhausted the master, however. They had not been there to halt or at least slow the march of people who came to him seeking every imaginable favor and cure. He was wearing himself out and he knew it. Sometimes he tried to catch his breath, and that was when he would ask Peter to help him slip away.

Peter planned those escapes with relish, either into the hills or to the other side of the lake, depending on where they were. He had not always managed them as smoothly as he did now. One of their first escapes very nearly ended in tragedy. He blushed with shame to think that it had happened on his lake, on Gennesaret.

It was one of those days of sweltering heat and tumultuous crowds. Jesus was exhausted. He could barely make himself heard, let alone answer the crowd's questions. He came up to Peter and said, "Let's cross over to the other side". Either he was overheard or Peter gave his men the order too loudly. At any rate, the people realized their intention. They surged after their master like locusts. Peter was at first too preoccupied with Jesus to notice them coming. He helped him into the first available boat and settled him down comfortably in the prow with a coil of rope under his head. When he turned around, he found the boat crammed with people, with more following. He tried to plead with them to leave, there were other boats. He may as well have been talking to the lake, because no one budged. He had felt a strong urge to take each one by the scruff of the neck and dump him over the side, but with Jesus aboard he did not want to make trouble. He glanced up at the sky: it seemed clear and calm enough; maybe they would make it all right. He fought his way through the crush of passengers to the helm. Now, if they could only break away before more clambered over the side. His men strained to pull away from all the hands clinging to the sides, holding them back. Slowly, laboriously they picked up speed. He breathed a sigh of relief. Over in the prow, Jesus was asleep. Peter looked around now to survey their situation–and his heart sank.

The boat was an old, large, flat-bottomed scow, designed for ferrying passengers, once sound and solid, but now worm-eaten and rotting, and barely responsive to the helm. It was so packed with Jesus' admirers that its sides were almost submerged. Peter shot another nervous glance at the sky. He dared not think what could happen. Even if there were no storm, if the people were to shift to one side. . . . It was madness to go out like this! He glowered at them, oblivious to the danger. His men were already hoisting the sails and trying to fix the oars. He shuddered as he watched them. He could hardly have picked a worse wreck.

Just when his nerves were beginning to settle, and he had convinced himself they would make it without mishap, he felt a cutting wind lash at his back. The water, smooth as glass until now, was suddenly rippled by wind into small choppy waves. Low ominous clouds rushed across the sky. The hairs prickled along Peter's arms. A storm was approaching. Fast. There was still hope that it might pass to one side of them, but a quick check of the wind direction and the speed of the clouds, and he knew—it was all over. It had happened before: a storm swooping down on the lake as suddenly as a bird of prey. Turning back was out of the question. The wind was blowing from behind them; it would mean a hopeless struggle against it. He still clung to the hope that they might get across before the onslaught, but he had scarcely finished shouting to the men to pull down the sails when the wind hit them full force. They were approximately in the middle of the lake. He threw all his strength and experience now into keeping the prow of the boat to the waves, which were swelling fiendishly before their eyes. But he knew his efforts could only postpone the disaster that was sure to follow. They had no chance. The boat was already furiously filling with water.

"Bail out!" he bellowed to the frightened faces, though he knew it was useless. Just something for them to do to keep them busy, distract them. Dark gray clouds eclipsed the sky, and covered the lake. Peter could barely make out the outline of the master. Why was he lying there so motionlessly? Could he possibly still be sleeping? Perhaps he had lost consciousness; the tossing and careening had begun in earnest. The roar of the waves increased with a vengeance. The boat climbed each new towering hill of water, creaking unmercifully, only to plunge down again from the crest like so much dead weight. The people were drenched from the violence of the waves. Peter was horrified to see that at any moment the boat would gather water, and the waves simply wash Jesus overboard. He wanted to rush over, wake him, shield him, save him, but working the helm might be their last hope. He gripped the lever until it hurt and peered into the murk.

Water stung his eyes. The wind took his breath away; he had
to turn his head to gulp air. White, terrified faces all turned
to him. He could see it—the verge of panic. And when it
erupted, it would be over in a flash. A child's cry pierced the
air. Like the signal for hysteria. The panic broke loose—
wailing, crying, shoving, clawing.

"Wake the master!" he shrieked over the wind and panic.

It was as if they all suddenly remembered that Jesus was
among them. They surged forward to rouse him, find rescue
in him. Peter held his breath as he watched to see if the next
wave would swamp the heavily weighted prow and engulf
them all. But the craft appeared sturdier than he imagined.
It withstood the next wave, then another, and another. Tense
to the point of rigidity, watching assault after assault and
expecting the worst, Peter failed to notice that the gale was
suddenly subsiding. Before he knew it, the sun was shining
out from behind the disappearing clouds. He could not believe
his own eyes, he was amazed at the sudden shift in the storm.
Dazed, he watched the people hugging and laughing and
wringing out their clothes. He shook his head. The lake was
like that sometimes, contrary and capricious as a young lass.
All the fishermen said that. They were lucky this time.

He heard a boisterous commotion coming from over by the
prow. He shouted for everyone to return to their places before
they all drowned. The ferment continued.

"What's happening?" he called out impatiently.

A flushed, excited passenger explained, "We awakened the
master, calling out to him, 'Lord, save us, we perish!' And
when he awoke and saw what was happening, he extended
his arm and cried out, 'Peace! Be still!' And the tempest
subsided!"

Peter glared angrily at the man. One more, he thought to
himself. They would all have murdered him out of love.
Exasperated, he turned back to the helm. He could not wait
to get to the other side and rid himself and the master of this
riffraff. Next time he would throw them overboard.

But the incident disturbed him for another reason. If Jesus
could sleep through a storm like that, if they actually had to
rouse him, then he was far more exhausted than he had

imagined. How much longer could he go on like that? What if he became seriously ill or, God forbid, died? What would become of them all? What would become of him? Where would he go? He could never show his face in his family if something happened to Jesus. And what about the priests—would they forget his association with Jesus? He felt secure around the master. The thought of being without him was terrifying. He resolved all the more to spare and safeguard him.

Now whenever he thought Jesus needed protection, he took to ordering the disciples to form a cordon around him. Sometimes Jesus objected to his Draconian methods. Like the time he overheard some women pleading with the disciples to let them through so he could at least lay his hand on their children. They would not ask for anything, they promised; he did not have to say anything, just please let Jesus place his hand on them. When, following Peter's adamant orders, they refused to let the children near Jesus, the master protested: "Leave them alone and do not forbid them to come to me; for of such is the Kingdom of Heaven".

But what disturbed Peter most were the secret night visits of strange people, people unknown to him. Jesus did not invite him to join these private meetings. Well, if the master did not invite him, then it was not his concern. He kept his distance. Until the night Jesus' relatives arrived. They made it abundantly clear that they did not want any of the disciples to be present. Somehow Peter just did not like them. He was curious as to why they had come and why they had made such a point of not being overheard. He crept up as close as he dared and watched, concealed. He saw them close around Jesus in a ring. Only fragments of their conversation reached him—they were speaking in undertones, obviously afraid someone might be listening. He heard one of them say: "Leave here and go to Judea, that your disciples there may also see the works that you do."

That was surprising—had his relatives finally begun to believe in him? But something about their tone of voice bothered him. It was too sweet. And too dangerous: urging him to go to Judea, when they must have known that his principal enemies were there, and the greatest threat to his life. Jesus appeared to be resisting their pressure. Peter heard a voice raised impatiently: "No one does anything in secret when he wishes to be known publicly. If you do these things, show yourself to the world."

There was a long silence. Finally he heard Jesus' voice: "My time has not yet come. But your time is always at hand. You go up to the festival."

So, Peter thought excitedly, Jesus saw through their motives. He was right, he disliked their sugary sweetness from the start.

He heard Jesus go on in a hard voice: "The world cannot hate you, but it hates me, because I bear witness concerning it, that its works are evil. I will not go up to this feast because my time is not yet fulfilled."

They must have realized that it was pointless to argue with him. They turned and left in a huff. Peter barely jumped out of the way in time, they nearly stumbled over him.

That episode confirmed his view of their perilous situation: under no circumstances could they go to Jerusalem and allow themselves to be trapped. But it was also alarming in another respect: did it mean the rats were abandoning the sinking ship? Jesus family was turning its back on him, even acting to his detriment. Did it mean his predicament—their predicament—was critical?

So Peter took to eavesdropping. Gradually he learned to distinguish the friends from the enemies. He discovered that, among Jesus' friends, scribes and Pharisees could very often be found; and that the reverse was also true—that among his disciples, very often predators could be found. It was not just curiosity that prompted him to eavesdrop; he felt he had not only a right but a duty to be well informed on what was happening around them. Yet, although he justified his actions as personal responsibility for Jesus' safety, in his heart the real reason was different: fear for himself. True for Jesus too, but Jesus could manage for himself. But what about him? He did not wish to die.

The more he listened furtively to reports brought to the master by a strange assortment of emissaries, the more his fears burgeoned. Their position looked grim. To his utter amazement, however, Jesus appeared not to even want to know about it. He made nothing of it, dismissed it nonchalantly. Slowly Peter pieced together a realistic picture of their situation. The temple was increasingly alarmed by and hostile to the teacher. The preists were reckoning on his coming back to Jerusalem, but there were two groups among them: those who were eager for his arrival so that they could settle accounts with him on their own territory and those who were afraid that, on entering Jerusalem, Jesus would be in an ideal position to seize power. These last wanted to stop him from entering the city at all costs and, somehow, dispose of him in the provinces. This solution gained the approval of the Highest Council, although Peter could not ascertain how they intended to carry out their plan. As if to confirm his analysis, ominous events began to take place.

First he got wind of rumors blowing through the countryside—Jesus of Nazareth was "queer in the head." He paid them no mind: people talked; eventually they would stop talking. But the exact opposite occurred: the slanderous rumors did not diminish, they intensified. Until they took on the worst possible image: Jesus of Nazareth possessed by a devil. And then Peter understood that it was not simply people's idle talk, but an organized campaign by the Pharisees to disseminate such reports in the synagogues throughout Galilee. He gained an inkling one evening of how things might end for them.

Word was brought to them, hurriedly, that some Pharisees had arrived from Jerusalem and were preaching in the synagogue and saying that Jesus of Nazareth was possessed, and that he cast out devils by the power of Beelzebub, prince of hell. In a twinkling the town became divided into two camps, the adherents of Jesus and his antagonists. His closest followers, outraged, were ready to spill blood in his defense. Jesus recognized the danger and, in order to prevent trouble, disappeared from view into somebody's house. Then, when passions had cooled and the tension lessened, he summoned Peter, and in the most ordinary way in the world, as if he were instructing him merely to go out and get some bread, told him to take someone with him and go to the synagogue to invite the scribes from Jerusalem over to the house.

Peter flinched—it was a seething cauldron over there. Jesus must have noticed, because he added that he would gladly go himself, but for one thing, they would not allow him into the synagogue, and for another, his appearance would precipitate new disturbances. Peter tried to wriggle out of going—it would be a waste of time to invite them, because they would refuse the invitation anyway, so why bother? But there were was no getting out of it. He took two other disciples and went. The instant they stepped into the synagogue, they were greeted by uproar. Peter kept his composure, although he was quivering inside. Very coolly he delivered Jesus' proposal. Just as he said, they rejected it disdainfully. But when he retorted that they were just plain afraid to meet him, pride got the better of one of the scribes and he announced that he would go.

And so he returned with a whole cluster of indignant scribes to the house where Jesus was waiting for them. Peter had to wonder at their sudden courage. But it very quickly became apparent why they had agreed—they had come with the clear intention of denouncing Jesus and inciting his followers to defiance and rebellion against him. From start to finish they addressed, not Jesus, but his hearers, trying to persuade them that he cast out demons with the help of Beelzebub.

Jesus heard them out in silence, then began to speak in his turn—the way he usually did, slowly, patiently reasoning with them: "Now how can Satan cast out Satan? Every kingdom divided against itself shall not stand. So if Satan is also divided against himself, how shall his kingdom stand? How can anyone enter into the house of the strong and rifle his goods, unless he first binds the strong? Then he can rifle his house."

Hearing this, his listeners began to applaud and laugh and point their fingers at the Jerusalem scholars who, seeing their humiliating defeat before these simple people, stole away from the room. the atmosphere had been loosened, the tension relieved, and the people began to disperse.

The only problem was, situations of this nature seemed to

crop up with increasing frequency. But with certain differences. The provincial Pharisees and Scribes were by no means anxious to meet with Jesus and discuss things with him. They knew they were no match for his rhetorical mastery. No, they concentrated their energy on destroying him before he arrived in their districts. And their efforts often brought results. Like the time at Gerasa, when Jesus cast evil spirits out of a possessed man. A delegation of townspeople came and asked him to depart and stay out of the town. The way they stared at him—as if they were seeing, not a prophet, but the prince of hell himself. Yes, the Pharisees knew their sheep well and how to get to them. They maligned Jesus and showered abuse after abuse upon him; they derided his greatest signs and miracles, and continued using that ugliest of weapons: he is possessed!

It may have been all the insult and vilification, plus the sad knowledge that even his relatives had cut themselves off and were hostile to him, that made Jesus visibly despondent and perhaps seek support in them, his closest companions. They were outside Caesarea Philippi when he suddenly shot them a question he had never posed before: "Whom do men say that I am?"

It was not at all like him. Peter felt sick at heart. He did not wish to hurt Jesus' feelings and repeat the scurrilous rumours the Pharisees were spreading. One or two of the disciples spoke up first, sparing him the pain of relating to what some of the people were saying. But neither did they tell everything—no one mentioned about his being demented and possessed by demons. Jesus listened in silence.

". . . . Some say John the Baptist, and some Elijah, and still others Jeremiah, or one of the prophets."

Peter watched Jesus nervously. The disciples exhausted their catalogue of celebrity.

"And who do you say that I am?"

It dropped like a stone. Silence. No one answered. Peter thought frantically, in another second he will look me in the eye. He quickly dropped his gaze to the ground and held it there. It was too quiet, the suspense was too great. He looked up—Jesus' eyes were on his. He felt as if Jesus were directing the question now to him personally: And what do you, Simon, think of me? He was cornered, he alone had to answer. He represented the whole group; the master had made him its leader. His mind raced to find the right words, the words that would best convey what he felt—how he believed in him, how he trusted in him.

They came in a flash—the titles he used so often to describe himself. But which one: Son of Man, Son of God, Messiah, Son of David? Which was most fit, most accurate? The answer burst from him in a rush: "You are Christ, the Son of the living God!"

Relief spread over him like a draught of cool water. He blinked around at his companions, seeking their approbation. Then he heard Jesus' words addressed to him.

"Blessed are you, Simon Bar-Jona, because flesh and blood has not revealed it to you, but my Father who is in heaven. And I say to you: that you are Peter, and upon this rock I will build my Church, and the gates of hell shall not prevail against it. And I will give to you the keys of the Kingdom of Heaven. And whatsoever you shall bind on earth, it shall be bound also in heaven; and whatsoever you shall loose on earth, it shall be loosed also in heaven."

Though he was baffled by Jesus' response to his outburst, he did not ask for an explanation. He did not want to know. He was afraid of those prophetic words.

Many times after that incident, Peter mulled over why he had given the answer he had: "You are Christ, the Son of the living God." He could not quite decide why he had blurted that out in particular. Because, frankly, he really didn't know what to think of Jesus—though he walked at his side day after day, though he watched everything he did, heard everything he said, though he knew him as few men did. He knew Jesus was simple, open, brotherly, just. Yet in some of the things he did and said, he revealed a depth so great that it dazzled the mind. Who was Jesus really? He kept coming up with the same answer: he must be a prophet. That seemed the best way to define him. He acted just like the prophets of old, undoing what men had done to Revelation: weeding, cutting, pruning, grubbing up the parasites—like a good gardener. Like the Prophets, he echoed back to what God had revealed to Abraham and Moses: to the greatest command-ment of love of God and neighbor. Tirelessly, incessantly, he explained to the prople that the Law and the Prophets cen-tered around that, and not around holocausts and sacrifices.

There came a day when Peter's definition of Jesus-as-Prophet suddenly disintegrated. They were in Capernaum in late autumn, on their way to Jerusalem for the first time. It was unusually cold. A light drizzle was falling. Jesus had been invited to stay at someone's house on the way. His fame had already spread far and wide. Some scribes arrived at the house to debate with him. News of Jesus' arrival flashed like lightning around the town, and from every quarter people squeezed in such numbers into the house that there was scarcely room to breathe. When the din and confusion of pushing, arguing, and occupying of places finally quieted down, Jesus commenced speaking. He had no sooner begun than a new commotion broke out, as of people trying to push their way into the room against the angry protests of the occupiers defending their hard-won places. With an ear finely tuned to signs of danger, Peter strained to follow the move-ments of the intruders. First he thought he heard a ladder being placed against a wall; a few moments later, the unmis-takable sounds of people climbing up the ladder to the roof— heavily, as if under strain, as if carrying something. He felt a flutter of apprehension in the pit of his stomach. Could someone be planning an attempt on Jesus' life? What could be easier than to drop a beam or rock on him from the roof? He scanned the room anxiously to calculate the possibility of coming to his aid. There was very little. If panic broke out, the people would trample themselves to death trying to get through the narrow door. He tried to reason logically: an assassination attempt made no sense; there were Scribes sit-ting right next to Jesus. But what if the assassins were pre-pared to sacrifice even their lives, if only to kill Jesus? They could be a third party, which did not scruple about the lives of a few Scribes.

They were on the roof now. Their footsteps resounded

loudly in the room below. Loosened plaster fell from the ceiling. Everyone craned their necks warily. Peter was terrified to see the tiles begin to move. He sprang to his feet and began to force his way through the crowded room toward Jesus. A face suddenly poked through the widening hole in the roof. A voice called down: "We are letting down a man with the palsy. Master, heal him."

The whole room seemed to exhale in relief. Peter gave a nervous laugh, then everyone broke into light laughter. The operation was begun to lower a man in a bed. They came dangerously close to spilling him off his pallet on to the heads of the crowd. Somehow room was made in the squeeze, and the invalid found himself lying at Jesus' feet. The levity subsided. Everyone watched the gaunt face lined with suffering, the eyes full of supplication directed toward Jesus. From the opening in the roof, now crammed with faces, came a chorus of entreaties to the master to heal the man.

Jesus studied the sick man closely. An expectant hush fell over the room. Suddenly he said to him, "Son, your sins are forgiven you".

Everyone froze. Instinctively Peter glanced at the scribes. They were stiff with outrage. He felt his own dismay creep over him—what on earth was he saying? How could he say that? "Your sins are forgiven you." Who forgave him his sins? Could Jesus be referring to himself? Only God himself could forgive sins.

In the appalled silence, the master's words rang like a bell: "What is it you think in your hearts?" He was facing the scribes. "Which is easier to say to the sick of palsy: Your sins are forgiven you, or, Arise, take up your bed, and walk?"

So, Peter was not the only one who thought that in his heart. They all did.

Jesus went on. "But that you may know that the Son of Man has power on earth to forgive sins—" Here he turned to the paralytic—"I say to you, Arise, take up your bed, and go to your home."

Before their very eyes, the man who had been condemned to a life in a litter simply got up, gathered up his bedding and stretcher, and made his way to the door. It took a dumbstruck moment or two, and then the pandemonium erupted. People weeping, laughing, cheering for joy. Peter thought the roof would cave in. Yet, as he pondered the incident, he was less struck by the healing, which had sent the onlookers into paroxysms of joy—he had seen greater miracles—than by the words Jesus had used to the sick man: "Your sins are forgiven you".

Who was this teacher from Nazareth whose company he kept now for so long? A blasphemer? Could a blasphemer perform such miracles? Who was he?

It was not the first time Peter had failed to understand the master. Sometimes he felt he did not understand him at all. Especially in the beginning. There had been times when he wanted to dump the whole idea and return home; when he had had all he could take of lamenting, wailing, begging, crying; of open, ulcerated sores, festering wounds, scabs, pus, and blood; when he could no longer stand the company of bloated bodies, the blind, the lame, the palsied, the deaf, and above all else, the lepers—why, Jesus even touched them; when he thought he would lose his mind from the sight and stench. They flocked from every conceivable place and region—as if they were all the sick and all the lame of all the world. He never dreamed there could be so many in Palestine. And Jesus went about healing them: bending over them, and putting his hands on their sores, and on their maimed, turgid limbs. Why, they were unclean! The very fact of contact with them made Jesus unclean! But he would smile and say, "The girl is not dead, only sleeping", and proceed to pick up a corpse from the sheet.

Not that Peter was scandalized by the sick themselves; it was Jesus' curing them that outraged his moral sense. Until now, everything had been clear to him: misfortune and disease were a punishment from God, and one had to suffer it patiently. Man had only himself to blame, he had to pay for his deeds. So, then, let the leper live in isolation, driving off the unwary with a warning rattle of chains, and pray that God shorten his misery. But Jesus went around curing them. He was disrupting God's order.

Until Jesus started healing those unhappy wretches, Peter

had been secure in the knowledge that the man of wealth, of status, of good fortune was so because God had blessed him. Whoever was poor and miserable was so because God was punishing him for sins. Maybe not always for his own sins, maybe sometimes for the sins of his parents, or grandparents, or relatives, or ancestors. Peter also knew that God did not take care of someone for nothing: one had to offer sacrifices, holocausts, give tithes and first fruits; one had to keep the commandments of the stone tablets of Sinai. He had experienced it on his own life when he was a fisherman. God had blessed him—he had prospered. But then he never dodged paying his taxes, or shirked offering sacrifices. The same applied to his health. He was healthy because he lived an honest life, he and his father both.

He watched Jesus' healings with distaste. If he had only done it once in a while, for friends, or in a few extraordinary cases; but some of his acts were little short of provocation. He acted as if he wanted to heal all the sick, help all the poor, as if he were bent on bothering God in his just order. It was open opposition to God's will. Frankly, in the depths of his heart, he was not all that surprised by what the priests and Pharisees were saying about him. If an evil spirit lives in a man, it was man's own fault!

So he waited for an explanation. He took an opportunity of asking Jesus about it when a blind man was brought to him. He asked him then, "Lord, is he to blame for this infirmity, or his parents?"

"Neither he nor his parents are to blame," Jesus answered.

Peter did not understand. He asked again, "If he is not to blame, then why is he punished?"

"That the glory of God may be shown."

And then he cured him.

He thought that someday Jesus would explain it to him, but he never returned to the question.

But if Peter managed to put up with the cures of the sick, he could scarcely endure what went on with sinners. Their presence was nothing short of personal indignity. He had his own faults and shortcomings, but at least he was a decent, honest man. Their company made him physically ill, how-

ever. He simply could not come to terms with having to
associate with them—even eat with them. At mealtimes he
always tried to find a place away from them. He was ashamed
of their company before others, for himself and for Jesus. It
stung him to hear the Pharisees jeer: "Your master eats with
sinners and publicans—glutton, drinker of wine!" What could
he say, when at heart he had to admit they were right? If
someone wanted to be a sinner, fine, let him be a sinner, it
was his business. But why did he want to go poking his nose
around honest folk? Peter's resentment soon came to boiling
point.

They were passing through Jericho one day, surrounded
by a crowd of disciples and spectators. They stopped abruptly
under a tree. Peter saw Jesus peer up into the branches and
call out to someone tangled in them:: "Zacheus, make haste
and come down. Today I must stay in your house."

Peter could not imagine which Zacheus he was talking to.
He never dreamed it could be that notorious chief of the
thieving publicans, who flayed the skins off the poor and
caused so much misery to people. He stood alongside Jesus,
staring curiously up into the branches. Then he saw him—
the selfsame dwarf, slithering down from the tree. He was
aghast, he thought he would split open with fury. That's
right, that's right, it was not enough for Jesus to receive
sinners, converse with them, eat with them; now he was
seeking them out, inviting himself into their homes. He could
not understand Jesus. Nor was he taking kindly to Zacheus.
He watched the dwarf's beaming face as he escorted them to
his house—he would have gladly twisted his thick neck. But
what drove him to frenzy was Zacheus' pronouncement at
the end of a lavish feast—a feast paid for by ordinary people's
blood, sweat, and money: "Lord, half of my goods I will give
to the poor, and if I have wronged any man of anything, I
will restore it to him fourfold."

"I would just love to see him," Peter muttered to himself,
turn over half his possessions." And even if he did pass a few
trinkets to the poor, he had acquired it by stealing in the first
place anyway.

But perhaps the biggest grievance Peter had against the

master was Matthew. How could he? Why, the man was a publican! And not only that, a veteran tax collector, too! Or if he had only come to Jesus, begging to be received. But the master while Matthew was sitting there in the custom house, simply walked up to him and said, "Follow me". If it had only ended with that, with Matthew just following Jesus—but so many sinners followed. Then the master chose him for their Twelve! Matthew the publican, the closest companion and most faithful friend of Jesus—did that not sound fine! Even if the tax collector was holy Jesus should not have done it. What would people say? Not his friends—they managed to swallow much worse than that—but his enemies, who were waiting for him to stumble. After all, it was not just a question of Jesus, any more; he was making prey of them all. And although so much time had elapsed since that day in the custom house, Peter still could not come round to liking Matthew. He still suspected him of some kind of ulterior, self-seeking motives.

He felt much the same about Mary Magdalene, although he had to admit he could not imagine their group without her. She was indispensable among the women who followed and helped Jesus, a girl who would, he was sure, follow Jesus unto death. Yet in spite of that, to his mind she was still a sinner. He could not forget her past conduct—which was what he failed to understand about Jesus. Contempt lingered in him, and a sense of expectation—when will she finally give up this "adventure" and go back to her real way of life?

Why did Jesus conduct himself like this? It could not be just to spite the priests and Pharisees. And certainly not to spite the Lord God. Finally, unexpectedly, he came to the conclusion that Jesus believed in a different God. He saw this confirmed one day when some Pharisees accosted Jesus and reproached him for receiving and eating with sinners. As so often, he did not answer them directly but told them a parable.

"Which man of you who has a hundred sheep, if he should lose one of them, will not leave the ninety-nine in the desert and go after the one which was lost until he finds it? And when he has found it, lay it upon his shoulders, rejoicing?

And coming home, call together his friends and neighbors, saying to them: Rejoice with me, because I have found my sheep that was lost? I say to you, that even so there will be joy in heaven upon one sinner who does penance, more than upon ninety-nine who do not need penance."

And without even pausing for a reaction, Jesus went right into the story about the prodigal son.

No one had ever spoken this way before about God. Not even the prophets. A God who hurries out to meet a wastrel, who kisses him, drapes him with a coat, puts a ring on his finger, and throws a great feast of rejoicing. Though he considered himself the man closest to Jesus, he found it hard to reconcile himself to such a picture of God. The son was profligate, a squanderer. The father was wrong. The elder brother was right to get away and refuse to enter the house.

The more he thought about it, the more astounded he was that the God of Jesus was a God who does not wait for a sinner to come crushed and repentent to him, but seeks him out, hurries out to meet him; a God who does not avenge sins, neither by misfortune nor by sickness, but just the opposite—a God who is with the sick, the suffering, the hungry, the thirsty, the oppressed; a God who assures men that whoever renders help to such as these, renders that same act to himself. Peter did not understand it, but he did know one thing: if the priests and Pharisees heard that, if that reached them—and why should it not reach them when everything else did so—it would mean disaster. How long would they tolerate Jesus portraying a totally different God from the one they taught about in the temple and synagogues? A God who does not want sacrifices, a God who only wants love for one's neighbor, and especially for the poorest among them. Jesus must perish or the temple would die—and the temple would never die, that he knew.

But was Jesus right? Was God really like that? Because if he was the way Jesus said he was, then it followed logically that those who believed in him would have wholly to change their lives.

Once he asked Jesus, "Lord, if my brother offends against me, how often should I forgive him? Till seven times?"

Jesus answered him, "I do not say to you, till seven times, but till seventy times seven times."

Peter did not wish to accept it. Though he understood it. In the end, it was logical. If God was so good, then man, too must be as good.

". . . And if a man will contend with you in judgment and take away your coat, give him also your cloak. And whosoever will force you to walk one mile with him, two. . . ."

Logical, but at the same time madness surely? Who was right, Jesus or the priests?

In the meantime, the temple adopted a method of enduring Jesus: see nothing, notice nothing, take no interest; shun all contact and discussions of his opinions with him; treat him like empty air, like a dead man. There was no sign of its ever acknowledging Jesus as the Messiah. Quite the reverse: his miracles, popularity, and teachings only intensified its implacable hatred.

Peter was all too often reminded of the Pharisees' fuming epithets: "Uneducated, self-taught, a carpenter! How could he possibly comprehend what was contained in the Scriptures? How dare he put himself on an equal footing with those who spent their entire lives studying the Scriptures! Charlatan! Seducer! He preys upon the ignorance of the masses. Madman! Satan son of Beelzebub!"

It was becoming alarmingly clear to Peter that Jesus meant to climb the steep hill of Jerusalem, which seemed to rise more and more unattainably before him. The teacher was not satisfied with his success among the simple people. He wanted to convert the whole nation to the path of truth, the temple included. He sought a confrontation with the scribes, Pharisees, and priests. His vision of the Kingdom of God required a restructuring of the whole enormous institution that was the temple. If the truths Jesus proclaimed were to survive him, then the temple would have to acknowledge his teachings. But the temple refused to notice him, and maintained a contemptuous silence. After the incident in Nazareth, Jesus was not allowed access into any of the synagogues. No one would speak to him—at least, no one who was anybody. True, there were polemical exchanges with emissaries from the Sanhedrin or the temple, but these were quick, strike-and-retreat sallies under the guise of private, personal initiative or chance meetings, which the temple ostensibly did not underwrite.

It was this conspiracy of silence that drove Jesus to his greatest outbursts of indignation. Like the time he fired words at a group of Pharisees: "Serpents! Brood of vipers! How will you flee from the judgment of hell? Behold, I send you prophets, and wise men, and scribes. Some of them you will put to death and crucify, and some you will scourge in your synagogues, and persecute from city to city, until upon you will come all the just blood that has been shed upon the earth, from the blood of Abel the just, even to the blood of Zacharias, the son of Barachias, whom you killed between the temple and the altar. Amen I say to you, all these things shall come upon this generation. Jerusalem, Jerusalem, you that kill the prophets and stone those who are sent to you, how often would I have gathered together your children, as the hen gathers her chickens under her wings, but you would not? Behold, your house shall be left to you desolate."

After those awful threats fell, Peter felt his terror before the Sanhedrin's revenge tightening like a noose around his neck. It was madness! He wanted to live! They would never forgive Jesus those words; they would never forgive him. The Sanhedrin would never yield, never admit Jesus was right, in spite of any and all arguments, in spite of any and all of the miraculous things he did to support his position.

At the same time, Peter could only stand by helplessly in the face of Jesus' pertinacity. The master was arranging an official entry with his disciples into the city: go there, preach there, force the temple to a confrontation there, corner its representatives into taking a stand before him there. That was the decision Peter feared most. Among the priests, there were those who were just waiting for his arrival in order to settle old scores there in the capital. Hence the dire warnings from Jesus' friends: if he goes, he will be tried and killed. But Jesus appeared oblivious to the warnings and determined to take the risk of death.

The precariousness of their situation kept Peter awake at nights. He wanted to stay in Galilee where they were safe, but he lacked the courage to tell it to Jesus directly. So he tried another means. Once, while they were resting beside the road, he started to clown—ostensibly for the benefit of his companions, but really to communicate his thoughts to Jesus. He began to mimic the Galilean villagers and their dialects, which he knew as few men did.

"Why should we push on to Jerusalem? Because the capital is there? Whose capital? The Judeans', and no one else's. Why, the rest of the descendants of the chosen nation lives in Galilee and Samaria. Jesus can remain with his disciples in Galilee. That would last them for the rest of their lives. Why go to Jerusalem? Because the temple is there? So what if it is? What do they need it for? To offer sacrifices? They can offer them before every tent or before every house, or, if they're so choosy, they can offer them before a synagogue, or in the fields. The way their fathers did before them. Because the Judeans dreamed up the idea of offering sacrifices in Jerusalem? They dreamed it up for business. Just look at all the money they make on lambs and vegetables, and in offerings for killing sheep. And what does it all amount to?"

He shot a glance at Jesus. The master made no sign of disapproval, so he went on. "Why, you yourself teach that the sacrifice God wants is love, and that the offerings of lambs and calves are in themselves empty without love behind them. If you want, we'll build you a temple right here. It does not have to be as big as the one in Jerusalem. It can be quite small, and everyone in Galilee can offer his sacrifices right here. He won't have to travel so far as to Jerusalem. And there won't be any more quarrels with the Samaritans, who always get ruffled when the Galileans pass through their country. And why shouldn't they get angry when strange people tramp through their pasture lands, scare their herds, trample their grass. Sometimes maybe a chicken or lamb goes missing, or even a calf or two. Sure, if they are frightened, they get lost, sometimes in a crevice, sometimes over a precipice. And the Samaritans say the Galileans steal them. What do we need all these troubles and years of despite for?

Then the Galileans curse the Samaritans because they don't go to the temple. Well, perhaps they're not so stupid. They set up their own altar on the hill of Gerizim and offer their sacrifices there. Their money stays with them, in their own land. Maybe we can find a hill like that, too. We have so many beautiful hills in Galilee, more beautiful even than Gerizim. We could set up a sacrificial altar there. It would be closer, and our money would stay at home. We wouldn't have to pass through the land of the Samaritans. And what if the Judeans do get angry? Let them. Maybe they'll lose some of the fat they've put on with our money."

He looked pleadingly at Jesus. "Do we have to go to Jerusalem?"

Jesus did not answer.

Eventually Peter dropped the subject. Evidently Jesus considered his entry into Jerusalem inevitable. But Peter could not conceal the fact that he was afraid of Jerusalem. He was born a fisherman, a man of the sea and of the village. The city was always something alien and artificial to him, somehow dark, threatening, sinful. He always felt hemmed in by the city, and now there was real danger. At least, as he later learned, Jesus had decided to wait until the festival days. At least then there would be more people from the provinces, their people: the ones who listened to him on the shores of Lake Gennesaret, in Capernaum, in Caesarea; the ones whom he had healed and cleansed of devils and diseases.

Gradually Peter came around even to liking the idea of the Jerusalem trip—just so long as it was only for the duration of the festival days when they would be safe. He could drop in on friends and relatives, find out what was happening, tell them about his own successes, let them envy his adventurous life at the side of the great master from Nazareth. Until, that is, he noticed that Jesus suddenly appeared to lose heart for the trip. For some reason, he had started to take the threats from Jerusalem seriously; and one day he said to them outright, "The Son of Man will be betrayed to the chief priests and to the scribes. And they will condemn him to death and will deliver him to the Gentiles to be mocked, scourged, and crucified."

Peter was so taken aback, he did not know what to say. He stole a suspicious glance at Jesus. Where did he get an idea like that? A lot of things might be said against him, but one thing was certain: he was the elect of God. Regardless of what they called him or made him out to be, it was certain that God was with him. And now he was suddenly talking about death on a cross. You did not need to be a priest or scribe to know what that meant. Not a Jew in Palestine was unaware. It was clearly spelled out in Deuteronomy: He who hangs on a tree is accursed of God. How could Jesus even suggest such an abominable thing about himself? Did he want his followers to turn tail and abandon him? Anyway, the thousands of his followers would never permit a thing like that to happen. As long as they got out in time, moved with the tide of pilgrims returning to Galilee, they would be all right.

Peter counted on that gloomy mood leaving Jesus. Instead, the closer the holy days came, the more Jesus talked about how his stay in Jerusalem would end in arrest, trial, sentence, crucifixion. Peter couldn't stand to listen any more. It made no sense. If Jesus was so convinced that God would condemn him to death on a cross, then what were all his teachings worth? Finally, when Jesus alluded one more time to his impending death, Peter blurted out, "Lord, this will not come to you—"

He stopped short at the sight of the anger rising in Jesus' face. Then he heard something he never dreamed Jesus could say to him.

"Depart from me, Satan! You are a scandal to me, because you savor, not the things that are of God, but the things that are of men."

The words stunned—terrified—him. No one had ever called him Satan before. He never thought Jesus capable of such hard words. The stinging hurt welled up inside him. How could the master say such a thing to him? He didn't deserve it. He began to avoid Jesus, to hide, seclude himself behind the other disciples, and observe him only from a distance.

The incident kept him at arm's length from the master longer than he imagined. Jesus concentrated himself totally on realizing the plans for his stay in Jerusalem during the Passover. From what he could gather, Jesus wanted to get to Jerusalem not only well before the Passover, but for some prearranged appointments as well but Peter could only guess at this, because Jesus did not tell him about his plans. Nor did he assign him any important tasks. He was clearly excluding him from everything relating to the Jerusalem trip. So Peter, though he ardently desired to be helpful to Jesus, retired into the background. He waited for instructions from him, but Jesus passed him by.

Then he heard that Jesus was hurrying, not to Jerusalem, but to Lazarus, who had been taken ill. Though the master did not reach there in time to heal him, because they arrived three days after the funeral, he raised him to life from the tomb. It made less of an impression on Peter than it did on the others; he was too preoccupied to think about miracles. If it made him glad in any way, it was only in the sense that Jesus had given new and forceful proof of his miraculous powers. They did not leave for Jerusalem right away. Apparently Jesus felt that the city, which was still fairly empty of pilgrims, did not yet guarantee him safety. Together with his disciples he withdrew to a quiet area, as if he wanted to prepare himself for the holy days. He prayed a great deal. Then they returned to Bethany for a feast given by Lazarus in Jesus' honor. Again they waited out the next few days in solitude. Those were heavy, oppressive days, full of strained uncertainty for all the disciples. Peter thought he would have much preferred it if something—even something bad—were to happen, but finally Jesus decided they would set out for Jerusalem.

When they stopped before Bethphage to rest, Jesus called Peter over to him for the first time in a long while and, as if nothing had transpired between them, said, "Take someone with you and go into the village before you. On entering it, you will find a foal of an ass tied, on which no man has ever sat. Untie him and bring him here. And if anyone should ask you what you are doing, say that the Lord has need of him and he will immediately send him back."

Peter signaled to Andrew, and the two headed down the

road to the village. On reaching it, they searched around anxiously for the animal. There was no foal. They came to a crossroads. Peter was considering which direction to take when he spied a foal tied before the gate of someone's enclosure.

"It must be that one," he pointed. He noticed a group of men on a small square observing them. "Well, should we untie him?"

Andrew nodded. They approached the animal slowly.

"Untie him," Peter instructed his brother. He glanced cautiously around at the men watching them. Several walked unhurriedly toward them.

"Watch out," he whispered to Andrew.

Andrew stopped unknotting the rope and turned to face the men.

"Why are you untying the colt?" one of them asked quietly.

Peter repeated Jesus' words: "The Lord has need of it and will immediately send it back."

The men glanced at each other knowingly and turned the animal over to the disciples, then themselves headed in the direction of the city.

Then it began. The massing crowds, swelling with every step of the way. Jubilantly singing and cheering. Fervently enthusiastic. Spreading their garments before Jesus mounted on the foal. Waving palm branches over their heads. Confidently advancing on the city. As he watched, Peter could not help thinking how like the Messiah prophesied in the Scriptures Jesus looked.

The exuberant procession reached the temple steps. The instant they entered the interior, Peter saw how the sight of the booths and stalls of moneychangers and merchants uproariously disputing, bargaining, and laughing stopped the master in his tracks. Outrage rose hotly to his face. Within seconds he had a lash of ropes in his hand, and with a wide and angry sweep, beat it against the first table, and the second, and the third, pushing and overturning and scattering them every which way. The temple roared with the squeals of birds, the clatter of spilling coins, the curses of furious vendors. Finally Jesus halted. He stood breathing hard, glaring at the scurrying merchants who gestured threateningly at him. But no one dared to touch him.

Jesus' voice thundered: "Is it not written: My house shall be called a house of prayer to all nations? But you have made it a den of thieves!"

At first Peter thought Jesus was upset by the fact of business being conducted in a place consecrated to God. He thought he just wanted the whole noisy bazaar to move beyond the temple grounds. But it was more than that. His flesh crept to hear the master speak—his words and actions were nothing short of an assassination attempt against the temple. An attempt contained in the words of the prophet Hosea, so long repeated by Jesus: I want mercy, not sacrifices. In the past they were only words; now Jesus was putting them into action. He threw out the moneychangers and the vendors selling bulls and doves, because God did not require sacrifices of animals, or food, or money; he required men to turn away from their hatred and evil. Determinedly, dangerously, Jesus was restoring the temple to its true essence.

They spent the entire day in the temple with Jesus and forced all the vendors to clear out with their benches and stalls. Over and over, Jesus repeated the same thing: "My house is a house of prayer, says the Lord". He was the master of that house that day.

In the evening they departed for Bethany to spend the night with Lazarus. Peter lay down to sleep full of the blackest thoughts. He was not deceived by their triumphant march on Jerusalem. No matter how objectively he looked at it, Jesus' actions that day were a direct provocation—as if he were determined to force the temple to respond, to reckon with him and his popularity among the masses, to engage finally in open dialogue with him. He was answered with a stony silence. The priests did not react. Or if they or a few Pharisees did, it was only "coincidentally", "in passing", on their own initiative. All of Jesus' most pointed statements, pronouncements, and formulations struck at a vacuum—there was no opponent. The adversary did not trouble about truth; the adversary would not take up the challenge and engage in dialogue with Jesus but, rather, treated him as unworthy of such respect. All that day they had waited for the priests to come and open a discussion with him. No one appeared. The priests were avoiding all contact with the teacher.

Peter could only guess at how Jesus' actions must have kindled the Sanhedrin to white-hot fury. Sooner or later the priests' hatred and thirst for revenge would find an outlet. They would use every possible means to kill him, and he did not know how to help him.

At least Jesus did not appear to be blindly courting death. He wanted to live, or at least he wanted to live as long as he possibly could. During the day he was surrounded constantly by protective crowds. In addition, he always kept at least some of his disciples around him. He was never alone. And he was careful to choose safe places to spend each night. He preferred best the house of Lazarus, Mary, and Martha.

The events of the next few days developed with dizzying speed. They were back at the temple again, but this time without trouble. The merchants and moneychangers had not dared to take up their stalls again. On the other hand, an incredible thing happened: priests, Pharisees, and Sadducees—all rabid opponents of each other were uniting in a concerted attack against their common enemy: Jesus.

They came singly and in groups. At their approach, a hush fell over the throng, always greedy for the sensational and now sensing a struggle between Jesus and his antagonists.

The first question thrust at him was: "By what authority do you do these things? And who has given you this authority that you should do them?"

Peter could see Jesus warm to the question.

"I will also ask you one thing, which if you will tell me, I will also tell you by what authority I do these things. The baptism of John, was it from heaven or from men? Answer me."

Peter could not quite work out what the question was supposed to lead to. But the Pharisees seemed startled by it. They retreated into a tight little cluster. Curious, Peter sidled over to listen in on their furious whispering.

". . . . If we say, from heaven, he will reproach us, saying, 'Why, then, did you not believe him, for he pointed to me as the Messiah?' "

"And we cannot blunder and say, from men. What would the people say—those who consider John one of the greatest prophets?"

They returned to the teacher, "We do not know," they said. They retreated. There was no confrontation.

Suddenly Peter spotted some Pharisees in the company of a few Herodians, casually strolling by, but not looking. No doubt about it, here comes the next attack. The multitude, also reading them correctly, pressed tightly forward, heads craning to listen.

The question came loudly, unmistakably, so that everyone would hear: "Master, we know that you speak true and care not for any man, and that you do not regard the person of men, but teach the way of God in truth. It is lawful for us to give tribute to Caesar, or should we not give it?"

An ominous silence gripped the listeners. Everyone knew that here was a crucial contest involving the life and death of the teacher from Nazareth. The question was a brazen affront. Peter trembled in anger. He wanted to protest aloud—it was indecent to ask about such painful, yet obvious, things, especially in the presence of traitors like the Herodians. It was shameful to discuss the Jewish nation's greatest humiliation and disgrace—that it must pay tribute to its enemy, to its occupier. How could any orthodox Jew answer such a question, except to say "no". Yet, if such a man were to answer "no", he could expect to be imprisoned immediately as a rebel. But could Jesus answer in the affirmative? No, He could not, because he was an orthodox Jew, and if he did, then from that moment on, he could expect even his most loyal adherents to abandon him.

Jesus turned to them. He said, "Why do you tempt me? "Bring me a denarius to look at."

The request seemed to throw them into confusion and suspicious. Why did he want to look at a denarius? Was it possible he had never seen one? Still, they brought one to him.

"Whose is this image and inscription?" he asked them.

Warily, already sensing a trap, they answered, "Caesar's."

With devastating logic he said to them, "Render, therefore, to Caesar the things that are Caesar's, and to God the things that are God's."

The words brightened before Peter like a clearing sky. He was not expecting such ease and freshness on Jesus' part, considering how fatigued he appeared to be by the pressing throngs and the bouts with the Pharisees. One more excellent answer: simple, yet containing so much. Yes, of course, that was the whole truth, spoken undisguisedly. It was the whole tragedy of their nation. Because, who had brought the Romans into the land, if not the Israelites themselves? Yes, and now they had to pay for it. The bitter truth, but nevertheless, the truth.

But these questions were not relevant to the essential issues. They were deliberately pointless, meaningless. Jesus' opponents were obviously trying to occupy him with trivia, nonsense, distract his and the crowd's attention, divert them from the real issues. They were playing for time—though to what end and for how long, Peter could not guess. Once again, it was being made alarmingly clear that this was the method devised by the priests and Pharisees: ostensibly "chance" meetings to form a net in which to entangle Jesus, tire him out, render him harmless. The next ones were already closing in. Peter looked anxiously at Jesus. How long could he hold up against it? He thought of Galilee and how he would just be waiting for the master to say to him, "Simon, let's cross over to the other side". But this was the odious, seething city. How he longed for the green hills of Galilee. If only they could withstand the next three days and return there safely.

The next interlocutor was a Scribe. Peter had noticed him earlier; he was struck by the man's serious and genuinely attentive demeanor. Now he edged over to Jesus and questioned him.

"Master, which is the greatest commandment in the Law?" he asked.

This was no trick. Here was a genuine question to the very

heart of Jesus' teachings. Peter could see an almost incredulous look cross Jesus' face.

He answered, "The first commandment of all is, 'Hear, O Israel! The Lord our God is one God. And thou shalt love the Lord they God with thy whole heart, and with thy whole soul, and with thy whole mind, and with thy whole strength.' This is the first commandment. And the second is like it: 'Thou shalt love thy neighbor as thyself.' There is no other commandment greater than these."

"Well answered, Master!" the scribe exclaimed. "You have said the truth, that there is one God, and there is no other besides him. And that he should be loved with the whole heart, and with the whole understanding, and with the whole soul, and with one's whole strength. And to love one's neighbor as oneself is a greater thing than all holocausts and sacrifices."

Peter watched Jesus brighten at hearing the scribe's words. By the time he finished, his face was radiant with joy at having found a man among the wolves.

"You are not far from the Kingdom of God," he said to him.

Peter thought it was a good note on which to leave, so that Jesus could go somewhere and rest. But the master had no intention of leaving just when he had finally met with some goodwill, with a chance for genuine dialogue. He turned to the assembled pilgrims, and to the priests and Pharisees hiding among them. In a loud voice he asked them, "How do the scribes say that Christ is the Son of David? David himself says by the Holy Spirit, 'The Lord said to my Lord: Sit thou at my right hand, until I make thy enemies thy footstool'. David himself, therefore, calls him Lord. How, then, is he his son?"

He paused, waiting for an answer—at least from the one man who had summoned up the courage to speak with him sincerely. The crowd shuffled their feet. No answer was forthcoming. Even the scribe on whom Jesus was counting began to withdraw. He swept the crowd with his gaze. When he spoke, his voice vibrated with indignation.

"The scribes and Pharisees have sat on the chair of Moses,"

he began. "All things, therefore, that they command you, observe and do. But do not act according to their works, for they talk, but do nothing. For they bind heavy and oppressive burdens and lay them on men's shoulders, but not with one finger of their own will they move them. And they do all their works in order to be seen by men. For they widen their phylacteries and enlarge their tassels, and they love the first places at feasts and the front seats in the synagogues, and salutations in the market place, and to be called by men, 'Rabbi'. But do not you be called 'Rabbi'. For only one is your master, and all of you are brothers." He paused.

Not one more word, he should not say a single word more, Peter thought frantically. He had said much too much already. The Pharisees would never forgive him. But, in panic, Peter saw that Jesus was not finished. The Pharisees were demonstrably displaying their unconcern, imperviousness, standing with smug, scornful smiles on their faces, scoffing and sniffing at his words. It was too much for him. He pointed directly at them. He raised his voice and lashed out with a vehemence Peter had never yet seen in the master.

"Woe to you, scribes and Pharisees, hypocrites! because you shut the Kingdom of Heaven against men. For you yourselves do not go in, nor do you allow those going in to enter.

"Woe to you, scribes and Pharisees, hypocrites! because you traverse sea and land to make one proselyte, and when he has become one, you make him twofold more a son of hell than yourselves."

Peter withered inside. He wanted to shrink away altogether. Jesus was becoming more and more worked up.

"Woe to you, scribes and Pharisees, hypocrites! because you tithe mint, and anise, and cumin, and have left the weightier things of the Law: judgment, and mercy, and faith. These things you should have done, while not leaving the others undone. Blind guides, who strain out a gnat, and swallow a camel."

Jesus' eyes were flaming, his hair streaming in the wind, his arms thrown open wide and furiously.

"Woe to you, scribes and Pharisees, hypocrites! because you are like whited sepulchers, which outwardly appear beautiful to men, but within are full of dead men's bones and of all filthiness. So you also outwardly appear just to men, but within you are full of hypocrisy and iniquity."

Peter was stunned by so much invective. To compare men to a sepulcher full of dead men's bones—he would never dare say such a thing even to his worst enemy. But that was by no means the end of it.

"Woe to you, scribes and Pharisees, hypocrites! who build the sepulchers of the prophets and adorn the monuments of the just, and say, 'If we had lived in the days of our fathers, we would not have been their accomplices in the blood of the prophets.' Thus you are witnesses against yourselves that you are the sons of those who killed the prophets. You also fill up the measure of your fathers."

Finally he was finished. Spent, he started down the steps.

Peter did not have the nerve to go up to him. Suicide, what he had committed was suicide. That was not a speech, but an outburst, which accomplished nothing, solved nothing. Jesus' reproofs were justified, but why speak them? It was slamming the door behind him, severing all possibilities for contact in the future, terminating any and all dialogue. Well, at least it meant Jesus was in Jerusalem for the last time. He had nothing here to come back for.

Peter had observed the Pharisees' reaction to his outburst. Some of them turned and left in fury, others stood their ground ostentatiously; while others could barely conceal their satisfaction. These last were certainly thinking what Peter was thinking: that Jesus had compromised himself. He had ceased to be an opponent, he was leaving the arena. After what had happened, they should leave Jerusalem at once. The danger was at its height. Peter did not say as much; he didn't want to annoy Jesus. The master was wise enough anyway to realize what had happened. But he promised himself to keep a sharp eye on him and not leave his side for a moment.

Their return to Bethany reminded him of the retreat of survivors from a battlefield after a crushing defeat. Only a small company of the most faithful were returning. They were greeted by an anxious Lazarus, a collected Martha, and a frantic Mary. Jesus retired early. Peter sat up late talking late with Lazarus, recounting the episode in all its grim detail. Lazarus was visibly worried. After their conversation, Peter lay awake in bed a long time. His eagerness to get as far away from Jerusalem as possible kept him sleepless. He felt a sinking sense of death around him, around Jesus, around them all. It was almost daybreak by the time he dropped off to sleep.

Someone was standing over him. One of the disciples. His senses awoke sluggishly. He heard, "The master is looking for you."

He rose and dressed hurriedly. He found Jesus outside with Lazarus. Jesus motioned to him.

"Simon, take John and prepare the Passover for us," he instructed him.

"Where do you want us to prepare it?" he asked, surprised that the master was assigning this task to him.

"On entering the city, a man will meet you there, carrying a pitcher of water. Follow him into the house where he goes and say to the owner of the house, 'The master asks, "Where is the guest chamber where I may eat the Passover with my disciples?" ' He will show you a large upper dining-room furnished. There make ready for us."

En route, Peter learned from John, who was, as always, the best informed of all the disciples and the first to reveal everything he knew, that it was to be a very grand and ceremonious Passover feast, and that Jesus probably was keeping the meeting place a secret because he did not want them to be disturbed by the mobs that were always hounding him. Peter said nothing. He did not intend to worry the youngster with his own thoughts about why Jesus was exercising caution.

On entering the city, they halted at the gate. Immediately they spotted a man idly standing beside a small pitcher of water. Peter had never seen him before, but the man must have known them well, because the moment he caught sight of them he picked up the pitcher and started to move off. They followed him at a cautious distance through the twisting maze of streets of the old town. After much tortuous winding, they came to a wicket in a high wall. Beyond it, a courtyard, then up a flight of stairs to an upper floor. The man with the pitcher was waiting for them on the landing. He knocked on a door. It was opened by a man of genteel and graceful manner who introduced himself as the owner of the house.

Peter repeated Jesus' message: "The master asked, 'Where is the guest chamber where I may eat the Passover with my disciples?' "

The owner ushered them inside. The two disciples found themselves in a splendid, spacious chamber. Peter could not help wondering how it had been preserved in the city so unbearably squeezed by pilgrims.

While preparing for the feast, Peter learned that the master of the house, who was evidently a person of influence in Jerusalem, was well aware of the unfortunate speech against the Pharisees the day before. In his opinion, Jesus was in grave danger. The priests would not let him out of the city now, and would murder him any way they could, openly or in secret. Peter also learned of the priests' order to arrest Jesus, and about the reward posted for information regarding the place where he lodged. But perhaps the most unexpected news was that the priests' were spreading the rumor that Jesus was preparing an insurrection against the lawful authorities.

Only now did Peter fully appreciate their desperate predicament. Their only chance would be to escape with the protective tide of pilgrims after the festival days, or in the dead of night under cover of darkness—tonight, or another night very soon. But under no circumstances could Jesus show himself in public. He left the upper room determined they should leave for Galilee if possible, that very night, right after the Passover supper.

They arrived at the dining hall fairly early that evening. Jesus still appeared somehow dispirited, worn. Sick, or maybe disheartened by more bad news, Peter thought. He watched him with misgiving. From the start, everything about the supper was strangely different. All the Passover feasts he had celebrated with Jesus had not only been solemn and ceremonious affairs, but joyous ones as well. By his own example Jesus had taught them to offer the Passover gifts to God with great joy, and in union with them, their own selves—their lives. This evening's atmosphere was in no way reminiscent of those others. Peter wished they could get it over with and escape as quickly as possible.

Suddenly he noticed that Jesus had disappeared from the room. Some minutes later he reappeared carrying a basin of water and wearing some kind of linen apron around his waist. He walked over to where the disciples were all bunched together indecisively, stopped before Peter, and without a word, stooped to the floor. For one puzzled instant Peter could not imagine what Jesus was up to. Then it struck him—he wanted to wash his feet! Like a slave would his master!

"You shall never wash my feet!" he cried. He seized Jesus by the arms and pulled him to his feet. Then he saw his tense face and eyes.

"If I do not wash you, you will have no part with me." His voice was taut and even.

Peter dropped his arms. The words were categorical, not permitting discussion. He surrendered. "Lord, then not only my feet, but also my hands and my head."

"He that is washed needs only to wash his feet and is wholly clean. And you are clean, but not all of you." And he proceeded to wash his feet.

Peter could not understand how Jesus could bring himself to do something so humiliating. What was happening to him? He looked at his bent back kneeling at his feet, washing the dust from them like a menial. He felt the touch of his hands, the cool water, the rough towel. Tears ran uncontrollably down his face. Then, without straightening up, Jesus began to wash the feet of the disciple next to him.

Peter watched the startled reactions of the others. They looked around helplessly at each other, bewildered, uncertain like himself what it all meant. They made no objections, having seen their protests were futile.

Finally Jesus put aside the basin, removed the linen cloth, and faced them. "Do you know what I have done to you?" he asked them. "You call me master and Lord, and you say well, for so I am. If, then, I being your Lord and Master have washed your feet, you also ought to wash one another's feet.

For I have given you an example, what I have done to you,
so you also should do."

How was that? Peter wondered. Were they supposed to
wash each other's feet? He thought Jesus would explain further. Instead, they began to take their places around the
table: as usual, Jesus in the middle, John on one side of him,
Peter himself on the other. Now he could see how badly the
ordeal of these last few days in Jerusalem showed on Jesus:
his features were sharpened by fatigue, his eyes sunken behind
deep shadows; perspiration covered his forehead; he breathed
with difficulty. How was he going to make it to Bethany that
night? How would he be able to leave for Galilee tomorrow?

The supper was begun. Jesus took the cup. It grew very
quiet around the table.

"I have greatly desired to eat this Passover with you before
I suffer," he murmured.

Peter shuddered. He was talking about suffering again. All
Jesus' predictions before their trip to Jerusalem reared up in
his mind yet again. Was it really supposed to come to that?

Jesus went on, "For I say to you, that I will eat of it no
more, until it has been fulfilled in the Kingdom of God".

He said a prayer of thanks and handed the cup to Peter.
He took it, drank from it, and passed it to Andrew. He went
through the motions mechanically, blankly, so badly had
Jesus's words shaken him. In fact, nothing at all registered,
not their common prayers, nor their customary reading from
Scriptures. Nothing—except one sentence uttered unexpectedly, without prelude, in the same soft voice, almost to himself: "One of you will betray me."

The words dropped like a hammer blow. No, he must have
been mistaken, he must have misheard. But the startled
silence that fell over the room was unmistakable. "One of
you." That meant one of the Twelve at the table, one of the
Twelve grown close and responsible for each other as a family.
"One of you." It was as if he had said each one of them to
some degree. As if betrayal was in each of them. His words
were like a slap in the face to them all. Now he understood:
this was the reason for Jesus's disquiet, his sadness.

Slowly Peter's nerves settled; he began to reason coolly. A

traitor? He would take care of him now. The most important thing was that Jesus had found out about him. But who? He stole a glance at his companions around the table. Could it be Matthew? Didn't he have dealings with the Romans? Or Thomas? Couldn't his incessant questions and doubts mean something? Or what about Judas? Who was he, really? In that instant of scanning his fellows, Peter realized how little he really knew about the men he had joined. He was actually only sure of three: Andrew, John, and James. No one else.

After the initial stunned silence, the disciples recovered their speech and began to press Jesus about the traitor's identity. Peter joined in their entreaties: "Who, Lord? Is it I?"

Jesus was silent for some minutes, until finally, perhaps yielding to their noisy insistence, he answered them evasively, "He who dips his hand with me in the dish, he will betray me."

Peter searched the table fiercely. What did that mean, who dips his hands in the dish? It meant nothing—they were all dipping their hands.

In a remote voice, as if his mind were far from the room, Jesus went on, "The Son of Man indeed goes his way, as it is written of him, but woe to that man by whom the Son of Man is betrayed! It were better for him if he had not been born."

Why was Jesus saying all this now, why had he not said it earlier? This was no time to take care of such matters, right in the middle of the Passover meal. Or maybe he had only found out at the last minute himself and was telling them all now?

"Is it I, Lord?" Peter asked again over the din of pleas and protests. He was hoping Jesus would give in, name the culprit. But with his eyes resolutely fixed to the table, Jesus said nothing.

Peter refused to give up. He had to know the traitor's identity. After all, he was responsible for Jesus' safety. He swept the room with his eyes, looking for a hint. A sudden idea came to him when he looked at John. Frightened by the idea of treachery in their midst, the boy was nestled against

Jesus' breast. Taking advantage of the ferment, Peter reached behind Jesus' back and tugged at John. "Ask him who he means," he whispered.

John grew suddenly very grave. An intense look tightened his face. Interminable minutes passed; he seemed to be concentrating. Finally, leaning upon Jesus again, he asked him in an almost casual whisper, "Lord, who is it?"

After a moment of reflection, Peter heard Jesus whisper back to John, "It is he to whom I will give the bread dipped in wine."

Peter could hardly believe Jesus had agreed so easily to John's appeal. He was already dipping the bread. Who would he hand it to? Tensely he watched Jesus' hand. For a horrible, fleeting second, he was ready to believe Jesus would hand it to him, but with a single motion he leaned over the table and gave the bread to Judas.

Peter sucked in his breath softly. Ah, so it is you, you scoundrel. I never did take a fancy to you. Tomorrow I will punish you personally.

A number of things came back to him now about Judas: how he was never in a hurry to work, how he always managed to avoid apostolic work; and those sneering smiles of his that may have concealed any number of schemes. He was one of the Twelve, yet he always stood apart and rarely participated in the common life of the group. As if he were always a stranger. Peter was angry with himself for not having seen through him sooner. But he would not escape now. They were not going to harbor a traitor among them.

Suddenly he felt Jesus' gaze on him. He turned. From the look in his eyes, it appeared that he had only just realized that John had acted at his urging, and now he regretted having revealed the secret to them. Peter saw him turn abruptly to Judas. His voice was audible in the whole room. "That which you do, do quickly."

Peter opened his mouth to object—how could the master let a traitor go free? But, he reasoned, Jesus knew what he was doing.

Out of the corner of his eye, he watched Judas' reaction. Did he guess that the master knew? Probably. Looking unnerved, he rose without a word and hastened from the room. All talk around the table died; everyone was baffled by Jesus' curious instructions. What had happened that Judas had suddenly to leave the Passover supper? But in the end they shrugged, it was just another of those mysterious sayings of his that they could not understand.

Judas' departure, however, produced a noticeable change in Jesus—as if he had been impatiently waiting for him to leave. The moment the door closed behind Judas, he seemed to come alive. He rose as a sign that the feast could begin in earnest, took a scroll of the Scripture and began to read aloud.

While he read, Peter lost himself in his own thoughts. Jesus' behaviour was clear now: he had simply wanted Judas to leave, he could not bring himself to eat supper with a traitor— break bread with him, drink wine with him. For the life of him, he could not understand how it had come to this: how Judas, one of the Twelve, a longtime disciple of Jesus, could turn informer against him.

He awoke from his thoughts just as Jesus concluded his reading. It couldn't have been a very long reading, he thought. At least not as long as usual.

Now came the most important moment of their Passover gatherings. He tried to brush away the thoughts distracting his mind and concentrate hard on the celebration. He watched Jesus take the bread and offer it to God, and then break it and distribute it among all the participants. That moment always moved him anew—when he took bread from Jesus' hands into his own, blessed bread, the bread of God, to eat. It was Jesus who had taught him how truly to partake of the Passover feast. Through him, he came to understand that the essence of the Passover was union of oneself with the sacrifice offered to God—with God himself. He had learned how, in uniting himself with God, to unite himself with his companions at the feast and forgive all offenses, quarrels, jealousies, and annoyances that arose among them.

Unexpectedly, instead of the customary prayer, Peter was startled to hear: "Take and eat. This is my body, which will be given for you".

He stared around at the others. Judging from their faces,

they were as mystified as he was. There had never been a
supper quite like this one. It sounded as if . . . Jesus was
offering himself to God and inviting them to share in his
sacrifice. The washing of feet had been a prelude. Peter took
the bread from Jesus' hand—his bread, his life, himself. He
repeated Jesus' words to himself. He wanted to preserve them
in his memory as faithfully as possible. But that last part
. . . "which will be given for you". That word, "given." What
did it mean? To whom was Jesus to be given? And how given?
Betrayed? Ah, of course, by Judas. Oh, but Jesus did not
need to worry about him. He would take care of Judas.

The supper continued along its normal course. Gradually
the atmosphere thawed, the odd words were forgotten. Conversation around the table grew more free and animated;
sporadic laughter warmed the room. But all was not in order.
Peter observed Jesus: he seemed remote, not attentive,
strangely mute and grave.

Peter could not at first put his finger on the source of the
tension he sensed in the master. Then it came to him: Jesus
was in a hurry. He caught the quick glances cast around the
table at the disciples eating supper. Years of close and constant association had taught him how to read what was happening inside the master. No doubt about it, Jesus wanted to
leave as quickly as possible. That discovery somehow annoyed
him—the end already? They had only just begun. They had
time, they could stay at least until midnight. Everyone would
be sleepy during the night—the guards and sentries included.
It would be easier to leave the city then. But the master
probably wanted to finish so that he could rest. Peter looked
around the room. The feast was just coming alive, the disciples chattering spiritedly among themselves, eased and relieved in he back of their minds that they would soon be
returning to Galilee. He was unsure how he could help the
master—perhaps by pressing the others on. But he felt sorry
for them, it was their last day in the city. Their eyes were
closing drowsily. It seemed a shame to leave now.

Abruptly he saw Jesus take up the cup for the closing
prayer. The noise and festivity died around the table. In all
their Passover celebrations, this was the second most import-

ant moment. Jesus' words before the distribution of bread rang persistently in his ears. What significance would the master give to the act of blessing the wine that would close their supper? Tensely he listened.

"Take and drink of this. This is my blood of the New Covenant, which shall be shed for you and for many for the forgiveness of sins."

The room was as if thunderstruck—motionless, powerless, speechless. Peter felt the cool of the cup in his hands as Jesus passed it to him. He took a sip of wine, blindly passed the cup to Andrew. All the while, the master was conducting the feast as if it were his own sacrifice, the sacrifice of his life. The echo of his voice still hung darkly over the room. Blood . . . therefore, death. Chills curdled his skin. No, Jesus really was exaggerating with that Judas. The cup wandered around the table and returned to Jesus. He rose and recited the last hymn. The feast was over. He moved toward the door.

They rose sluggishly and filed out of the room into the black night. The cold air instantly stirred their drowsy senses. The heavy atmosphere of the supper—of danger and death— dissipated in the darkness. Once outside, the disciples felt as if they had one foot at home already. Their good humor returned—jokes and quips about the Judeans, noisy bombast about the superior Gaileans. Every few minutes Peter had to clap his hands over someone's mouth, or hush him to keep down the noise. He wanted them to pass through the city unnoticed. Not until some minutes later did he realize they were heading in a different direction. He caught up with Jesus.

"Where are we going?" he asked anxiously. "Aren't we going to Bethany?"

Jesus did not answer. Peter was about to give up—Jesus did not want to talk to him, fine—when finally Jesus said, "To the Garden of Olives."

"To the Garden of Olives? And we're going to have to spend the night there?"

What a disappointment. He had dreamed of sleeping comfortably in Bethany.

Jesus interrupted his dream of sleep. Softly, as if more to

himself than to them, he said, "You will all be scandalized this night because of me. For it is written, 'I will smite the shepherd, and the sheep of the flock will be scattered'."

Peter felt sorry for Jesus that he was so disheartened by Judas' having turned traitor. With a broad sweep of his arms, he clasped him to himself. He wanted to comfort him, reassure him.

"Even if all will be scandalized because of you, I will never be scandalized."

In answer he heard: "This very night, before the cock crows, you will deny me three times."

"Me?" He was completely taken aback. The very idea was impossible. He forced a laugh, confident he could refute the master. "Even if I should have to die with you, I will not deny you!"

The other disciples had been listening. They chimed in now, vigorously affirming their loyalty and attachment to Jesus. A miniature storm ensued, with the disciples all eddying about Jesus, assuring him, seizing on Peter's words— "Even if I have to die with you, I will not deny you!" Peter let them. He walked off to one side, troubled in his mind. What was happening to Jesus? He had never seen him like this. Daybreak was only a short time away, and he was telling him that on that very night he was going to deny him. Maybe he said it because he had failed to keep his eye on Judas. . .?

They left the knot of streets, passed beyond the belt of walls, and began the descent into the Cedron Valley. In the open the light of the moon made their movements easy. They crossed the dried riverbed over jutting rocks. In minutes they were ascending the steep opposite side of the gully, Peter supporting Jesus in the climb. They reached the other side. Now what Peter would enjoy most was a good sleep, but they had to keep moving. Why didn't Jesus want to spent the night in Bethany? True, it was a bit of a trip, but at least it would have been a roof over their heads—and warm.

A short distance, and they were at the garden. Jesus stopped them at the entrance. He gathered them around him in a circle and told them that he wished to remain in the garden to pray. He asked them to wait there at the gate.

Peter was just promising himself that he was going to stretch out on the grass to sleep when he heard he was to accompany Jesus with John and James. He did not know quite how to understand that: if Jesus did not trust him, why was he taking him with him? Or maybe Jesus thought he might run off and inform on him.

In Jesus' name, he instructed the rest to keep watch at the gate, and in the event of danger, to signal to him.

The four entered the silent depths of the garden. It was dark; here only a faint glow of moonlight penetrated the thicket of branches, covered with small silvery leaves. They had walked in silence for sometime when Jesus turned to them and said, "Wait here and watch."

The three disciples found themselves in a small clearing. They watched Jesus withdraw to a distance, his white garments glimmering fleetingly in the faint light. About a stone's throw from where they stood, he stopped near an enormous rock. Peter saw him kneel to pray. The sight moved him. And that must have been the last thing his eyes registered, because slowly, heavily, they began to close. He honestly meant to watch with him; he struggled to stay awake; but his muscles were limp and his eyelids unrelenting. He thought, what was the harm if he fell asleep for a few minutes? Who could possibly guess that Jesus had come here and not gone to Bethany? Anyway, all Jerusalem was asleep, and the others were guarding the entrance. If anything should happen, they would rouse him. . . . And that Judas would have to be taken care of tomorrow. . . . It wouldn't hurt to sleep a few moments. He lay down, covered himself with his cloak and was instantly asleep.

He could not be sure about what happened after that—whether he dreamed it or not. He thought he felt someone tugging at him. Then it must have been Jesus trying to awake him once or twice—he thought he saw the master's form bending over him in the moonlight; he thought he heard his voice . . . "Could you not watch one hour with me?" His head was so heavy, he simply was unable to stir himself from that deep primary sleep.

It was the flash of torchlight that brought him to his senses.

Dark figures were springing up on every side. He ran in panic to where he had last seen Jesus. James and John were there with him. He stood beside them, trembling with fear and the cold. The disciples who were posted at the gate were nowhere in sight. He wanted to ask John or James about them, but could not find his voice through the gagging tightness in his throat. In the garden, they could make out forms darting among the trees. Peter still hoped against hope that it was not Jesus they were looking for, but in his sinking heart he knew he was deluding himself. He looked around desperately: lights flashing everywhere. They were surrounded. No one had spotted them yet, but it was only a matter of a few more moments. What if they fought their way through? He grasped the hilt of his sword—how good that he had it on him. The sounds of shouted orders, oaths, cries, and laughter pierced the night. Peter could now see armed soldiers combing the undergrowth. There was no chance of escape. They could only wait in the hope that they escaped detection. Fury welled up inside him at his own stupidity, and at the others at the gate for not signalling to him. He cursed under his breath, that he had let himself be so stupidly caught off guard, that he had not kept watch. Now it was too late. One thing he could do—he gripped his sword fiercely—he would sell his and Jesus' life dearly.

Suddenly he thought he saw Judas's face among the trees. Could it be? Yes, it was him, wielding a torch high over his head, searching around carefully, examining the clumps of trees. The realization struck like a racing arrow: today was the day when Judas was to betray, not at some indefinite time in the future. And that was why had had left before the end of the Passover supper. "One of you will betray me. . . ." Jesus' words rang in his ears like a taunt. Then came the next stupefying realization: Jesus knew everything, knew that this betrayal—this assault—would take place today. And that was why he had said, "What you do, do quickly." Peter thought he would burst with angry, helpless frustration. How could he have been such a fool not to heed Jesus' words. But why had the master not been more explicit—they could have restrained the traitor then.

Judas stopped short—he had spotted them. For a moment he appeared to hesitate, peering intently at them. Then he broke into a run and bounded breathlessly up to Jesus, acting as if he had just run into him somewhere around the Lake of Tiberias.

"Hail, Rabbi!" He embraced him warmly and kissed him. He looked cool, calm, one could almost say joyful.

Peter was so surprised by Judas' manner that he stood numbly with his arms hanging at his sides. A greeting like that at such a moment? Bewildered, he turned to see Jesus' reaction. He hard him answer Judas quietly: "Judas, do you betray the Son of Man with a kiss?"

So, this was no comedy. The kiss must have been a prearranged signal, for at that moment the band of men who had been following Judas at a distance lunged forward to apprehend Jesus. They thrust John and James roughly out of the way and were about to shove Peter aside as well, when he leaped in front of Jesus to screen him and began to repel the attackers. Suddenly his eye caught the glint of a spear thrust in his direction. He tore out his sword and lashed out at the assailant, striking him a heavy blow on the side of his helmet. The blade slid down to the guard's shoulder and was stopped by his massive brassard. Peter was about to haul up his sword for a second strike when he felt the hard squeeze of a hand on his arm. Through the white-hot fury rushing in his ears like water, he heard Jesus' voice: "Put away your sword".

He pulled back his weapon with an effort at control, trembling and poised for the next attack. He glowered wildly at the ring of torches around them. Jesus' composed voice sounded beside him: "Whom do you seek?"

"Jesus of Nazareth."

"I am he."

He stepped into their midst and spoke to them. Peter caught fragments . . . having to do with releasing him, meaning Peter, and the others. Then the rest was drowned in an outbreak of bellowing, pushing, wrenching. For one more fleeting moment Peter saw the master's erect figure before he was hauled into the vortex of the mob and carried from sight in a sea of heads and smoking torches.

Night fell around him again; it grew suddenly dark and empty. It might all have been a nightmare, were it not for the dots of light flickering among the trees and the drone of voices receding in the distance. Instinctively he followed; he did not want to stay in the garden alone. He ran after them until he could see the flaring torches concentrated at the head of the column. Fear suddenly froze him in his tracks—he thought he saw a shadow flitting among the trees. He strained his eyes against the dark. With a release of breath, he recognized the nimble figure of John. He chased after him and caught him by the arm. John jerked away in fright before he recognized him, then threw his arms around Peter's neck in unashamed joy. "You're all right!" he cried. "I thought something had happened to you."

They approached the exit. Peter slowed his pace. He held John back by the arm. "Let's not rush. They might recognize us."

From where they watched, they could see the horde of soldiers spilling into the ravine.

"We must tell Lazarus about this," Peter breathed.

When the last soldier had disappeared from view, the two hurried down after them, and minutes later they were scrambling back up the other slope, safe in the shadow of the defense walls. They entered the city.

"Where are they taking him, do you know?" Peter asked in an undertone.

"Probably to the palace of Caiaphas. We'll find out in a moment."

Peter shook his head in disagreement, but to his surprise a moment later the assailants did indeed head in the direction of the palace of Annas and Caiaphas. A soft glow of activity was already visible there. They halted at a safe distance. The division marched through the gate, which closed swiftly behind them. The guards resumed their posts outside.

"What do we do now?" Peter whispered.

John, with characteristic initiative, whispered back, "Let's do this: I'll go inside and find out what's happening to Jesus— I know everyone in there—and then I'll bring you in."

Before Peter could object, John had run off and disappeared. He was back before very long. He grabbed Peter by the hand. "Come on."

Peter let himself be led. John knocked on a narrow door recessed in a shadowy wall. It creaked open. A few whispered exchanges between John and the portress, and they were in the courtyard.

"Wait here, I'll be right back," John murmured, and he was gone.

Peter sought cover in the deep shadows at the foot of a wall. Nearby a group of soldiers stood warming themselves around a fire. A short distance from them, closer to Caiaphas's palace, another group huddled around another blaze. The gate he had entered suddenly clanged shut behind him with a chilling rattle. It was then that he realized the trap he had walked into—through his own folly. He was locked in the courtyard of the palace of the High Priest. It was madness to have come here. The only way out now was through the gate guarded by armed attendants. He felt like a cornered rat. Even if Jesus had managed to get them off the hook in the Garden of Olives, sooner or later the priests were bound to come after his disciples as well. And how would the presence of Jesus' foremost disciple and defender in the courtyard of the High Priest be interpreted, if not suspiciously? "I can die in defense of Jesus," he muttered to himself, "but I have no intention of dying for nothing." He flattened himself against the wall. He was furious with himself for letting John lead him in like a calf. Where was he anyway? The minutes dragged interminably and still John did not reappear. He tried to suppress the cold fear rising to his throat for the lad's safety. It was taking him too long.

"You there," a voice called out to him. "Don't stand in the cold, come join us."

This was it. One of the men warming himself at the fire was calling him over. With every nerve in his body, Peter overcame the impulse to rush headlong in the direction of the gate and take his chance of escaping into the redeeming darkness. No, that would be suicide. He had a better chance here; maybe they would not recognize him. If he did not step forward soon, they would get suspicious and drag him over to the light—and that could be far worse. He drew his hood more tightly over his head, and with a pounding heart sidled over to the fire.

"Listen to what he's saying," the man said.

Peter grunted and took a place between two palace guards, flapping their arms at the flames. They hardly noticed him, so absorbed were they in a guard's breathless and loud account of the capture in Gethsemane. Peter listened closely. He was surprised to hear about the detachment that had encircled the house in which they had feasted only to spring into an empty dining room; and about another detachment that had been sent to intercept them on the road to Bethany. The rest he knew only too well, and he did not need to listen to the soldiers' sardonic banter to know that once Jesus was in its clutches, the Sanhedrin was determined to deal with him with finality. No one and nothing could help him now.

And he had warned him so many times. Their one chance had been to stay in Galilee and organize something there, some type of New Israel, like the one Jesus was always talking about. But no, he had insisted on coming to Judea—and now he had what he wanted. And he had called him Satan when all he wanted was his welfare. One thing was sure, there was not going to be any Kingdom of God, the one he had promised them and prepared them for. And the twelve of them could not now get that chance to judge the twelve tribes of Israel, that was certain, too. Nor would that other promise of his come true now: that whoever leaves father or mother, brother or sister in his name would receive a hundredfold more. And to think he had believed him. How naive he was! Yet, what was he to think about the whole affair really? Did Jesus lie to them, deceive them? Was he a seducer, the way the priests said he was? Or simply a dreamer, a fantasist who failed to grasp reality?

The shock of seeing Jesus led away by soldiers came back to him. He could not reconcile himself to what had happened. Until a very short while ago God had blessed him. By the power of God he had performed so many great miracles: he had healed, raised the dead, multiplied loaves of bread. And how often in the past had he overcome attempts on his life:

in Nazareth, when they tried to push him off a cliff and could not; in the temple, when they tried to stone him when he said, "Before Abraham was, I am," and they could not. He had always managed to escape. God was with him then. What happened now? If God had wished, he would have saved him tonight. If he could save the Israelites from Pharoah's vengeance and open up the sea; if he could save Daniel in the midst of lions, what was it for him to save his son? Jesus had met with God's wrath. God had abandoned him. Everything was over.

The world he had lived for and breathed for in the last few years—his pearl of great price, his treasure in the field, his friendship and enthusiasm for Jesus, everything—was suddenly coldly gone.

Another soldier joined the group around the fire. Amid peals of laughter he recounted the facile capture of the stupid Galileans fast asleep at the entrance to the garden. Peter simmered as he heard about the panic of the Galilean riffraff at being awakened from their drunken sleep to find before them not the face of their distinguished master, but the soldiers' knives under their noses. The guard's jokes unleashed a volley of jests about the seducer who fooled the simpletons from around Gennesaret with his cunning little tricks, and the wonder worker who couldn't save himself from capture. "We'll see if he can knit his bones when we break them," someone yelled. And everybody roared.

Peter could not bear to listen. Galilee, with its lakes and boats, loomed peacefully in his mind. Why did he ever leave and get himself mixed up with this madness? To build God's Kingdom? That Kingdom seemed so remote and distant now he could not even remember his own enthusiasm for it.

He felt suddenly uncomfortable, as if someone were watching him. He looked up. Across the fire, the woman who had let him in was staring fixedly at him. Perhaps curious to know what all the laughter was about, she had come over to the fire and had spotted him now in the glow. Peter saw her face change—the smile quickly faded, recognition, then anger took its place. He dropped his head, pretending not to have noticed her, hoping she would leave. She did not leave, she stood and stubbornly stared at him. He saw the hand go up and point accusingly, lethally at him. Over the gives and roars about the snared Nazarene, she shouted at him, "And you were with him!"

Paralysis numbed him. Death. But to die now? When he wanted nothing to do with Jesus any more; when he did not care about him any more? To die for him now?

The voices broke off around the fire; curious, unbelieving faces whirled around to him. He wanted to run while there was still time. Before the hands reached for him. But how? They would catch him, kill him. It was too late for anything. Somehow, all that day it had been too late for anything. He did not want to die. He had to say something. He shrugged stiffly, artificially.

"I neither know nor understand what you are saying," he retorted, with a show of indignation to cover the trembling in his voice.

He had better not idle there among the soldiers much longer—they would not let the subject drop now. Slowly, coolly he edged around the circle to the portress, as if he wanted to assure her, let her take a good look at him, see that she was mistaken. He took her by the arm and propelled her toward the gate. He spoke rapidly, meaningless words, gibberish, just to keep her occupied. Out of the corner of his eye, he watched to see if anyone was following. No one. Except the whites of their eyes gleaming in the blaze, following them curiously. It was still very quiet around the fire. He practically towed the portress behind him, toward the second group, hoping to get around or through them and out of the others' sight. Alarmed by his behavior, the woman began to resist. He rushed with her over to the other fire. Just when he thought he was safe, she broke free of his grip and ran up to one of the guards. "This is one of them!" she screamed.

Peter stopped dead in his tracks. The instant silence rang in his ears like a dirge. Everyone turned and stared. They knew at once what she meant.

He turned to the woman, that awful, hounding woman who shadowed him like an angel of death. "Woman, I don't know the man," he insisted.

It did not work. A voice from the fire boomed accusingly, "Surely you are one of them. You're Galilean, even your speech betrays you."

"Man, I don't know what you're saying," he stammered.

A strong arm grabbed him and spun him around toward the firelight. "Didn't I see you in the garden with him?" a husky voice demanded.

Nearly faint with fear, Peter choked, "I swear, I don't know this man you are talking about."

He knew no one believed him. He began to insist, louder and louder, calling God as his witness, swearing oath after desperate oath. Perspiration oozed out of his skin in a wave of heat. He pleaded, protested, swore, denied, as a hysterical garble poured from his mouth.

He stopped suddenly. No one was listening to him. All heads were turned toward the palace of Annas, from which a howling roar could be heard. Crowds of guards, attendants, scribes, and Pharisees streamed from the long rectangle of light from the open gate. They are bringing Jesus out, Peter thought in a flash. The excited mob spilled into the courtyard and in seconds absorbed them into their human tide, flowing across to the palace of Caiaphas. Now was his chance, when his persecutors had momentarily lost interest in him. Escape into the swarm swirling past him. He threw himself forward, and was instantly swallowed up by the secure, anonymous throng. He had to hurry. Bruised, jostled, he inched his way through the surge toward the desired gate. A few more feet and he broke free of the cauldron. The gate was open. He dashed past, and was gathered up by the comforting darkness. He ran as fast and as far as he could from that deadly courtyard. He ran until the clatter of his own footfalls beat unbearably in the hollow streets. Panting, unnerved, he fell against a wall and burst into weeping. It simply happened, as suddenly as everything else had happened that night.

Blinded by tears, he stumbled through the empty streets, crying for himself and for his misfortune, crying for Jesus, crying for everything he had lived for. He knew that in leaving Jesus behind at the palace of Annas and Caiaphas, he was leaving him forever.

He was alone and free now. He would do what he had planned to do all along: he would return to Galilee. He would blot out these last few years and start to live again like a normal human being; sail out in a boat on his beloved sea in the early mornings and the late nights; haul in the nets heavy with water and flapping, excited fish; ride in to markets full of the hubbub of buyers and vendors and gossip of the shore. Eventually people would forget about that peculiar episode in his life, when he joined some itinerant teacher from Nazareth, and he could take root again in the soil of his world, a world of simple people and simple problems, and full of the scent of the lake and cool winds and ordinary decent living.

He had to get out of Jerusalem as fast as possible, because by tomorrow they would be scouring the city for the disciples, especially for him. Quite possibly, Andrew, James, and the rest were already on their way home. He blundered his way to the city gate. Beyond it, he headed in the direction of Galilee, avoiding the main road altogether.

The night was bright. He recognized rock and cliff formations, trees and shrubs and trails between them, he had tramped this way before many times. The farther he walked, the more numb and indifferent he felt. He could scarcely shuffle his feet along. He did not wish to think about the past or the future any more. All he wanted was to stretch out peacefully and sleep. He fought back the urge to lie down in the fields: morning was dangerously close. People would be on their way to the city soon. It was best that no one should see him.

That was another thing that worried him, daylight. He ought to wait out the day somewhere, then continue his journey by night. The thought of Bethany popped into his head. Bethany. It came as something extraordinarily beautiful, yet already remote and alien. With a mild shock he realized that it was only yesterday that he had been there with Jesus. He hungered for that warmth and sincerity. Of course he could stop there and let them know what had happened to Jesus, then perhaps find refuge there for the day and continue on his way by night. He could sleep in peace and comfort there. . . .

Peter reached Bethany with the dawn. He was surprised to see everyone up and around—and armed. The servants informed him that Mary and Lazarus had gone, and that James and Judas had already come before him. Judas? They must have been mistaken. No, they insisted, it was really Judas, the one who had betrayed. It did not make sense. Finally Martha emerged, full of foreboding. She wanted to hear everything he had seen and heard.

Peter told the story as best he could, but omitting the part about his cowardice and denials. Of course, Martha had no doubt about why he had come to them. Obviously he had come to round up help for Jesus. In view of the noble motives she ascribed to him, Peter did not have the courage to tell her he was on his way back to Galilee. So he pretended he had come out of concern for the other disciples. For a panic-stricken moment he thought she was going to send him right back to Jerusalem to help Lazarus and Mary find help for Jesus among the Galileans there. But no, she decided he should wait there, because they might return any minute. So Peter went to sleep.

He was jolted out of a deep slumber by exploding thunder and lightning. Opaque dark clouds had turned day into night. He thought he had slept through to evening, but it was only three in the afternoon. Martha was beside herself with worry—Lazarus and Mary had not yet returned. She pressed Peter to go back to the city and find out what was happening; start with Joseph of Arimathea, she advised, they had gone to him first. Peter's heart sank at the prospect. But Martha insisted and he felt ashamed, and when the rain stopped and the sky cleared, he found himself trudging the wet road back to Jerusalem, cursing his brilliant idea of stopping at Bethany. Especially since, as opposed to Martha, he knew no one could help Jesus now. At least he agreed with Martha on one point: the whole affair would require some considerable time, because the priests would have to bring legal action against Jesus, and consequently would be searching around for witnesses.

He took his time, in the hope of running into Mary and Lazarus, or one of his people on the way, who could tell him what was happening in the city and save him going back. But he met no one.

The sight of the milling throngs at the gate made his stomach shrink like a closing fist. And the spies—priests and attendants innocently loitering along the walls and among the stalls, on the lookout for suspicious-looking individuals. He could not risk recognition; he decided to circle the city and enter the side rarely frequented. It was convenient anyway, because Joseph lived on the other side, in the direction of Golgotha.

As he picked his way around, he thought he caught a glimpse between roofs of some crosses jutting out of the hill of the skull. That was strange, he did not recall seeing them there in the last few days. In fact, he did not remember seeing them there last night when he was leaving Jerusalem. They must have just condemned someone to death. But no, that couldn't be, tomorrow was the Sabbath.

At the palace of Joseph of Arimathea, Peter walked into a strangely muted flurry of activity. He stood and waited to be noticed in the confusion. Finally he accosted a servant and asked to see Joseph.

"He's at Golgotha."

"Golgotha?" he repeated in surprise. "How can I get there?"

"This way." The servant pointed. "Straight through the garden."

"Through the garden?"

"Yes. It reaches right up to the hill."

Peter never dreamed Joseph's garden was so large and sprawling. He thought it would never end. All along the way he kept running into strange people. By their mien and hurry he could see something urgent was happening. A dread foreboding crept over him. No, he shuddered, it could not be. He refused to let himself think it. The thing was impossible. There had to be a trial first, with witnesses, and that would take days by the time they gathered all the evidence against Jesus.

From beyond a grove of trees he heard voices. He quickened his steps. Through the branches he saw figures stirring about what looked like a freshly-cut tomb in the rocks. A burial, they were concluding a burial—the stone was rolled across the entrance. Even when he recognized Mary Magdalene among them, still he refused to accept the truth. He crept closer through the trees. And then he saw Mary, the mother of Jesus, and a boy in tears clinging to her side. That was John. One after the other he recognized them: there was Salome, the mother of the sons of Zebedee; Nicodemus, and Joseph of Arimathea. And still he refused to believe it. There must be some mistake, it was impossible: this simply could not be Jesus' burial. Only a few short hours ago he had been with him, eaten with him. And though he denied it, he knew it—that someone freshly laid in the tomb, behind whom the stone was rolled with finality was Jesus, who had just died on a cross.

He felt faint, his legs wobbled uncontrollably. He could not bring himself to approach the group. He threw himself against the trunk of a tree, as if to hide from the sight, obstruct the reality, and burst into wrenching sobs.

It may have been minutes or hours or days even, that he stood like that. The light touch of a hand on his shoulder finally roused him. Mary Magdalene. Without a word, she took his arm and led him through the now darkened garden back to the house. Through a daze he heard Joseph instruct his servants to prepare a room for him and John. He slept fitfully between despairing bouts of weeping for the man who had been dearest to him in the whole world. Later John tried to tell him everything that had happened, but he didn't listen, it did not seem to matter now. He just sat before the tomb and stared into the stone that had irrevocably sealed off his world. He felt lost, orphaned, inconsolable. He was deeply ashamed of yesterday's flight. How could he ever think that way about Jesus and all the things they had experienced together. He could not imagine how he could go on living now without him.

And he grew increasingly bewildered by his grief. Because if ever there lived a decent man on earth, then Jesus was certainly that man. If ever there lived a man on earth who wanted to fulfill God's will, then Jesus was certainly that man. Why did God allow him to die such a horrible death? Or maybe Jesus was right, when by his words and cures he taught that the sick and maimed and destitute were not necessarily evil men, and that the rich and healthy were not necessarily good and virtuous. If that was what he wanted to say, he said it all too well. He lost against the temple, but he really had no chance against it, a monstrous machine, flawlessly whirring and revolving, for which the matter of liquidating one man required very little effort.

It must have been around noon when Peter was shaken out of his trance by the sound of marching steps. Soldiers here? Instinctively he scrambled behind some shrubbery and watched. A file of Roman soldiers marched up to the tomb. For a moment he thought they were about to roll away the stone. They did quite the opposite—affixed a seal to the tomb. Peter crept unseen to Joseph's house. He lingered outside for some time, afraid that someone responsible for the soldiers' presence might be inside talking to Joseph. One of the servants spotted him. "Don't be scared," he jeered. "You can go in, they've gone now."

Peter bristled, but said nothing. Inside, Joseph had a worried look on his face. Without looking directly at him, Joseph launched into a long-winded account of how the soldiers had sealed up Jesus' tomb. Peter wondered why Joseph was telling him all this, since he knew he was already aware of it. He fidgeted impatiently, until his attention was arrested by one sentence—"The priests are afraid someone might steal Jesus' body."

"Steal it? Who? For what?"

Joseph looked at him for the first time. "You." He corrected himself quickly: "We."

"We?" Peter exclaimed in astonishment.

Joseph smiled. "Do you think they overestimated you?"

Peter pretended not to have noticed the sarcasm.

"Why should we want to steal Jesus' body?"

"Apparently the priests know that better than you." He eyed Peter closely. "Reportedly Jesus once said—I didn't hear it, but it's what they say—that even if the priests killed him, he would rise from the dead."

"But why should we want to steal the body?" he repeated dully. He could see Joseph losing patience.

"Because you could simply carry off his body, and then spread the word that just as he predicted, he has risen from the dead."

He rose to indicate that the discussion was at an end. Peter was about to leave when Joseph lightly touched his hand.

"I beg your pardon, but I have one small favor to ask of you."

Peter already guessed what was on his mind.

". . . . You know that I invited you to my home and told you that you may stay as long as you wish. However—"

"Don't worry," Peter broke in. "I'll leave. Just as soon as the Sabbath is over."

Peter saw the frown of distaste cross Joseph's face at his having rudely finished what should have been left unsaid.

With his hand still on Peter's arm, Joseph said, I'm only concerned about your welfare. It will certainly be best for you."

Peter pulled away and was almost out the door when Joseph's voice reached him again.

"Oh, I almost forgot. . . "

Peter halted with his back to the room.

"Some of Jesus' disciples are staying at the upper room where you last ate supper."

"Who?" Peter asked without turning around.

"That, I don't exactly know."

He knows, he knows, Peter thought, but for reasons of his own, he does not want to tell me.

He went out into the garden. How peculiar Joseph was. They say he was such a great friend of Jesus. True, he did go to Pilate, and he did take care of the burial. At any rate, he shrugged, he grates on my nerves.

The news that some of the other disciples were in the upper room made him glad, and he was sincerely grateful to Joseph for telling him. He felt like dashing over there immediately, but the distance from Joseph's house exceeded several times the permissible Sabbath distance. He would rather not expose himself—someone might see him and accuse him of violating the laws by taking too many steps on the holy day. And then the trouble would begin. Now, if he were with Jesus, he would not have all these qualms about taking this many or that many steps; they would simply go. Jesus would not hesitate. But Jesus was gone. He would wait until morning.

For the first time since his headlong flight from Jerusalem, Peter's head was clear. He started to consider what he should do. Of course, he would prefer above all to return to Galilee. But it did not require much foresight to see that if the priests intended to arrest Jesus' disciples, nothing could be easier for them than to send messengers to all the synagogues of Galilee, and then pluck them from their homes like so many fish in a net. It was impossible to hide in a small town or village. Every man knew the business of every other. It was easier to lose oneself in a big city. On the other hand, Jerusalem was an alien city, with the enemy lying in wait at every turn. He could compromise: remain a while in Jerusalem until things cooled down, then return to Galilee. That seemed the most sensible thing to do. But stay where in Jerusalem? Not at Joseph's house, with the Romans standing guard there—and even if they were not Joseph had obviously had enough of his company. He did not have much choice.

Though he did not admit it to anyone, Peter nurtured a quiet hope that something would happen in the city. No, not disturbances, but at least some kind of protest, some kind of proof of attachment to the master from Nazareth on the part of the crowd. But the city was silent. At first he assured himself that news of the execution of Jesus had not yet reached them. But he very quickly came to the bitter realization that the people were simply afraid. Yet how could he blame them, when he, who had been closest to Jesus, had himself denied and fled from him. Now that he was dead, the people were stunned by the show of the priests' power. The fact that Jesus could have been so swiftly, so effortlessly condemned by them to death—Jesus the wonder worker, the marvelous teacher from Nazareth—had shocked everyone into a state of numbness.

Peter planned to leave Joseph's house early on the first morning after the Sabbath. The hours spent before Jesus' tomb were his farewell to him. He lay down late that night. Not surprisingly, sleep eluded him. He tried to ease his insomnia by talking far into the night with John. When he finally dozed off, it was only to be awakened what seemed mere minutes later by someone shaking him, trying to tell him something. He sat up, blinked his eyes. It was still dark. Mary Magdalene was tugging at him in tears, begging him to get up. Finally her sobbing words pierced his drowsiness: "They have taken the Lord's body!"

He sprang out of bed, threw something on, and shook John awake, repeating what Mary said, "They have taken the Lord's body". He raced through the garden. A faint twilight grayed the air, though it was still difficult to see. Halfway to the tomb, John overtook him and raced ahead. When he ran up, he found John, apparently afraid to enter alone, beside the yawning black opening to the sepulcher, and the stone cast away to one side.

"You can see the sheet," John whispered.

Peter took a quick look around first to see if he would find something peculiar, out of the ordinary. Then he brushed John out of the way and went in. The silence of the tomb unnerved him. The white binding sheets glowed faintly near the entrance, scattered, as if thrown aside. Little else was visible. He found the napkin that must have covered Jesus' face folded separately and laid aside. Jesus' body was definitely not there. John crept in behind him. They barely fit together in the tight crypt.

"Who could have done it?" Peter asked aloud when they emerged. "Where are the soldiers? They're supposed to be here." He examined the stone and the broken seals. "No, the soldiers couldn't have done this. But if someone else did, what happened to the guards. Murdered? Where are the signs of struggle, where are the bodies? We have to notify everyone. Joseph first. Maybe someone knows something, maybe someone saw something."

At the house, the servants were already moving about. Joseph came out to them, as usual fresh and ceremonious, as if he were on his way to an appointment with the High Priest. He asked Peter inside—no, only Peter for now. Could John please wait outside?

Peter went in. For the first time he saw Joseph visibly agitated. Immediately Peter suggested that he go and see what had happened to the tomb. No, he didn't want to go, and, anyway, he knew all about the empty tomb.

How was it he always knew everything right away? Peter wondered to himself.

For now, Joseph said, he would rather hear what he, Peter, had to say about the matter.

Peter did not like the sound of that. "What do you mean, what I know 'about the matter'?" he demanded.

"About the matter of that empty tomb."

"What is this, an interrogation?"

Joseph dropped his gaze. "Did I say it was an interrogation? I only want to find out what you know about the matter."

Chafing from the implication, Peter gave him a curt account of the events from the moment he had retired to bed, through his awakening by Mary Magdalene, right up until his return to the house. Finally Joseph raised his eyes to him and asked, "Is that everything?"

"Everything."

"May I ask you one other thing, then?"

"Ask," Peter snapped.

"If you recall, yesterday I told you that a number of disciples are staying in the house where you last ate supper with our master."

It infuriated Peter to hear him call Jesus "our master".

"Did either you or John communicate with them?" he pressed. "Were you there to see them?"

Peter was not sure what he was getting at. "When could I have gone to see them?"

"During the night, for instance."

"During the night? But it was still the Sabbath. We're not permitted to walk such distances on the Sabbath, it's unlawful."

"Well, yes, but Jesus taught us not to pay attention to

trifles, didn't he? A few steps more or less are unimportant. The commandment of love is important, am I right?"

Peter quivered with anger. He was beginning to understand. "Yes," he hissed between his teeth, and he wheeled around and left.

"One more disciple of Jesus," he muttered outside to himself. "One more Pharisee with the gall to call Jesus his master. I wonder how long he'll be calling him master, and if he talks about him like that in the Sanhedrin."

Flushed and indignant, he was automatically heading toward the tomb, when from out of the depths of the garden, Mary Magdalene came running toward him—hair flying, arms thrown open wide, laughing, crying, almost hysterical with joy. He watched her in alarm. She practically hurled herself at him and threw her arms around his neck.

"I have seen the Lord!" she cried.

So it had finally happened. The master's death had been too much for her—Mary had snapped.

"Who?" he asked calmly, disengaging her arms.

"Jesus!" she exclaimed.

He grabbed her roughly by the shoulders and shook her. "Get a hold of yourself."

"But yes, I saw him!" She stopped suddenly and peered suspiciously into his face. "You think I've gone mad, don't you? Listen to me." She wiped her eyes and tried to collect herself. "I lost Salome and Mary of Cleophas somewhere in the garden," she mumbled half to herself.

"How's that? You weren't here alone?"

"No, I came with the other women."

"So early? For what?"

"To anoint Jesus' body."

"Anoint his body?"

"Yes, of course. Everyone was in such a hurry Friday evening, the sun was setting, there was no time to do it. So we determined to come first thing after the Sabbath and anoint it—bury him like any other decent man."

"Where are the others?"

"I don't know."

"Tell me everything from the beginning," he said, confused.

"Well . . . we came, we looked . . . the stone was rolled away and the tomb wide open. We were terrified, we didn't know what it could mean. I left them behind when I ran to wake you. I returned to the garden, but the other women were gone. I thought maybe his body might be lying somewhere in the bushes or the rocks, that possibly someone wanted to desecrate it. I circled around, searching everywhere—nothing. From a distance I saw you and John enter the tomb. Then I saw you both leave. I kept looking around for him. Suddenly I saw the gardener coming toward me, the one who was wandering around here all day yesterday. I thought to myself, he might know something, or maybe even he did it for some reason. I walked toward him, but then I saw that it was not the gardener at all, but someone else—it was still fairly dark and I could not make out his features. I was a little frightened, but I asked anyway, 'Sir, if you have taken the body of Jesus, tell me where you have hid him.' And that's when he called me by name, that's when he said, 'Mary'. Then I recognized him—it was the master!"

She burst into sobs of joy. Tears streamed down her face, and she was trembling badly.

Peter clasped her to him. "Calm down, calm down."

"Wait, I haven't finished. When I recognized him, I fell at his feet. He told me not to detain him, because he has to go to the Father. Then he disappeared."

"What do you mean 'disappeared'?" He stared at her in disbelief.

"He simply disappeared, he was gone."

"If he was there, then he should be there the whole time." He tried to reason with her, make her see reality.

She shook her head adamantly. "He disappeared."

"Let's leave," he said, changing the subject.

"And go where?"

"To the guest room where we ate the Passover with Jesus. Some of our people are there. But I don't think it's wise for the two of us to go together. We might attract attention."

"What! Are you afraid? Of whom? Jesus is alive! They're the ones who should be afraid!"

He changed the subject again. "Do you want to tell Joseph what you just told me?"

"I could. . . ."

Magdalene went inside to tell Joseph. She did not come out for a long time. Peter paced nervously outside. The idea came to him to go straight to the priests and inform them about what had happened. By doing so, he would give them to understand that he had nothing to do with it. But he was afraid to go alone. What if they did not believe him and accused him of violating the tomb? And Joseph would not go with him, that was certain—Joseph was practically convinced that he had stolen the body.

Finally Mary emerged. She looked considerably more composed, except that she had an odd, incredulous smile on her lips. "Do you know what Joseph said to me?"

"I think I can guess. He told you it was you who had carried off the body," he joked.

"Not exactly in those words," she answered seriously, "but basically that was it. Or if it wasn't me, then at least I took part in the conspiracy together with the other women and I don't know who else. He said I should immediately tell him everything, or even march over to the priests and tell them."

So, Peter thought to himself, I wasn't the only one to think about going to the priests. Joseph was, too.

"Is that all?"

"No. . . ." She hesitated. "He tried to insult me. He told me to stop fabricating and stop pretending to be mad, because it looks unconvincing. Oh, and one other thing—he wanted me to promise I wouldn't breathe a word to anyone about what I told him. Not even our people, if—as he put it ironically—they don't already know that the tomb is empty and that Jesus is alive."

"What did you say to that?"

"I refused. What gives him the right to talk to me that way? Then he softened and said, all right, I can tell Jesus' disciples—he repeated that they probably know anyway—but no one else. I still refused. Then he warned me: you'd better not mention it to anyone, if you know what's best for all of you. If the priests find out that you're spreading news like that, they'll sweep you all off the face of the earth. Well, then I conceded. I promised that at least for today, I wouldn't tell anyone else. But as for the future, I couldn't promise anything."

Peter felt ashamed for Joseph. "Let's leave," he said.

They turned and were leaving when Joseph's voice called to them from behind. "I would like a few more words with the two of you."

He stood in the door watching them. They approached him reluctantly.

"If I may request one other thing, then I would like you, Peter, to remain here at my house today. And you," he nodded to Magdalene, "go to the upper room and let them know that Peter is here. In keeping with our agreement, say nothing else."

"Why should I stay here with you?" Peter asked.

"I'm afraid you could be arrested on the way to the upper chamber. I would rather you didn't show yourself on the street during the day. You're far too well known to be able to pass unmolested through the city. Wait until evening, then you can go. You'll be safe here."

Peter was unsure how to interpret Joseph's proposal. For the moment he agreed.

The day passed without incident. Joseph made every effort to accompany him everywhere. If he had to leave, even for a moment, a servant materialized instantly in his place. It was explained to him: all out of concern for his safety. But Joseph's underlying motives soon become apparent to him—he simply suspected that Peter, together with the other disciples, planned to engineer an overthrow, or insurrection, or some other mad scheme on the strength of the empty tomb, on the principle—Jesus did not manage, but maybe his disciples could bring it off. Peter was helpless in the face of such suspicions; it was futile to argue or explain. The few times he tried, Peter met with the same cold, ironic smile. He gave up, resigned himself to Joseph's suspicions. For that matter, he knew that if he had not agreed to stay, he would instantly have had Joseph against him and the others. And Joseph knew too much about them. If he went over to the side of the priests, it would be the end for all of them. The best thing to do was simply let himself be observed, let Joseph see for himself that he had nothing up his sleeve.

From the pieces of conversation he picked up, he learned that some priests and Romans had come around, and not just anybody—individuals of rank and station. He tried to find out what was happening. His inquiries were answered with silence. From fragments he overheard, he deduced that people in the streets were starting to ask about what had happened. Apparently, in spite of all precautions to keep it quiet, news of the empty tomb had leaked into the city. No one was permitted to enter the garden. The gates were tightly barred, the servants given the strictest orders to let no one in.

That evening Peter approached Joseph. "Can I assume that my private arrest is over?"

Joseph smiled and said nothing.

"Did you manage to satisfy yourself that I had nothing to do with the whole affair?"

Again silence and the smile that said nothing.

"May I leave now to join the others?"

"Of course, you always could. You were only here for your own protection."

It was Peter's turn to smile ironically and say nothing.

He crossed the city without incident. More disciples had assembled in the upper room than he had expected, and they made a sorrier sight than he had expected—dejected, sullen, mute, hunted. He was received coldly, as if were personally to blame for everything. He could scarcely draw more than a few reluctant grunts out of them. Eventually he pieced together their story. Most had come there straight from the Garden of Olives after Friday's tragedy and had spent the Sabbath there, immobilized by the holy day. A few had left for Galilee that morning, but the majority had stayed behind, held back by the news the women had brought them. They were simply afraid to leave.

"It doesn't look like it, but they were waiting for you to

come," Andrews assured him. "They wanted to consult with you about what to do next."

So they were waiting for him. He was still in charge. Ignoring their stony faces, he repeated his conversation with Joseph about the threat hanging over them. The empty tomb was not only a fact, but a cause for arrest. The crime of stealing the body was one charge; the second was spreading news about a risen Jesus. Of course, the best thing to do would be to expose the perpetrators, but since in all likelihood, the priests had done it themselves, there was, practically speaking, little room for action. He advanced his arguments in favor of returning to Galilee and in favor of remaining in Jerusalem. They agreed with the wisdom of staying the city for a period of time to lessen the risk of danger to themselves and their families. They would simply have to make the best of their situation on the one hand, return to their homes was cut off, on the other, they were fugitives in a city where every emergence on the street could be dangerous. Even their hideaway there would not long go undetected by the priests.

Their discussion was abruptly interrupted by a pounding at the door. All eyes flew questioningly to Peter. The looks were reassuring—he was still leader of their group. The door was opened. In stepped two disciples, Cleophas and a companion. They had left that very morning for Emmaus and now they were back—tired, dusty, perspiring, but to the astonishment of everyone, radiant and overjoyed.

"We saw Jesus," they piped in unison.

"How could you have seen him?" Peter snapped. "Neither of you were anywhere near the tomb."

"No, we weren't at the tomb. We were going home," Cleophas said, with a hint of shame in his voice.

"And what?"

"Nothing. We were walking in the direction of Galilee, and we thought the best road to take would be through Emmaus—

"I'm asking you about Jesus," Peter broke in impatiently.

"In a moment. We'll tell you about Jesus in a moment. We were very troubled and grieved, and were asking ourselves how it all could have happened. And then the master suddenly came up to us."

"What do you mean, came up to you?" Peter shouted. He was losing his patience. It seemed everyone around him was losing his mind. First Magdalene, now these two.

"He just joined us and started to walk the road with us."

"And what did you do?"

"Nothing. We didn't recognize him."

"Well, if you didn't recognize him," Peter said more calmly now, "then why do you claim it was him?"

"He joined us and asked us why we were so sad. We asked him, hadn't he heard about what had happened in Jerusalem? Then we told him about Jesus of Nazareth, who was a prophet, mighty in words and works before God and all the people, and how our chief priests and rulers delivered him up to be sentenced to death annd crucified him. . . ."

Peter let them ramble on. Poor fellows.

". . . . And we told him how everyone had been hoping that he would redeem Israel, and that this is the third day since he died. And how certain women of our company had frightened us, because they went to the tomb before it was light and didn't find his body, but told us they had seen a vision of angels who said that he is alive—"

"Which women?"

"Salome and the others who were at the tomb this morning."

"I don't know anything about any vision."

"Then you can find out. They're upstairs," someone told him.

Peter gazed around the room suspiciously: there was something going on here, something outside of him. This was no collective hallucination. It had all to be prearranged. So, Joseph was right, after all. There really was a conspiracy of some kind. But who could be behind it? So far he had these two, a couple of women, and Mary Magdalene. Somehow, of all of them, Mary did not fit in. But it had to be a conspiracy. Because, really, he might suspect Cleophas and his companion of many things, but certainly not of having succumbed to mass hysteria. He watched their lips mouthing the words, and he did not believe any of it.

". . . . Then he told us we weren't too smart, because everything had been spoken of by the prophets earlier. And beginning with Moses and with all the prophets, he explained to us all the things written in the Scriptures that pertained to the Messiah."

"Was that when you recognized him?" Peter asked sarcastically.

"No, we didn't even recognize him then."

"Then when?"

"Only when we reached Emmaus. We always stop there at a certain inn for supper. He wanted to continue on his way. But I said to him, 'Stay with us, because it is getting toward evening, and the day is now far spent.' He agreed. We all three went in. The hall was empty. There were only three of us. That's when I recognized him, at the table."

"Why then?"

"It was when he took bread, blessed and broke in, and handed it to us that I recognized him."

"And?" Peter pressed, in spite of himself.

"And nothing. He disappeared."

"What do you mean, disappeared?"

"He was gone, there were just the two of us left."

For a conspiracy, it was not very convincing. He encouraged them: "And what did he tell you to do? To go to the priests, or to the people and announce that you have seen him?"

"No, he didn't say anything at all about that."

Peter eyed them warily. "What happened next?"

"We rose immediately from the table and returned here to Jerusalem to tell you of this."

Peter could see he wasn't going to get any more out of them. He turned away. Now for the women. He had to have a talk with them.

They came down in a group, looking very sunny and serene.

"What happened this morning?" he fairly growled.

One of them began, "Early, before light, we went to the tomb to anoint Jesus' body—"

"There was no time Friday because of the Sabbath," another interrupted.

"As we walked, we asked ourselves, who will roll back the stone for us? But as we approached the tomb, we saw that the stone was already rolled away. We peered into the sepulcher, and there on the right side was a youth sitting. He was dressed in a white robe. We were greatly puzzled: what was a youth doing in there? Then he spoke to us. 'Do not be afraid,' he said. 'You are looking for Jesus of Nazareth, who was crucified. He has risen, he is not here. Behold the place where they laid him. But go, tell his disciples and Peter that he goes before you into Galilee. There you shall see him, as he told you.' We were seized by fright then, because we realized that this was no youth, but an angel. We fled from the tomb."

"What did you do?"

"First we looked for you and John, but didn't find you in your room. So we went to Joseph."

"And you told all this to Joseph?"

"Yes."

So that was how Joseph knew everything—and he said nothing to him. "What did he say?" he asked.

"He upbraided us and forbade us to speak of it to anyone. We obeyed him at first, but later we came here and told everyone, because, well, Jesus instructed us to."

"How did they react?" he pressed, hoping to pinpoint the conspirators.

"They didn't believe us. They were terrified that someone had taken the master's body."

"No one seemed happy with the news?"

"No, no one."

The trail stopped there. The street that should have led him straight to the conspirators turned out to be blind. He dismissed the women. The two disciples from Emmaus were still trying to convince the others of what had happened to them on the road. Peter shook his head wearily. Better to occupy himself with preparing supper. That responsibility was now his above all others.

The room was in nearly total darkness. He instructed the

disciples to light some oil lamps—not too many, just to be safe. As he looked around at them huddled in the room, he was reminded of the storm at sea—there was the same fright in their faces, and the sea of hatred surging around them, eager to destroy them. He felt the way he had them at the helm, responsible for them. Responsible, and at the same time helpless. Except that it was different then—Jesus was sleeping in the bow of the boat.

With a heavy heart he asked them to take their places at the table. Three days ago they had done the same. He noticed that they kept the same places they had at their last supper. Jesus' place was left vacant. It was time to rise, recite the hymn, and break bread. Jesus always discharged that function; now the distinction and duty fell to him. Jesus had taught them that their suppers in common should unite them, with themselves and with God. But how could they share this supper when they were divided, at variance, hostile, and uncaring toward one another. There seemed no sense in his trying; he felt empty, helpless, limp. He cried out inside, in anger and in sorrow—Why did you leave us like this?

Through the low murmur around the table, a voice reached them from the direction of the door.

"Peace be to you."

He shook himself. It was not possible. A delusion? But no, the others had heard, too. In the gloom he could see their white faces turned towards the door. An uncanny silence filled the room. He held his breath and stared hard into the shadows. Nothing, it was too murky, the oil lamps barely stretched their light to the darkness around the door. He strained his eyes until they hurt. Then he heard—they all heard—his unmistakable voice again.

"Peace be to you."